Regionalism and global integration

D1549402

This scholarly and interdisciplinary volume sheds much-needed light on the relationship between national policies, regional integration patterns and the wider global setting. It covers regional patterns in Europe, Asia and the Americas. Individual chapters focus on topics ranging from industrial and financial policies to social welfare regimes, as well as broader assessments and comparisons of regional arrangements in a global context.

The chapters point to the diversity of regional patterns in the world economy and the continuing importance of national regulatory structures, yet they also point to the common pressures of globalization felt by all, especially in the domain of capital markets. With broad coverage and clear but sophisticated analysis this new book will be vital reading for all those seeking to clarify their understanding of the contemporary regional/global paradox.

William D. Coleman is Professor of Political Science at McMaster University. **Geoffrey R.D. Underhill** lectures in the Department of Politics and International Studies at the University of Warwick.

90 0391502 3

Regionalism and global economic integration

Europe, Asia and the Americas

Edited by William D. Coleman and
Geoffrey R.D. Underhill

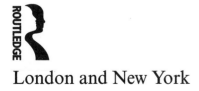

London and New York

First published 1998
by Routledge
11 New Fetter Lane, London EC4P 4EE

Simultaneously published in the USA and Canada
by Routledge
29 West 35th Street, New York, NY 10001

Typeset in Times by RefineCatch Limited, Bungay, Suffolk
Printed and bound in Great Britain by
MPG Books Ltd, Bodmin, Cornwall

British Library Cataloguing in Publication Data
A catalogue record for this book is available from the British Library

Library of Congress Cataloging in Publication Data
A catalogue record for this book has been requested

ISBN 0–415–16247–5 (hbk)
ISBN 0–415–16248–3 (pbk)

This volume is dedicated to parents, pupils and teachers of the Suzuki violin method everywhere. We and our children have enjoyed every minute.

Contents

Contributors

William D. Coleman is Professor of Political Science, McMaster University, Hamilton, Ontario, Canada.

Yves Dezalay is Directeur de Recherches, Centre National de la Recherche Scientifique, Paris.

Kenneth Dyson is Professor of European Studies, University of Bradford, Bradford, UK.

Kevin Featherstone is Professor of European Politics and Jean Monnet Chair of European Integration Studies, University of Bradford, UK.

Richard Higgott is Professor of International Political Economy and Director of the Centre for the Study of Globalization and Regionalization, Department of Politics and International Studies, University of Warwick, Coventry, UK.

George Michalopoulos is Senior Research Officer, Department of European Studies, University of Bradford, UK.

Helen Milner is Professor of Political Science, Columbia University, New York City, USA.

Jonathon W. Moses is Associate Professor of Political Science, University of Trondheim, Trondheim, Norway.

Martin Rhodes is Senior Research Fellow, Robert Schuman Centre, European University Institute, Florence, Italy.

Monika Sie Dhian Ho works at the Netherlands Scientific Council for Government Policy, The Hague, The Netherlands.

Richard Stubbs is Professor of Political Science, McMaster University, Hamilton, Ontario, Canada.

Diana Tussie is Senior Research Fellow and Co-ordinator of the International Relations Programme, FLASCO, Buenos Aires, Argentina.

Geoffrey R.D. Underhill is Lecturer, Department of Politics and International Studies, University of Warwick, Coventry, UK.

Klaas Werkhorst works in the Monetary and Financial Affairs Directorate, Ministry of Finance, The Netherlands.

Andrew Wyatt-Walter is Senior Lecturer in the Department of International Relations, London School of Economics and Political Science, London, UK.

Acknowledgements

This book began its life as a set of papers presented to a workshop in the Joint Sessions of the European Consortium of Political Research held in Madrid in April 1994. Several of the chapters appeared subsequently in a special issue of the *Journal of European Public Policy* in August 1995. Noting the growing importance of the interrelationship between globalization and regionalism, the editors sought out several other papers to provide depth to the special issue. The contributions by Yves Dezalay, Richard Stubbs, and Diana Tussie serve this purpose. In addition, Richard Higgott provided a new paper that built on his earlier work, but extended considerably the comparison of European integration and Asia-Pacific regionalism. All of the remaining chapters were updated and revised by the authors.

This volume would never have seen the light of day if it had not been for the European Consortium for Political Research and its welcome practice of inviting proposals for workshops around defined themes. This practice frequently has the fortunate result of bringing together a diverse group of scholars who are interested in a set of problems but approach these problems from various perspectives. This workshop brought together specialists in international relations, comparative public policy, and European politics from both sides of the Atlantic. The intellectual exchange and generous Spanish brandies in the evening helped create a constructive atmosphere for further research and writing. The editors wish to acknowledge the contributions of all of the workshop participants and to thank the contributors to the volume for their willingness to participate in this exercise.

Introduction
Domestic politics, regional economic co-operation, and global economic integration

William D. Coleman and Geoffrey R. D. Underhill

Global economic integration is one of the most pronounced developments of the late twentieth century. The liberalization of domestic economies, the strengthening of (basically liberal) co-operative regimes in international trade and finance, and the transnationalization of corporate structures have all contributed to this dramatically accelerated growth of globally integrated market structures.

The 'globalization' thesis can be taken too far, however. It is undoubtedly premature to announce the disintegration or even emasculation of domestic state institutions as a significant focus for economic management and change. The policies of nation-states continue to structure the market domain, liberalizing some aspects, yet retaining tight control of others. Likewise, global market integration has been accompanied by different patterns of institutionalized regional economic co-operation.

That various regions of the global economy should manifest distinct patterns of integration within the larger global context is hardly surprising. Geographical proximity is the likely starting point of this phenomenon. Unless there is a forbidding enmity between peoples (and sometimes despite it), one trades with one's neighbours first before moving further afield. Shared historical experiences among states of a particular region develop over time (not always pleasant ones), and the cultural affinities which facilitate commerce are more likely with neighbouring peoples than with those from afar. What is more remarkable, and more difficult to explain in the late twentieth century is not, then, the mere fact of different regional patterns, but the trend towards formalization of these regional patterns into a series of co-operative arrangements to facilitate regional economic integration of various kinds.

Most pronounced in this regard is undoubtedly the European Union as it moves, with some trepidation, towards a single currency. The implementation of the Single European Act and the conclusion of the Maastricht Treaty have greatly accelerated the process of European integration. A significant number of public policy issues in the EU member-states are now managed to a greater or lesser extent through co-operative processes at the regional level. The movement towards a single market for goods, services and capital in the European Union has, furthermore, been accompanied by parallel regional integration processes elsewhere in the world economy. Most notable was the recent conclusion of the North American Free Trade Agreement (NAFTA) embracing Canada, the United States, and Mexico. Greater regional integration has also developed in East Asia between Japan, the 'Four Tigers', and other members of the ASEAN group. The larger Asia-Pacific Economic Co-operation forum (APEC), which includes the antipodes, ASEAN, Japan, as well as the US and Canada, has also declared its intention of setting in motion a co-operative economic integration project based on free trade. The trans-Pacific interlinkages between the US and the Japanese economies are already well known.

These regional processes have accompanied important international co-operative measures which involve integration at the global level. The Uruguay Round GATT negotiations establishing the World Trade Organization (WTO) were successfully concluded with considerably expanded jurisdictional coverage, aiming to liberalize trade in services and to regulate other aspects of global trade unrelated to the traditional domain of manufacturing and primary goods. Central bankers in the Basle supervisors' committee have developed a nascent global regime to regulate international banking activities. Similar developments are occurring in areas as diverse as managing environmental pollution and telecommunications services.

What is less clear is the relationship between the development of global markets in many sectors and these evident steps towards greater and more institutionalized economic integration at a regional level in the world economy. This volume is a systematic attempt to look at the interrelationships between national policy arrangements, regional integration processes, and global economic integration. These relationships are examined primarily from the perspective of the European Union, NAFTA and APEC.

In order to illuminate this set of linkages across three levels of analysis, this volume has sought to pose a number of questions and to answer them through comparative assessments of regional economic integration, case studies of monetary, financial, welfare, and industrial policy issues, and an examination of public regulation in multi-level governance systems. First, to what extent do regional integration policies force convergence at the national level in policy areas where national policy styles were traditionally highly distinctive from one another? Do additional globalization pressures hasten this convergence process or slow it down? Second, how do regional integration projects compare the one to the other? Third, how compatible is extensive regional integration of markets, and corresponding policy co-ordination among participants, with attempts at liberalization at the global level?

The chapters also address a number of more specific questions. What is the relationship of global financial integration to regional currency zones like the European monetary system? Does the creation of large regional free trade areas mark a step towards a new kind of protectionism against global multinational firms operating in world-wide markets? Or are these areas a necessary stepping stone to the establishment of an even more integrated world economy? What are the implications of both kinds of changes for the future of industrial policies at a national level? Are anticipatory industrial policies based on indicative planning and state allocation of credit destined for the same museum that houses the Gold Standard and nationalized industries? Or is it simply an approach destined to be shifted to newly constituted regional authorities? Next, what impact will greater regional integration in a global liberalizing context have on the less advantaged strata of society, particularly on those dependent upon the social welfare safety net? Do both regional economic integration and globalization of markets favour the removal of defences for the less advantaged? Or do these economic changes promise an improvement in the quality of life for these groups? Finally, what effects do culture and the different forms which capitalism appears to take in various regions have on the process of integration? Are we moving towards an era of competing regional capitalisms and a 'clash of civilisations?' (Huntingdon 1993). Or are the cultural underpinnings of the variants of capitalism less meaningful in the long term? This question is particularly relevant because of the apparent clash between the neo-liberal idea of globalized capitalism and both the capitalist model in Asia, with its very distinct cultural traditions and open debate on democratization and 'Asian values', and that in continental Europe with its welfare state traditions of social justice and state intervention.

In short, the relationship between regional economic integration as illustrated by the Single Market in Europe, APEC, and the North American Free Trade Agreement on the one hand, and the rapid development of global markets on the other, is unclear in comparative public policy studies and in research on international political economy. Nor do we yet understand well the range of effects these two sets of integration processes have on the content of domestic policies and the structure of domestic policy communities and policy networks. The chapters in this volume investigate carefully these relationships and offer assessments of their impact on national autonomy in the areas of industrial, financial services, legal services, social welfare and macroeconomic policies, and on the resulting economic fate of the less advantaged sectors of society.

In analysing the relationship of global to regional integration patterns, this volume also addresses a number of debates in the converging comparative public policy and international political economy (IPE) literatures. In IPE, hegemonic stability theory, traditional realist analysis and radical political economy have all sought to understand the twin phenomena of regionalization and globalization by focusing on trade and money/finance issues. Depending on the theoretical approach, greater or lesser emphasis is paid to the role of large transnational firms, to changes in international regimes, and to more traditional assessments of national power. Considerable research has been devoted to trade issues in this regard. This volume contributes to the idea that there are intimate linkages between state policy processes, the private interests of market actors, and the emerging global/regional patterns of integration in the world economy (Underhill 1994: 17–21). Neither globalization nor regionalization are dynamics devoid of politics.

Work on the international monetary system also provides examples of subareas of international political economy highly relevant to issues addressed in this volume. The considerable IPE literature on financial services globalization also relates to the chapters in this book. Several of the chapters provide some assessment of the astonishingly widespread effects of the globalization of financial markets. The new GATT agreement extends the liberalization in financial services even further and the EU and NAFTA have, in turn, pushed regional financial integration to still more liberalized levels.

Another important debate in IPE and the broader international relations literature concerns transnational economic interdependence and the question of levels of analysis. Traditional international relations perspectives have usually insisted on a clear contrast between the nature of domestic and international politics. The obvious interlinkages, however, among the global, regional, and domestic levels of politics which are revealed in the chapters of this book call into question this sharp domestic–international divide. Transnational interdependence means that state and non-state actors alike become interrelated across three levels of political institutions: global co-operative processes, regional institutions like the EU, and the traditional national level. There is a continuity in policy and institutional terms across the levels of analysis.

Likewise, the book has relevance for those doing research on international regimes and who are assessing the importance of policy and epistemic communities in the establishment of those regimes. The development of international regimes in the areas of international banking and international securities markets involve complex interactions among national governments, regional organizations like the EU, and global intergovernmental forums like the GATT, the Basle Committee on Banking Supervision and the International Organization of Securities Commissions (IOSCO). The politics of these multi-level games is an increasingly important phenomenon and one that is not yet well-understood.

Specialists in comparative public policy who have traditionally focused their attention at the national level also find themselves forced to take increasing account of the relationships between the creation of regional economic arrangements like the EU and globalizing market developments. These specialists, whose interests cover a broad range of sectors like high technology industries, financial services, and professional services to name but a few, find that they no longer can explain and evaluate policy at the national level without examining carefully developments at the supranational regional level and at the global level. Conceptual tools like policy networks and policy communities which were well-suited to domestic policy studies need considerable refinement if they are to explain these more complex policy developments. By trying to consider the interaction of domestic, regional and global factors, the chapters in this volume provide some groundwork for pursuing refinements in policy community approaches. Similarly, public choice theory and its examination of outcomes from regulatory competition in federal states has now been turned to consider similar issues in supranational governance systems. Several chapters indicate some of the complexities in moving from the domestic to the international level in this regard.

Finally, as a prelude to these empirical case studies, this introduction will examine a crucial set of issues related to democratic politics. The case studies provide us with an excellent overview of the institutional consequences of interactions between global, regional and national levels. It is important to remember that these institutional changes present important challenges to the persistence of democracy.

GLOBALIZATION, REGIONAL CO-OPERATION AND DEMOCRACY

We have already noted that the phenomenon of increased, institutionalized regional economic co-operation coincides with a new era of globalization. Highly developed economic relationships on a global scale are not new to the world economic system. During the latter part of the nineteenth century and ending in 1914 with the First World War, the world's major economic powers participated in a remarkable period of global trading and international financial flows under a fairly stable international monetary system based on sterling and the gold standard. None the less, each globalizing era has its own specific features and this era, the last three decades of the twentieth century, differs significantly from those of the past.

First, goods production has become integrated on a world scale. Multinational corporations earlier in the century relied principally on direct investment in branch plants to expand their operations in the world economy. Over the past three decades, global corporations have moved away from this model to one where plants are built wherever in the world the overall efficiencies and production costs seem the most favourable. The products of plants from a number of different countries are then brought together in still another country for final assembly of a finished good. Thus a Nissan Quest minivan might be built in Tennessee for a Japanese company but will include parts not only from the US and Japan, but also from Mexico, Canada and the UK, to name but a few countries. Associated with these processes is a move away from hierarchical firm structures to flexible production organized through subcontracting and other network relationships (Cerny 1995: 613–14; Hollingsworth *et al.* 1994). Information technology facilitates the creation and maintenance of such networks on a global scale.

Second, the present era has seen an unprecedented expansion of financial transactions on a global scale. Whereas in the past, financial transactions tended to follow and support expanding goods trade, in the present the movement of capital and financial products on the global plane outstrips by far goods trading. Estimates put the volume of financial transactions to total twenty to forty times the value of merchandise trade (Cerny 1995: 617). In fact, to the degree that the movement of capital and money reflects speculation about future investment possibilities, it can increasingly determine where future goods production might take place. This financial globalization includes several distinct phenomena: the rapid growth of international banking, securities, and equities markets, growing interdependence and linkages between domestic financial services markets, and the deepening and diversification of domestic markets (Coleman 1996: 5–8). Each of these developments is again greatly facilitated by the availability of communications technology which enables information to be transferred almost instantly from one market or country to another.

The relationship between these changes in the structure of the world economy and the political institutions of the nation-state is remarkably complex. Nor can we expect this relationship to be the same for all states; some are more internally coherent, powerful, and higher in the world order than others. On the one hand, nation-states took the political decisions that reduced protectionism in goods trading, that liberalized capital movements, and that ended the segmentation of financial services markets (Pauly 1995). They did so, it is true, under significant economic and political pressure from powerful economic actors who stood to gain from hyper liberalization. But states have not been passive; they have created the new world order in tandem with the many private interests which are integrated into state policy-making institutions and processes (Underhill 1996a).

On the other hand, this new order is having a profound effect on states in return. They are becoming part of a larger and more complex political structure that is the counterpart of the production and financial systems (Cox 1987: 253). Global interconnectedness is creating 'chains of interlocking political decisions and outcomes' which are transforming national political systems themselves (Held 1991: 158). Cox (1987: 253ff.) captures this set of changes with the concept of the 'internationalizing of the state' which comprises three elements. First, there have developed processes of interstate consensus formation regarding the needs or requirements of the world economy that take place aided by an increasingly shared ideological framework. Second, participation in this process of consensus formation is hierarchically structured, with the US, Japan and Germany playing the leading roles. Third, national governments have responded by reforming the internal structures of states so that they can best transform the 'global consensus into national policy and practice' (Cox 1987: 254). As Cox concludes, the accountability structure of states changes from an accountability *within* to an accountability *without*. Their responsibilities are no longer to defend domestic interests against disturbances from the outside, but to facilitate the adjustment of domestic actors to the new global economic order.

Regional economic co-operation is a fundamental component of these political changes. Although this book details some of the very important institutional differences between the European Union, the North American Free Trade Agreement, and APEC, all represent attempts by states to engage in consensus formation on a supranational scale. All as well seek to ensure that their signatory states become more responsive to the world economy (they are more liberalizing than protectionist), all the while attempting to secure advantages for their members in this new order. These regional institutions also fit into global political connections. The EU negotiates for its member-states in the international trade regime, and its President now attends the G7 Economic summits. But EU states also participate directly in other global institutions organized under the auspices of the IMF, the World Bank, or the Bank for International Settlements.

These developments encompassed in the concept of globalization pose serious and difficult questions for democratic politics. Held (1991: 139) points out the contradictions between democratic theory and recent economic and political changes. Democratic theory assumes that nation-states can be treated as self-contained units and that they can be clearly demarcated from one another. This demarcation is particularly important with regard to the fundamental socio-economic choices regarding the mechanisms of wealth generation, the scope of market institutions, and the distribution of 'national' product. According to democratic theory, the changes that take place within democracies can be understood largely with reference to the internal dynamics and structures of the nation-state only. Thus political leaders are assumed to have the capacity to implement policies they deem necessary to ensure their political legitimacy in a democratic context. Citizens can hold these leaders to account for these decisions. Through political parties or interest groups, citizens can also participate individually in attempting to influence the actions of political leaders. This participation assumes, in turn, that citizens have access to the information needed to understand and evaluate policy proposals. In short, democratic politics is assumed to be the expression of the interplay of 'forces operating within the nation-state' (Held 1991: 139).

These assumptions have always been somewhat problematic given the persistence of socio-economic interdependencies across the borders of nation-states. With globalization, however, they become open to even more serious question. First, to varying degrees depending on their place in the hierarchy of nations, states are losing the capacity to control changes within their borders and to design and implement policies in various sectors. Cerny (1995: 608–9) distinguishes three kinds of public goods traditionally provided by the nation-state: regulatory public goods which establish a workable market framework for the economy, productive and distributive goods such as the provision of public infrastructure and public services, and redistributive goods including those associated with the social welfare state. He notes that under globalizing conditions, nation-states have difficulty supplying all three types. For example, the control over fiscal and monetary policies that was necessary for a Keynesian full-employment macroeconomic policy has weakened considerably (Scharpf 1991); in other respects, financial globalization has severely compromised the policy-making autonomy of states, whether Keynesian or not (Underhill 1995). In fact, effective implementation of macroeconomic policy objectives rests increasingly on co-ordination at the international level (Webb 1995). This loss of national control over macroeconomic policy also weakens the ability of nation-states to design and control social welfare policies. Under the rubric of 'subversive liberalism', Rhodes (Chapter 5) underlines these pressures while Moses (Chapter 6) details some of the broader economic factors that account for these changes.

Second, these questions about capabilities of nation-states point to increasingly serious problems with democratic accountability. As citizens of democracies, individuals still look to hold political leaders to account for policy changes (increases in interest rates, high unemployment) that they may no longer be able to influence. Or, even more troubling, for an increasing range of decisions, no accountability mechanisms are available to citizens. For example, the Bundesbank raises its discount rate which increases the attractiveness of the German Deutschemark. This move leads investors in Canadian government securities to think about switching from buying securities denominated in Deutschemarks rather than in Canadian dollars. In response, the Canadian central bank raises its interest rates to ensure that adequate funds remain available to Canadian governments. But this change in the cost of money triggers in its wake a further weakening of the jobs market in Canada. How do citizens of Canada worried about employment hold the Bundesbank accountable? Even German governments have difficulty in this task!

Once again, the problem is perhaps most acute in relation to the globalization of financial markets. Increasingly, the regulatory policy processes associated with global financial markets are escaping the traditional mechanisms of democratic accountability. Relatively closed policy communities with control over crucial knowledge and expertise (Coleman 1996) are involved in transnational policy processes which not only attend to 'technical' problems of safety, soundness, and systemic stability but also effectively promote financial globalization through the harmonization of domestic regulatory requirements and the promotion of the liberal market values of liquidity and efficiency (Underhill 1996b). The greater the transnational integration of capital markets, and the greater the mobility and volatility of capital, the more crucial choices concerning the mix of government macroeconomic policies depend on the responses of financial market actors (often foreign) for their success. These developments pose a fundamental problem of democratic accountability and indeed political legitimacy in general. States find it increasingly difficult to choose to be different, however important a particular policy stance may be for resolving a state's individual problems of economic development and socio-economic stability.

Not surprisingly, during the public sector work disturbances of the autumn of 1995, some French labour leaders characterized their job action as a strike against globalization. This frustration highlights the consequences of a lack of democratic accountability structures for many of the newer international activities. If the global financial system is now commonly depicted as 'governing' important components of the lives of citizens, and this view is replete in the popular press, there is going to be a problem of legitimacy (Pauly 1995: 371; Held 1995a: 102–3; Held 1995b: 17–18). Democracy presumes that significant changes take place *after* political leaders secure the consent of their citizens. But political leaders have not normally sought the consent of citizens to their decisions to participate in the changed global system. In fact, some leaders may have consciously sought to restrict the powers of domestic state intervention by committing their governments to global liberalization (Helleiner 1996). With these decisions taken, and with the economic, political and legal interconnectedness among states that has resulted, mechanisms for securing consent are weak to non-existent.

The hierarchy of nations exacerbates these problems. Developing countries do not meaningfully participate in some of the most crucial international policy processes such as the G7, the OECD, and the Basle Committee. Wherever possible, powerful states like the US will often prefer to operate through bilateral agreements in international economic matters which allow it to maximize its own power. Smaller states can pool their power and sovereignty better in multilateral regimes. In the crucial world of international finance, the US Securities and Exchange Commission has often preferred the bilateral mode for these reasons (Porter forthcoming).

In short, in the absence of consent, the international financial system will lack legitimacy. Without legitimacy, Pauly (1995: 388) cautions, global institutions and practices become useful targets for extreme right political movements who use them to promote other xenophobic goals.

Finally, the absence of accountability procedures in international institutions and regimes is accompanied by significant barriers to citizen participation. Participation depends on citizens' accessibility both to decision-makers and to information. But international institutions ranging from meetings of the G7, the IMF, the World Bank, and international regimes such as those governing banking at the Basle Committee, securities at IOSCO, and telecommunications all tend to restrict accessibility. They are highly secretive in their deliberations. Information is scarce and, where available, is often highly technical. Technical information and knowledge become sources of power and control. Only those with 'expertise' will normally have the knowledge necessary for codifying and interpreting the information. Too often this expertise remains in the hands of finance ministries, central banks, transnational corporations, and international corporate lawyers. Under such conditions, democratic politics is not possible.

The problems for citizen participation are exacerbated further by the frequent recourse to self-regulation in the international sphere (Porter forthcoming). Ironically, self-regulatory practices became increasingly subject to more intensive state oversight at the domestic level after 1960 (Moran 1991; Vogel 1986). As Streeck and Schmitter (1985) have argued, 'private interest governments' require a strong state watchdog if they are to realize their promised efficiencies and still work towards the public interest. Otherwise, they become robbers' coalitions conspiring to particularistic interests only. Many of the international regimes that have emerged during the current globalizing era have taken the self-regulatory form (Porter 1993, forthcoming). Unfortunately, these regimes lack a global government partner to discipline self-interested behaviour. Just as they did on the domestic plane, therefore, these global self-regulatory structures become an affront to democracy.

One possible solution to these interrelated problems of legitimacy and democratic accountability lies at the intermediate or regional level. By pooling sovereignty and by developing quasi-federal institutional arrangements for co-operative regional economic management, regional integration can attenuate some of the democratic deficit at the same time as it helps individual states to confront the pressures of globalization. Historical experience should leave one with no illusions, however. Political integration and the formal abrogation of national prerogatives is the single most difficult hurdle in regional integration. There is indeed no smooth progression from integration on technical economic issues to political integration as the neo-functionalists once argued might be possible. Former EU Commission President Jacques Delors has expressed in vain the view that the implementation of Maastricht requires forthright attention to developing the political institutions of the EU.

At the very least, a legitimating balance between the regional/global on the one hand, and the domestic level on the other hand, must be struck. If not, an arrangement such as NAFTA is unlikely to endure should it emasculate the cultural identity of Canada and its welfare/labour market institutions, or if continental integration sparks a repeat of the 1995 peso crisis for Mexico. The APEC process is as yet in its infancy as Higgott argues (Chapter 2), but the debate on 'Asian values' is surely a premonition of the obstacles as Stubbs (Chapter 3) shows. The recent turmoil in Asian Currency and securties markets will also have an undoubted impact.

Certainly the experience of the EU, by far the most formalized and institutionalized of the major regional integration efforts, demonstrates this problem. Many such concerns about supranational economic integration and its impact on democratic politics were raised following the Single Market programme when worries about a 'democratic deficit' intensified. The Danish electorate initially rejected the Maastricht deal on precisely these grounds. Some, but not all, have also been articulated by developing countries as their position as 'policy-takers' has become more pronounced. Unless they are addressed soon, they may lead to frustration by citizens and add support to anti-democratic movements.

Certainly, the globalization process has not fostered a sense of common human purpose and values. If anything, it has been associated with a reinforcement of the significance of identity and difference (Held 1991: 149). Ethnic nationalism is resurgent in many parts of the globe and long dormant regional identities under the Westphalian nation-states system have surfaced with surprising force over the past three decades. Although some of these movements profess concern about democracy and the place of the citizen, many others have concluded that democracy is a failure and that stronger, sterner political arrangements are now necessary. The political stakes, it would seem, are high, and the lessons of the interwar period may yet have to be learned over again.

ORGANIZATION OF THE VOLUME

The volume is divided into three sections. The first section looks at contrasting patterns of regional economic co-operation in the global economy. Helen Milner's chapter leads off with a comparative explanation of the motivations for regional integration in the movement towards the EU's Maastricht agreement and the NAFTA. This chapter focuses on two related questions: why did the countries involved choose to co-operate economically, especially in the face of difficult domestic politics?, and why were they able to reach an agreement and to secure domestic ratification? Milner argues that more emphasis needs to be given to domestic politics than is normally found in realist or neo-liberal institutionalist theories in international relations.

Richard Higgott's chapter picks up on these same theoretical issues, and adds a consideration of constructivist theory and the role of ideas. His chapter examines the recent efforts at economic co-operation in the Asia-Pacific, with particular emphasis on the Asia-Pacific Economic Co-operation forum (APEC). He then compares APEC and other Asia-Pacific economic pacts with the approach to regional integration taken by the EU. The comparison is a fortunate one because it challenges some of the conventional wisdom about 'blocism' and raises the question whether regionalism follows different logics in different parts of the globe. Higgott suggests that the Asia-Pacific will follow quite a different path towards institutionalizing economic and political integration than the EU. Where the Europeans have *pooled* sovereignty, the Asians seek to *enhance* sovereignty through market-led regional integration. Globalization, it would appear, does not bring convergence at the regional level – at least not yet.

Richard Stubbs amplifies on the differences between regional integration in Asia and the patterns in North America and Europe. He argues that Asian governments have come together to try to forestall attempts by proselytizing Western government officials and academics to impose a neo-liberal version of globalization on the Asia-Pacific region. He underscores Higgott's analysis by adding that a distinctive form of capitalism is emerging in the Asia-Pacific which will not only encourage greater regional integration, but also may set the region apart from the other major economic regions of the world. His chapter sets out the characteristics of this particular form of capitalism and shows how it differs not only from the neo-liberal model that has become increasingly associated with globalization, but also from the corporatist, social market form of capitalism to be found in some member-states of the EU.

Diana Tussie brings the first section to a close with a consideration of the impact of regionalization on some developing countries in Latin America that are 'outside the loop'. She notes the possible contradiction between the trend towards regional economic integration on the one side and the development of the multilateral trade regime on the other. While the latter may offer some advantages to developing countries, these advantages may be overturned by the behaviour of regional economic blocs such as NAFTA and the EU. She notes that this concern has helped trigger a growing regionalism of its own in Latin America. She adds that the new regionalism in Latin America and elsewhere in the global economy may carry with it the solution to a reinvigorated and updated multilateralism. These regional arrangements are not associated with the aspirations of US-led multilateralism. Rather, somewhat in line with Higgott's and Stubbs's arguments about Asian regionalism, the new regional deals are 'bottom up' integration processes based on the attraction of markets, not 'top down' government decisions. They are serving to integrate North and South in ways GATT never did, providing Latin America with the access to markets the WTO was never built to guarantee.

The second section of the volume examines the interaction between globalization, regionalism and domestic policy change with a series of policy case studies. Martin Rhodes begins by noting that the welfare states in Western Europe are extremely diverse and that each has responded in different ways to the problems of cost containment. He then argues that these choices are increasingly constrained by the need to avoid an excessive fiscal burden on the middle classes and by the growing interdependence that comes from market integration and liberalized capital movements. Consequently, European states experience a loss of control over many traditional policy instruments and are experiencing common pressures for convergence towards a reduced and more market-sensitive welfare state regime. The chapter by Jonathon Moses which follows continues the discussion introduced by Rhodes by focusing on whether the social democratic agenda of full employment and a full-service welfare state remains viable in the new global economic environment. Moses develops a formal analytical model to examine how increased capital mobility might affect the traditional policy matrix of social democratic regimes. He discusses this problem in relation to the difficult choices faced by Nordic states with respect to EU membership.

Andrew Wyatt-Walter observes that the European Community has tended to allow foreign-owned (i.e. non EU owned) firms substantial access to several of its key industrial policy programmes on technological research and development. Such access might seem surprising because one might have expected that Europe's desire to compete effectively as a region with

Japan and the United States would have led to a more protectionist policy. Wyatt-Walter fashions an explanation for this surprising outcome, noting that conventional accounts tend to leave out the important factor of corporate preferences, particularly those of global, transnational firms. Global alliances and connections between transnational firms will have an important impact on the industrial policies of Europe and perhaps on those of other regions as well.

Monika Sie Dhian Ho and Klaas Werkhorst examine a sometimes forgotten, but very important, instrument of industrial policy: export credits and export credit insurance. This policy instrument brings together in obvious ways the intricacies of interaction between domestic, regional and global policies. The authors show that nation-states are reluctant to give up export credit insurance as an industrial and trade policy tool. These strong domestic preferences come into opposition with the logic of European regional integration, rendering policy change slow to emerge. Regional concepts, in turn, must always be balanced by global relations. The authors show that EU decision-makers resist the logic of their own treaty if it means disadvantaging member-states *vis-à-vis* the US and Japan. But, they add, the existence of a global process at the OECD does allow a member-state like the UK to break ranks and use the global forum to place pressure on the EU policy process. Autonomous domestic industrial policy-making is an increasingly rare phenomenon it would appear.

Finally, Kenneth Dyson, Kevin Featherstone, and George Michalopoulos look at the questions of why central bank independence has become an integral dimension of the new European Union and what role central bankers will play in the new arrangement. They argue that central bank independence is a key institution for managing the contradictions between changes in global financial markets, the building of a regional economic union, and retaining a domestic presence. In explaining this development, the chapter opts for external factors including the structural power of the Deutschemark, the changes in the nature of capitalism, the policy style of the EU, and the particular relationship of central bankers to the state.

The third section of the volume focuses on some of the legal complexities that arise out of attempts to regulate markets on a regional and global scale. Here the interactions between domestic political styles, nascent regional governance systems, and global markets still lend themselves to big power politics. States remain important, but the domestic, the global, and the regional remain difficult to disentangle. Yves Dezalay observes these political struggles through the prism of the legal profession, a profession that has a place front and centre in emerging regional and global governance systems. His chapter argues that the globalization of the market for legal expertise has decoupled traditional professions from their historical milieu and identity, a process which takes place simultaneously at the global, regional, and national levels. The opening of borders means a reconversion/restructuring of national legal elites. Competition between styles of governance at the global

level puts pressure on older forms of 'collegiality' and introduces a financial
rationality born of the global market. His analysis reveals that this restructuring of professional hierarchies and corresponding discourses takes place
across regional variants: the spread of the major (and multinational) US
firms leads to the importation of the model of the American Lawyer. Leading
global centres (New York, the City of London) push this restructuring into
Europe. The French legal profession undergoes considerable change as it
confronts US pressures.

The second chapter in this section by William D. Coleman and Geoffrey
R.D. Underhill, examines the same confrontation between the US and
Europe, and between globalization and regionalism, but from the perspective
of changes in regulatory policies for securities markets. They investigate the
interrelationships between the attempt of the EU to construct a common
regulatory regime for securities through the Investment Services Directive
and the related Capital Adequacy Directive and the initiative of global organizations to accomplish the same objective on a broader scale. The chapter
notes that there is a measure of convergence between the two efforts somewhat consistent with a thesis developed by Michael Moran. None the less,
convergence is by no means uni-directional or linear in this complex global/
regional nexus. One must take into account the interests of the EU as a
regional actor competing with the US and Japan and seeking to preserve and
enhance the position of its financial markets in the world sphere. Such competition opens the door to the process of 'regulatory arbitrage' among political jurisdictions and pressure on the US to adapt to emerging EU and global
standards.

The phenomenon of regulatory arbitrage is not new to policy studies;
extensive investigations of the possibility of regulatory competition and its
effects have occurred in federal states, particularly the US. In the field of
public and social choice theory, alternative theories have been developed
that argue in favour and against the value of assigning regulatory authority to lower level governing units in multi-level systems. Will such an
assignment lead to the unwelcome phenomenon of a 'race to the bottom'
or a more acceptable 'race to the top?' These questions have already been
raised in the context of studies of legal regulation in the EU and have
increasing relevance for institutional design in nascent global governance
arrangements.

These observations bring us full circle back to the question of globalization
and democracy. Assigning authority to higher or supranational level bodies
does not necessarily enhance democracy. If the fundamental principles of
democratic governance remain in operation only at the level of the nation-
state, then governance becomes a matter of 'experts', lawyers, and technocrats. Only the global players will be heard in such arrangements. Citizens will
be left with the options of filling the streets to register their concerns, or
voting for parties opposing globalization and integration. These parties, of
course, are too often the vehicles for xenophobia, racism, and exclusionary

politics. Democratic deficits at the regional and global levels pose dangers for citizens and governments everywhere.

REFERENCES

Cerny, P.G. (1995) 'Globalization and the changing logic of collective action'. *International Organization* 49: 595–626.

Coleman, W.D. (1996) *Financial Services, Globalization and Domestic Policy Change: A Comparison of North American and the European Union*, Basingstoke: Macmillan.

Cox, R. (1987) *Production, Power and World Order: Social Forces in the Making of History*, New York: Columbia University Press.

Held, D. (1991) 'Democracy, the nation-state and the global system', *Economy and Society* 20: 138–72.

—— (1995a) 'Democracy and the New International Order', in D. Archibugi and D. Held (eds) *Cosmopolitan Democracy: An Agenda for a New World Order*, Cambridge, UK: Polity Press.

—— (1995b) *Democracy and the Global Order: From the Modern State to Global Governance*, Stanford: Stanford University Press.

Helleiner, E. (1996) 'Democratic Governance in an Era of Global Finance', in M. Molot and M. Cameron (eds) *Canada Among Nations, 1995*, Ottawa: Carleton University Press.

Hollingsworth, J.R., P.C. Schmitter and W. Streeck (1994) 'Capitalism, sectors, institutions, and performance', in J.R. Hollingsworth, P.C. Schmitter and W. Streeck (eds) *Governing Capitalist Economies: Performance and Control of Economic Sectors*, New York: Oxford University Press.

Huntingdon, S. (1993) 'Clash of civilizations', *Foreign Affairs*, 72(3): 22–49.

Moran, M. (1991) *The Politics of the Financial Services Revolution*, Basingstoke: Macmillan.

Pauly, L. (1995) 'Capital mobility, state autonomy and political legitimacy', *Journal of International Affairs* 48: 369–88.

Porter, T. (1993) *States, Markets and Regimes in Global Finance*. Basingstoke: Macmillan.

—— (forthcoming) 'The transnational agenda for financial regulation in developing countries'. in L.E. Armijo (ed.) *Financial Globalization in Emerging Markets* Basingstoke: Macmillan.

Scharpf, F.W. (1991) *Crisis and Change in Social Democracy*, Ithaca, N.Y.: Cornell University Press.

Streeck, W. and P.C. Schmitter (1985) 'Community, market, state and associations? The prospective contribution of interest governance to social order'. in W. Streeck and P.C. Schmitter (eds) *Private Interest Government*, London: Sage.

Underhill, G.R.D. (1994) 'Conceptualising the changing global order', in R. Stubbs and G.R.D. Underhill (eds) *Political Economy and the Changing Global Order* London: Macmillan, 17–44.

—— (1995), 'Keeping governments out of politics: transnational securities markets, regulatory co-operation, and political legitimacy', *Review of International Studies* 21: 251–78.

—— (1996a) 'Financial market integration, global capital mobility, and the ERM crisis 1992–1995', Global Economic Institutions Research Programme Working Papers, no. 12, Economic and Social Research Council.

—— (1996b) 'Private markets and public responsibility in a global system: conflict and co-operation in banking and securities regulation', in G.R.D. Underhill (ed.) *The New World Order in International Finance*, London: Macmillan, 17–49.

Vogel, D. (1986) *National Styles of Regulation: Environmental Policy in Great Britain and the United States*, Ithaca, N.Y.: Cornell University Press.

Webb, M. (1995) *The Political Economy of Policy Coordination: International Adjustment Since 1945*, Ithaca, N.Y.: Cornell University Press.

Part I

Regional economic integration in the global economy

1 Regional economic co-operation, global markets and domestic politics
A comparison of NAFTA and the Maastricht Treaty[1]

Helen Milner

INTRODUCTION

Global economic interdependence has created incentives for greater international economic co-operation. In many instances, these incentives have led
states to accept important and controversial co-operative agreements, despite
other constraints. A crucial element of contemporary international economic
policy co-operation is the development of regional patterns of economic
integration. In the early 1990s, regional economic co-operation took two
large steps forward. In 1992, the US, Canada and Mexico signed the North
American Free Trade Agreement (NAFTA). In 1993, the Maastricht Treaty
initiating a process of monetary union among the twelve European Union
(EU) countries came into effect. These agreements represented significant but
costly co-operative measures. In both cases, the countries agreed to give up
substantial policy autonomy and some measure of national sovereignty.
These agreements also provoked much domestic opposition. Indeed, Prime
Minister Brian Mulroney of Canada faced a major challenge in the 1988
elections because of his backing of Canadian-American Free Trade Agreement (CAFTA), while political leaders in Europe, such as John Major in the
UK and Paul Schulter in Denmark, suffered electorally for their support of
monetary union. Policy-makers thus faced significant costs in accepting both
NAFTA and Economic and Monetary Union (EMU).

The central question asked by this chapter is why did these countries
choose to co-operate economically, especially given the costs they faced. This
question is addressed in three parts. First, why did political leaders initiate
these negotiations? That is, given the costs of such far-reaching economic
change as the accords involved, why were leaders interested in pursuing them?
Free trade agreements in North America and monetary union among European Community (EC) countries had both been attempted before, and had
failed. While different leaders were in power by the early 1990s, these earlier
events still should have alerted them to the potential costs involved. Why did
political leaders initiate these negotiations?

The second issue is why were the countries able to reach agreement? A
number of factors, such as the end of the Cold War in the late 1980s and the

economic difficulties experienced by the advanced industrial countries after 1987, could easily have undermined such co-operation. Finally, the chapter asks what made domestic ratification and implementation possible. For each of these agreements, the political leaders who negotiated them had to obtain domestic approval from either their legislatures or electorates. Ratification proved to be a problem in both agreements, as did implementation, particularly in the case of Maastricht. The NAFTA accord faced a difficult fight in the US Congress, and then the new Canadian prime minister almost vetoed the agreement. It took two years to ratify the Maastricht Treaty; Denmark failed to pass it the first time; Britain and Denmark passed it only with significant amendments; France barely ratified it in a popular referendum; and the Germans were the last to implement it only after a constitutional court ruling. These three phases of the international agreements – their initiation, negotiation and ratification/implementation – are the focus of this chapter.

The argument is that the answers to these questions lie in the intersection of domestic and international politics. Like arguments about two-level games, it stresses the linkage between domestic and international events (Putnam 1988; Evans *et al.* 1993). Unlike such games, the argument here emphasizes more the domestic logic of these agreements. International economic co-operation results from the calculations of political leaders, whose first priority is getting re-elected, and is constrained by the need for domestic ratification of any agreement negotiated. These domestic factors are, however, linked to international ones. The political calculations of leaders about initiation and ratification depend on the extent of international economic ties that a country possesses. A country's degree of international economic openness importantly affects the policy options available to leaders and the distribution of costs and benefits associated with co-operation.

Furthermore, the costs do not end with successful ratification of the agreements in question. The uncertainty for political leaders continues with the implementation process. John Major's own party, when facing a likely electoral disaster in 1997, remained severely divided on the question of EMU and the single currency. Pitched battles raged in the cabinet and wider parliamentary party, leading to a challenge to Major's leadership in the summer of 1996. As stage three of EMU approaches and, in particular, the date on which EU member countries must qualify for entry approaches (1 January 1998), conflict is far from abating. The Maastricht agreement will figure prominently in the upcoming campaign. Both the French and German political systems are experiencing similar turmoil. The NAFTA implementation process has been somewhat less turbulent, but in the recent campaign which saw the re-election of Bill Clinton, trade issues and 'globalization' continued to dog both main candidates. Environmentalists and trade unionists have not forgotten the claims they made in the ratification debate concerning the harmful effects of NAFTA on US and Canadian labour standards, or on standards of pollution control. It is a safe bet that the politics of global economic interdependence as illustrated in the two cases developed here will continue to raise ongoing controversy.

The chapter proceeds in two steps. First, it presents a domestic politics argument. This argument links the logic of elections to that of co-operation and spells out the conditions necessary for domestic ratification. It emphasizes the role of national political leaders in launching co-operation, and the way international and domestic concerns interact in shaping international negotiations. The second step is to examine the argument as it relates to the two cases. The initiation, negotiation and ratification phase of each will be explored. It should be noted, however, that this chapter does not claim to be a thorough and systematic test of this theory. Given the large number of variables and few cases, it cannot possibly constitute a valid test. But it can provide some initial evidence.

A THEORY OF INTERNATIONAL CO-OPERATION: ELECTORAL AND RATIFICATION POLITICS

This chapter presents an argument about the interaction of domestic and global influences on international co-operation. It draws on arguments from the 'second image reversed literature', two-level games and 'intergovernmentalism' (Gourevitch 1978; Milner 1988; Rogowski 1990; Putnam 1988; Moravcsik 1991, 1993; Frieden 1991). It argues that the existence of national political leaders (executives) who have a preference for such co-operation is a necessary precondition. It spells out why and when political leaders might have such an interest, thereby linking preferences back to international factors. Second, it shows that the structure of domestic preferences – both societal and political – matters crucially. Divided government, where the policy preferences of the legislature and the executive are far apart, is a recipe for failure. Finally, the institutions of ratification matter. In particular, changes in those procedures in the course of an international negotiation can be fatal for co-operation, and the implementation process holds further pitfalls in store. Global, domestic, and regional factors interact continuously in attempts at international co-operation.

The argument here uses a game-theoretic, rational choice model. It assumes that actors are rational and seek to maximize their utility, but that they can only do this contingent on the actions of others. It also assumes that actors, like the executive branch, are unitary. These assumptions are all questionable. Indeed, over the years numerous challenges to the basic assumptions of rational choice theory have arisen (Simon 1955; Tversky and Kahneman 1981). None the less, rational choice theory still seems to have at least heuristic value. It allows one to articulate clearly the microfoundations for individual action and to examine systematically the results of strategic interaction among actors. It is hoped that these advantages outweigh the costs of such assumptions.

The domestic model

International negotiations to conclude regional co-operative agreements and domestic politics are intertwined. In most countries, the executive branch – that is, the prime minister or the president – controls foreign policy. It has the authority to begin negotiations with other countries to reach co-operative agreements and generally controls the international policy agenda. The legislature, however, is likely to have a say in accepting international agreements. In some countries, such as the US, international treaties must be ratified by the legislature. Even where there is no constitutional right to ratify, parliament usually needs to approve any changes in domestic laws and/or the constitution that are a result of these agreements. Votes on these matters will in effect be motions to ratify or reject the international agreement. In some countries, parliament may be bypassed through a popular referendum. In all cases, anticipated reaction will be at work: the prime minister or president and the foreign country will always try to negotiate agreements that the parliament and/or public will ratify. This means that domestic considerations will affect the international negotiations even before they begin, and by implication they will continue after ratification is complete and implementation the main concern.

Parliament's role in this process is often constrained. First, parliaments cannot initiate and conduct international negotiations; they must accept the agenda-setting role of the executive. Second, parliaments are usually constrained in how they can vote on international agreements. They seldom can do more than accept the agreement as made, or reject it. Amending the agreement would force renegotiation at the international level. This is also true for popular referenda. Parliaments may have some capacity to affect or constrain implementing legislation despite the fact that they are limited by the broad outlines of the ratified treaty itself.

In this game, the executive and foreign country negotiate and propose an agreement, anticipating the reaction of the legislature, which in turn disposes. In such a situation, the executive has much power to shape the outcome in favour of its own preferences. The legislature, however, is not without influence. The proposal can be rejected by the legislature, thus forcing a reversion to the status quo or no-agreement point. This reversion point sets the limit on how much of a compromise the legislature is prepared to make. The legislature cannot be pushed to accept an agreement that lies beyond the no-agreement point. If the proposal's utility is less than that obtained from this reversion point, the legislator will rationally reject the proposal. The status quo, or no-agreement point, is thus crucial to the game. Its location critically affects whether co-operation can be achieved.

In this game the role of societal groups, like labour and capital, is not formally modelled. These groups are assumed to affect the internal and external negotiations through the political actors. That is, the preferences of domestic interest groups shape the preferred policies of executives and legislators. Since these political actors are concerned with (re-)election, they must take into account the preferences of important social interest groups. How domestic groups react to international agreements is important for the executive since this may well affect the willingness of legislators who depend on these interest groups for campaign contributions or votes to ratify the agreement. Keeping domestic interest groups happy may be a central goal of the executive in negotiating an international agreement, and this concern will continue all the way through to eventual implementation. Domestic interest groups thus affect this process of executive–legislative bargaining indirectly through the pressures they exert on political actors to take their preferences into account.

A key point of this simple game is that the executive must be willing to initiate negotiations in the first place. The model suggests that the willingness of the executive to initiate depends on her preferences about the agreement, especially relative to those of the foreign country and her own legislature. She must be 'dovish' enough relative to both of these other actors so that some potentially profitable agreement exists.

Preferences of political actors

Why would political leaders ever initiate international negotiations to co-ordinate economic policies? More directly, when will executives have preferences that are 'dovish' relative to both their own legislature and to the foreign country? As argued above, if the executive does not initiate negotiations, no matter what the preferences of other domestic actors, international co-operation will not occur. It is critical then to understand what might induce political leaders to favour co-operation over unilateral policy-making.

There is at least one central reason: if we assume that the political actors making this choice are politicians who must be (re-)elected to office, their reasons can be related to electoral concerns. If politicians want above all else to remain in office and their re-election depends on economic conditions, politicians will worry about the economy. They will be concerned with the prospects for economic growth, employment and inflation. This is a fairly standard set of assumptions, but it says nothing about why co-ordinated, multilateral policy-making should be preferred.

The choice of co-ordinated policy-making depends on the degree of a nation's economic openness. Openness refers to the extent of integration between a country's economy and the world economy. The growth of economic openness for a state means that other countries' policies have greater reverberations on that country's economy. Greater openness means that a country's prices of goods and capital are increasingly constrained to the level of world prices. Only by co-ordinated action with many countries can this constraint be overcome. 'The gains [from co-operation] are supposed to come specifically from taking into account externalities, or "spill-over" effects, that one country's policies have on other countries' economies, which the countries would have no incentive to do in the absence of coordination' (Frankel

1988: 354). Rising openness means greater economic externalities. As these externalities grow, so do the gains from co-operation, and hence so do the incentives for it.

> Differences between countries in the expansiveness of macroeconomic policy spill over into trade balances ... Thus, as international trade becomes more important, countries face larger international payments imbalances as a consequence of divergent macroeconomic policy choices, and each government's interest in international policy coordination to reduce its burden of adjustment increases.
>
> (Webb 1991: 316)

What this means is that a country's level of economic growth, employment and/or inflation may depend critically on the behaviour of other states, rather than just on one's own policies.

If countries' economies are tightly woven together through trade and capital flows, they may not be able to achieve their economic goals without other states' help. If rates of growth, employment, and/or inflation in one state depend on the policies chosen in other states, politicians' re-election hopes are tied to the behaviour of these foreign countries. Getting them to alter their policies to promote the economic outcomes that you desire may require a co-ordinated approach to policy-making. For example, in an interdependent world economy, one country's efforts to increase growth may be unsuccessful without the co-operation of other states. The cases of the US in the late 1970s and France in the early 1980s suggest that this is true, regardless of the exchange rate system in place. Co-ordinated reflationary policies may be political leaders' only choice.

A similar, but slightly different, version of this argument is related to the *prevention effect*. If political leaders in one country believe that another country will adopt policies that are likely to have negative effects on their economy, they may need to block it from doing so. International co-ordination may be a way to prevent externalities or spill-overs from other countries from hurting one's electoral chances at home. The home country may have to give up something in return, but this should be worth the price of binding the other actor. This argument assumes that externalities are important, or are perceived as important, so it is part of the openness argument.

Another aspect of this argument involves the *binding effect*. If domestic groups want politicians to take actions perceived as deleterious for the economy as a whole, politicians may seek to insulate themselves from domestic pressures. International co-operation may be one way for political leaders to commit themselves to not doing something. For example, national leaders may avoid sectoral pressures for trade protectionism by forging international agreements that lock free trade policies into place. Similarly, in the macroeconomic area, 'participation in the ERM [may have] introduced an external discipline and thus reinforced the hand of institutions and interstate groups inside a country fighting for less inflationary policies' (Tsoukalis 1993: 201).

The European case is telling. Levels of trade and capital flows among the West Europeans have increased dramatically since the 1950s. In the mid-1980s trade accounted for an average of 30 per cent of EU GDP, up from 15 per cent in the early 1960s (*European Economy* 1987: Tables 26, 30; Cameron 1993: 37). Intra-EU trade has also grown dramatically for these countries, reaching 60 per cent of their total trade on average by the late 1980s (Tsoukalis 1993: 214–15). The creation of vast Eurocurrency markets since the 1960s and recent capital market liberalization have generated unprecedented levels of capital mobility among the EU countries. This rising openness seems strongly linked to the EC's new resolve after the mid-1980s to complete the single market and to move towards monetary union (Gros and Thygesen 1992; Tsoukalis 1993: 214).

In all cases, political leaders must believe that the benefits from international co-operation outweigh costs. In the face of non-co-operation, the domestic economy would be worse off, and hence their re-election chances would be worse. It is only when the costs of co-operation are expected to be less than the benefits that political leaders will initiate co-operative agreements.

What are the political costs of co-operation? The central cost seems to be the loss of a policy instrument. International co-operation means that political leaders are prevented from manipulating some policy variable that they otherwise could. Co-operation might mean that trade policies like quotas are outlawed or tariffs on goods are 'bound' to low levels, which cannot be changed without new international negotiations. In the macroeconomic area, the policy instrument lost is often exchange rate control. Monetary union, which goes even further, means the loss of one's own money and monetary policy. The costs of the loss of these instruments are both real and symbolic. In the future, a political leader may pay an electoral cost when she cannot improve the economy before an election by changing monetary policy or when she cannot politically appease potential supporters by raising trade barriers. The symbolic cost may entail a loss of 'sovereignty' in the eyes of constituents. These costs may be very high – so high that political leaders would not rationally choose co-operation.

What can this argument tell us about the conditions under which political leaders might be more favourable to initiating co-operation? When will they be 'doves'? Clearly, the argument suggests that higher levels of economic openness should make for more dovish leaders. The greater a country's openness, the more favourable its leaders should be towards international economic co-operation, regardless of their partisan identification or personal ideologies.

The ratification/implementation process

This discussion of political leaders' preferences concentrates only on their electoral considerations. But the decision to start international negotiations also depends on the chances of ratifying an agreement at home. Leaders decide whether and how to negotiate internationally with the ratification process always in mind. They must anticipate the reactions of their legislatures and important societal groups. The executive thus must make two sets of calculations. It must decide whether co-operation could improve its electoral chances by improving the economy, and it must estimate whether and which international agreements will be ratifiable domestically. It is very costly to leaders to negotiate an international agreement only to have it turned down domestically; this may be the worst outcome from an executive's point of view, as the Norwegian prime minister discovered in late 1994. The implementation stage was never in fact reached in that case.

The electoral and ratification/implementation calculations are different because they involve distinct constituencies. Elections for national political leaders involve the entire national electorate. Even in parliamentary systems, where the prime minister is elected by vote of the parliament, the party of the prime minister usually must win enough local constituencies across the nation to obtain the necessary parliamentary support. In coalition governments, and especially in minority coalitions, this support tends to be less broad nationally. For ratification, the relevant groups are different, except in the case of a popular referendum. According to the model, the key to ratification is obtaining the support of both the median legislator and of crucial societal interest groups affected by the negotiations. It is the preferences of these groups that matter for ratification, and hence for the course of the international negotiations.

In particular, the degree of divided government matters. The degree of division in government is a function of how much the preferences of the prime minister or president differ from those of the legislator who will make the deciding vote in the ratification contest, whether the vote represents a simple or supra- (e.g. two-thirds) majority. The challenges to John Major's leadership, intimately related to his understandable unwillingness to repudiate the Maastricht Treaty he after all helped negotiate, is a case in point. In presidential systems, where the executive is elected separately from the parliament, these preferences can differ greatly, as is currently the case in the United States following the re-election of Bill Clinton facing a Republican majority in both houses of Congress. But they need not; the president and the median legislator can come from the same party.

In parliamentary systems the median legislator and the executive can also differ greatly. In a two-party plurality system, like the British one, it may be the case that the prime minister's preferences are very close to those of the median legislator.[2] In a multi-party parliamentary system, however, coalition government is likely, and hence the median legislator and the prime minister may have quite different preferences. Divided government may even be more common in parliamentary systems than in presidential ones. Most parliamentary systems have multi-party systems and coalition government (Budge and Keman 1990: 209). Moreover, minority coalition governments, which most closely resemble divided government in presidential systems, have also been common, accounting for about 37 per cent of all parliamentary governments in the 1945–82 period (Laver and Shepsle 1991: 254; Strom 1990).

In cases of minority or coalition government, the prime minister came from a different party than the median legislator and had to rely on a coalition in parliament to pass legislation, including international agreements. While a vote against the government can have serious consequences for a legislator – which is less likely in presidential systems – ratification votes need not be votes of confidence. In addition, the prime minister in such situations may have to appoint members of other parties to cabinet posts. This can divide government even more since the prime minister may not control these ministries, as it does in a single-party majority government. Negotiations occur both within the executive branch and between parliament and the executive over policy in coalitional systems.

In addition to divided government, the form of the ratification vote matters. Whether ratification takes place through a simple legislative majority, a two-thirds majority or a popular referendum affects which groups will determine the outcome. In a referendum, the legislature will not be involved; hence the median voter will probably be the same as for the national parliamentary elections. Under different institutions, the median voter is different. Hence the calculations of the executive about what type of agreement can be ratified at home will be different. If the executive begins the international negotiations assuming a simple majority vote in the legislature, she will negotiate an agreement that the median legislator will support. A different ratification process logically implies a different agreement. The problem for the executive arises when the institutions of ratification are changed after the fact. That is, if the country decides after the agreement is made that a referendum instead of the parliamentary vote is necessary, the executive has a problem. The agreement negotiated may not be one that the public will support, implying its rejection. Hence opponents of an international agreement should try to change the institutions of ratification after the fact. Any change in the ratification process after an agreement is reached will make ratification and thus international co-operation less likely. The current debate in a number of European countries concerning potential referendums to approve the actual introduction of a single currency (even though Maastricht as a treaty has long been ratified) is a case in point.

A number of predictions about the initiation, negotiation and ratification/ implementation of international economic agreements can be drawn from this domestic politics perspective. First, national political leaders should be the ones initiating international agreements, and they should initiate only under certain conditions. In particular, leaders of highly economically interdependent countries should be more favourable to international co-operation. Leaders of economies that do not depend much on the world economy will be more likely to be 'hawks'. Second, the international negotiations will be affected by domestic politics. The conditions that domestic leaders will accept in the negotiations will depend on what terms they can get ratified at home. The negotiators will always be looking over their shoulder at how the proposed agreement will be accepted domestically. Finally, ratification will be more difficult under two domestic conditions. Highly divided government will be inauspicious for co-operation. Changes in the ratification procedures after agreement is made will also be negatively correlated with successful ratification. If ratification has been shrouded in controversy, then implementation may yet prove difficult.

THE CASES: NAFTA AND THE MAASTRICHT TREATY

Two cases of co-operative agreement are examined in the following section to see whether they lend support to the theory. Each phase of their progress is analysed to evaluate whether the variables discussed here seemed important.

NAFTA

Initiation

In early 1990, Mexico and the US began discussions about a possible free trade area (FTA). The idea for bilateral negotiations between Mexico and the US came from the successful conclusion of the CAFTA agreement in 1988. A Mexican government initiative, such negotiations were proposed to the Bush administration. In September 1990, President Salinas de Gortari officially asked the US to begin negotiations on a bilateral treaty (*Financial Times*, 10 September 1990; Pastor and Wise 1994). The official negotiations, however, could not commence until June 1991, following US congressional approval of their start and the 'fast-track' ratification process that the president wanted. To obtain this, Bush had to agree to add negotiations about labour and environmental issues to NAFTA and to allocate funds for worker retraining, issues which would continue to dog even the implementation process.

As the model above suggests, it was national political leaders – Salinas in particular – who initiated. Also the ratification process on the US side was already interfering with the negotiations, for Bush had to obtain congressional authorization to begin them.

What were the motivations of the leaders for initiating NAFTA? What gains did Salinas (and Mulroney with CAFTA) expect, and why did the US acquiesce? Why were they interested in further opening their markets despite likely political costs? As the initiator, Mexico is of particular interest. For practically the entire twentieth century, Mexico has employed a very protectionist system of import-substituting industrialization (ISI) as its central development strategy to avoid increased economic dependence on the US. The proposed FTA went completely against these long-held principles.

Interestingly, the end of Mexico's protectionism and ISI strategy commenced before the NAFTA negotiations. Unilaterally, the Mexican government began a massive economic reform programme in the early 1980s. After the debt crisis of 1982 and the second oil shock, Mexico in 1983 launched a comprehensive reform programme that eliminated virtually all quotas and reduced its high tariffs to around 10 per cent on average (Schott 1989: 255–60). In the absence of this internal decision to liberalize trade, Mexico would have had no interest in NAFTA. Indeed, NAFTA became the logical next step. As one analyst noted in 1989, considering the rapid pace of Mexico's import liberalization 'it is hard to imagine an immediate movement toward a freer trade regime without some concessions on the part of Mexico's main trading partner' (Schott 1989: 267). Moreover, NAFTA provided a means to lock in the trade liberalization strategy that had been undertaken unilaterally. By joining a FTA, Mexico could not unilaterally change its policies and return to protectionism, at least not without incurring substantial costs. 'NAFTA could help cement the trade reforms already implemented in Mexico by better allowing its policymakers to resist protectionist pressures at home' (Calvijo 1993: 386). This increased the credibility of its policy moves and hence their effectiveness.

Mexico's unilateral trade liberalization policy from 1984 to 1988, which preceded the initiation of NAFTA, was a central catalyst for the free trade agreement. Interest in both stemmed from the same considerations, which fit the model sketched above. Many agree that by 1982 the Mexican economy was in shambles; there was little growth, high inflation, capital flight and very low productivity. These economic problems in turn caused political ones for the ruling party, the PRI. Challenges to their unbroken rule were arising as the economic situation deteriorated. Given this set of conditions, a free trade strategy seemed one of the few ways to revive the economy and to ameliorate the PRI's political problems. By the early 1980s,

> with a low price for oil and with the absence of foreign funds that followed the debt crisis, a more open foreign trade strategy seem[ed] to be one of the few options for attaining a rapid and sustained resumption of economic growth in Mexico.
>
> (Schott 1989: 258)

This option of trade liberalization and NAFTA was favoured in large part because of the extensive openness of Mexico's economy. 'The Mexican economy is too small to support an efficient industrial sector under an autarkic scheme. Some specialization and foreign trade is thus necessary to attain an efficient scale of production in many industries' (Schott 1989: 257). Moreover, an agreement with the US was particularly important since most of Mexico's trade (70 per cent) was with the US; hence, trade liberalization in Mexico meant more trade with its northern neighbour. The point is that NAFTA was initiated by leaders in an interdependent economy facing poor economic conditions. In this situation, freer trade appeared as a primary means to revitalize the economy and political fortunes of the ruling party.

The domestic political and economic consequences of NAFTA played an important role for all three leaders. Salinas saw the pact as promoting his party's interests in Mexico. Bush and his advisers believed that there were economic and political benefits to the programme. The American administration saw NAFTA as 'crucial to a more efficient, competitive and export-oriented economy' (*Wall Street Journal*, 7 August 1992). The administration was counting on it as 'a vote-winner for President Bush' (*New York Times*, 12 August 1992: 1). The prospect of increased growth, competitiveness and jobs motivated political leaders. Domestic politics also shaped the Canadian government's attitudes: 'Like President Bush, Mr Mulroney is expected to use positive features of the trade agreement in his own bid for reelection' (*New York Times*, 13 August 1992: 4).

Negotiation

The official NAFTA negotiations lasted over the fourteen months from June 1991 until August 1992. The actual negotiations, however, began earlier, probably in mid-1990. While the negotiations were intended to create a free trade area with the elimination of all trade barriers between the three countries, the actual result, according to many, was more of a trade agreement with many sectors being exempted or treated specially (Whalley 1993). The central concern of the negotiations were these 'exceptions' from the overall principle of free trade.

A number of so-called 'sensitive' sectors were the focus of attention throughout the entire fourteen months, and some even after the agreement was signed. 'Autos, textiles, agriculture and petrochemicals are the sectors where negotiations seem to have been the most intense' (Whalley 1993: 357–8). For each of these sectors, the problem for the negotiators was domestic politics. In each case, firms or the entire industry strenuously objected to trade liberalization in their sector. Political leaders were often forced to listen to these complaints because they might need the support of these groups to win ratification. The Mexican government faced pressure from its banking, energy and certain agricultural sectors for continued protection, while the US administration was under strong pressure from its auto, textile and apparel, and various agricultural groups to obtain exemptions. These domestic pressures critically shaped the international negotiations. The opposition of domestic sectors and the need for ratification combined to shape the international talks.

In addition, the Bush and then Clinton administrations were forced by Congress to initiate negotiations over issues tangential to the accord. 'In order to gain Congressional approval for fast-track negotiating authority for the talks with Mexico, President Bush submitted an action plan to Congress in May 1991' (Whalley 1993: 375). This plan entailed beginning negotiations with Mexico over issues of environmental and labour standards, which were important for certain groups in the US whose support was necessary for ratification. Since the US government was divided with the Democrats in control of Congress, Bush, as a Republican, needed some of their votes. Appeasing American labour and environmental groups would allow some Democrats to vote for NAFTA. Once more, the international negotiations were heavily influenced in advance by the domestic politics of ratification.

Ratification and Implementation

Many theories of co-operation, including realism and neo-liberal institutionalism, would lead one to overlook the domestic ratification process entirely. Only a domestic politics argument lays emphasis on ratification and its eventual sequel, implementation. Hence, a central issue is whether ratification domestically was important.

In at least two of the three countries, ratification was a crucial issue. For the US and Canada, ratification was not a foregone conclusion. Up to the last minute, no one knew if these two would accept the deals they had negotiated internationally. The negotiations hinged on the anticipated effects of the politics of ratification. In the US, the Bush administration, which depended on Democratic votes, had to devote funds to worker retraining and develop a plan for negotiating environmental and labour issues with Mexico before Congress would authorize the NAFTA negotiations. The Bush administration realized at the conclusion of the talks that 'The hard part comes next. Having thrashed out the path-breaking accord with America's neighbours, the Bush administration now must sell the deal to a Congress and an electorate that seem more concerned with job losses than with liberalized trade' (*Wall Street Journal*, 7 August 1992).

Clinton, once President, took the extreme step of reopening negotiations with Mexico to deal further with these two issues of the environment and labour standards, largely because he needed to appease members of his own party so they would vote for NAFTA. Besides these two side-agreements and the exemptions for sensitive sectors, Clinton was also forced in the end to make several special deals with Mexico to ensure ratification (*New York Times*, 14 November 1993). A large worker retraining package, a development bank, and an environmental commission also had to be negotiated with Congress as a price for obtaining majority support.[3] After all of this, the US finally secured ratification of NAFTA, but the debate on the environment and labour standards has refused to go away. As the accord becomes an apparently permanent feature of the landscape in the US, these questions continue to affect the debate over American trade policy.

Even though US ratification appeared assured, the Canadians endangered the accord. The Mulroney majority government was reduced to a miserable rump in the Canadian general election, and the change of government in late 1993 brought Canadian ratification into doubt. Only after receiving various assurances from the US did the Canadian government pass the accord. The ratification process (sixteen months) took longer than the official negotiation process (fourteen months). While the implementation process has proceeded somewhat unperturbed in an atmosphere of relative economic recovery in Canada, trade issues and the pressures of global economic interdependence are seldom far from the political debate.

Ratification was thus a major issue throughout the negotiations and afterwards. The key concerns for the countries were domestic, not international. Few in any country complained that another country was obtaining better terms than it was; the relative gains concerns which are central to many international level analyses were muted. Rather, the problem was the effect of the accord domestically; the concerns in Canada and the US were that absolute gains were non-existent. 'Much of the focus of public debate, however, has centred on a few broad questions: whether American jobs will be created or destroyed, whether American wages will fall and whether the Federal budget deficit will grow' (*New York Times*, 14 November 1993). This emphasis on domestic concerns, especially those connected with jobs, underlines the linkages among international negotiations, electoral politics and the ratification process. While the other approaches ignore this aspect, the argument here highlights the way ratification and its potential aftershocks affect the entire process.

The Maastricht Treaty and EMU

Initiation[4]

In early 1988, the French government, led by Edouard Balladur as finance minister and Mitterrand as president, presented a report calling for further moves towards monetary integration in Europe, especially creation of a European Central Bank (ECB).[5] This report was favourably received by Germany's foreign minister, Genscher, who also called for an ECB (*Financial Times*, 21 January 1988 and 27 February 1988). The idea was, however, opposed strongly by both Kohl, the Chancellor of West Germany, and Pöhl, the head of the Bundesbank. In June 1988, the twelve EU countries agreed to set up a commission to study the mechanism for moving towards monetary union, headed by Jacques Delors, the President of the European Commission, and submitted its report in April 1989. After further discussions among the countries, official intergovernmental negotiations began in December 1990 over a modified version of the Delors report.

This initiation process, like the one for NAFTA, shows the 'weaker' partner as the prime mover. Germany, which could be seen as a regional hegemon, was divided over this issue. Genscher supported EMU, while Chancellor Kohl, Finance Minister Waigel and Bundesbank president Pöhl were much less enthusiastic, if not overtly opposed. It was largely French pushing aided by Genscher that placed the issue on the EU agenda (*Financial Times*, 21 January and 27 February 1988). Moreover, it was national political leaders who generated initial momentum for the negotiations. Without the firm support of Mitterrand, Balladur and Genscher, EMU probably would have gone nowhere. This is not to diminish the role played by Delors and the EU Commission in moving the idea forward. Monetary union had been agreed upon before within the EU – for example, in the Werner report of 1970. This report lay dormant for almost twenty years, however. National political leaders' interest in monetary union was what brought the issue back to life.

Why did France initiate the EMU process? France's interest in EMU was tied to its domestic political situation and its international economic position. Much like the Mexican case in NAFTA, the impetus for co-operation depended on prior changes in domestic politics. In 1984, the French government announced a major set of policy reforms for the entire financial system, the central one being the elimination of all capital controls by 1990. This decision came in the aftermath of the economic crisis of 1981–3, in which France had imposed draconian capital controls to stem its outward flow in the face of expansionary policy. The failure of those controls and the pressure exerted by industrial and financial interests within France against such controls led to the government's reversal of position (Goodman and Pauly 1993: 73–5). As with Mexico and its move to free trade, the French decision to open its capital markets represented a major policy shift away from its traditional dirigiste direction (Loriaux 1991).

Two points are crucial. Without this unilateral step in 1984, the French would never have initiated EMU in the late 1980s. 'The shift in favour of capital mobility [in France] eventually tied in directly with plans for European Monetary Union, and France became a key promoter of the idea. The freedom of capital movements across member states of the prospective union, indeed, was a prerequisite' (Goodman and Pauly 1993: 75; Tsoukalis 1993: 117–22). This unilateral French financial reform programme was the key event in prompting its interest in reviving EMU. Second, this reform programme had internal roots. It was motivated by concerns among French officials and businessmen about French competitiveness and jobs.

> More subtle and ultimately more decisive pressure [for financial reform] emanated, however, from the boardrooms of large French firms and financial intermediaries. In the French case, direct threats of exit were muted by the fact that virtually all of these firms were owned or controlled by the state. In this environment, such an option was transmuted into rising concerns of government officials regarding the competitiveness of those firms relative to their rivals. Jobs and investment were seen to be leaving France and migrating to less restricted markets.
>
> (Goodman and Pauly 1993: 74)

French policy-makers thus realized the extent of their economy's exposure to the international, and especially the European, economy. This recognition of their interdependence had three consequences. 'In effect, as international financial integration outside France accelerated, French policymakers came to the conclusion that their preference for national monetary autonomy was unrealistic' (Goodman and Pauly 1993: 75). They also recognized that capital controls had become less useful and more costly. Finally, they realized that restrictive financial market regulations reduced the competitiveness of French industrial and financial firms, thus hurting economic growth and job creation. The experience of 1981–4, when the French government was forced to reverse its policies in the wake of huge capital outflows and trade deficits, brought home the extent of its openness. The 1984 programme, begun by the Socialists and continued by both Conservatives and Socialists after, was fuelled by its leaders' growing acceptance of the fact that economic growth and elections now depended on co-operation with its neighbours.

French interest in EMU may also have arisen from its attempt to reduce the externalities imposed by independent German and American policy-making. The initiation of EMU has sometimes been attributed to European frustration with American policy (Tsoukalis 1993: 184). The EMU may have also represented an attempt by French policy-makers to constrain autonomous German policy-making. This would be particularly important for France in the emerging post Cold War climate of the time, wherein Germany would no longer be constrained by the Four Power agreement on Berlin and other features of the provisional settlement which followed the Second World War. Quite apart from this larger context, many have argued that Germany held the dominant role in European economic and especially monetary affairs after the early 1970s (Andrews 1992:13–14; Giavazzi and Giovannini 1989: 63–83). France and some other states saw EMU as an opportunity to alleviate the asymmetric performance of the European monetary system (EMS), which gave Germany a privileged position in Europe (Gros and Thygesen 1992: 325).

> [T]he drive toward EMU came ... from France and other states that wanted a greater say in EU monetary policy-making than they enjoyed in the EMS ... In the late 1980s, French leaders chafed under what they saw as German dominance of the EMS. They proposed monetary union because it would increase the voice of France in the format of EC monetary policy.
>
> (Sandholtz 1993: 27)

In general, it was the deepening of French and other European states' openness in the 1980s and the domestic political repercussions of this that prompted them to search for co-operative ways to realize their internal policy objectives.

Negotiation

The official international negotiations over EMU lasted one year, from December 1990 to December 1991. The unofficial negotiations began in 1988 when the idea was first broached. The negotiations centred around four issues: the timing of union, the preconditions for union, the status and role of the ECB, and the irreversibility of union. A number of northern European creditor countries with good inflation records, led by Germany, preferred a long or unspecified period to effectuate union, with economic convergence prior to union and an independent ECB ruled by a price stability mandate. The other group of mainly Latin debtor countries with poor inflation records, led by France, negotiated for a shorter, more specific timetable for union, that was irreversible and preceded convergence, and a more political ECB controlled by a council of European central bankers. While countries in both groups agreed on the need for union, Britain under Thatcher was the only one which explicitly rejected this idea. For the British government, national, democratic control of its macroeconomic policy remained a key demand throughout. Despite Britain's resistance (which would continue and indeed strengthen in the ratification and implementation stages), the EU signed the Maastricht Treaty in early 1992 after the December summit.

The divisions in the EMU negotiations reflected domestic concerns, in particular worry over ratification. The two countries that seemed most reluctant to move forward were the UK and Germany. For the UK, Thatcher and a bloc of Conservative Party members opposed union on the grounds that it would be an unconstitutional relinquishing of national sovereignty; they were 'hawks' in our terms, and their opposition would initiate a costly and growing split in ruling Conservative Party ranks. Losing national monetary control would make it harder to reach domestic goals, like low inflation, deregulation and strong economic growth. Thatcher's opposition was also attributed to domestic electoral concerns (*Europe*, 26 October 1989). As others have pointed out (Gros and Thygesen 1992: 256–9; Tsoukalis 1993: 214), Britain was less interdependent in both trade and monetary affairs *vis-à-vis* the Community than the other major states, making it easier for it to pursue an autonomous monetary policy. In the negotiations Britain blocked progress on every move and finally negotiated an 'opt out' clause for itself (*The Economist*, 29 October 1988; *Financial Times* 11 December 1991: 2). Despite John Major's evident hope that the opt out would provide a safety valve for opposition to Maastricht from within his own parliamentary, indeed cabinet, ranks, the issue continues to destabilize his government in the run-up to a general election.

In Germany too, the concerns of a dominant domestic player affected the negotiations. The opposition of the Bundesbank, led by Pöhl, changed the negotiations. The German government realized that it needed the Bundesbank's support for EMU to be ratified. The Bundesbank was thus able to set conditions for EMU that the German government had to fight for internationally if it wanted domestic support (*The Economist*, 22 September 1990). The Bundesbank insisted that the ECB replicate its structure: that is, it be politically independent and have price stability as its main goal. In addition, the Bundesbank wanted all central banks to be made independent before the ECB was created. It also demanded that tough convergence conditions be met by all countries prior to proceeding with EMU (*Financial Times*, 7 November 1991), conditions that, ironically, Germany itself is finding it difficult to meet in the implementation process. The French government and others opposed these conditions. In the end, however, since the Bundesbank's endorsement was essential to German support for the agreement, the demands it made were largely met in the treaty.

The real issue in the negotiations was how and when EMU would occur. On these questions, the EU was split into two groups, each of which had different ideas and preferences. There were no technical economic solutions to these issues; indeed, economists disagreed on them. Bargaining among the states was driven in large part by concerns about domestic political consequences.

Ratification and implementation

Most theories of co-operation, including realist and regime approaches, imply that domestic ratification of the treaty should not be an issue. But the agreement nearly came apart as a result of a failure of ratification. The first country to attempt ratification, Denmark, ended up rejecting the treaty. The British had major problems ratifying it, and it took them over a year to do so. The process ended in a nail-biting but ultimately positive vote in the House of Commons. The French public almost rejected the treaty in a referendum after a tortuous battle in parliament against the agreement. The Germans were the last to accept it after a Constitutional Court ruling in November 1993, almost a full two years after the agreement was signed. The ratification process again lasted longer than the official negotiations, and it resulted in significant amendments to the treaty. It seems clear as the prospective introduction of a single currency approaches (the decision must be taken in January 1998) that popular opinion opposes the idea of EMU in most EU countries. The implementation process is proving at least as difficult as ratification.

Domestic politics drove this difficult process. Party competition and divided government played significant roles. With elections on the horizon – or, in fact, to provoke them – the parties competed using the Maastricht Treaty. For instance, in Denmark in 1992, the government was divided. It was a minority conservative–liberal coalition, which had won less than a third of the votes in the December 1990 elections (Cameron 1993; *Financial Times*, 15 October 1992: 3). Two small parties on the left – the Socialist People's Party and the Progress Party – opposed EMU, while leaders in the largest party, the Social Democrats, voiced support. In the end, however, the Social Democratic voters and the supporters of the left parties overwhelmingly rejected the treaty. The minority government was unable to obtain ratification. Only after it had fallen and been replaced by a majority coalition led by the Social Democrats could the public be persuaded to ratify Maastricht. This coalition also attached new conditions to the treaty, including an 'opt out' clause.

In Britain, party competition and divisions in the government also created difficulties for the government. In 1992, the Conservatives, led by John Major, had a majority in parliament. But his party itself was riven by dissension over EMU. A group of about forty Conservatives, led by Margaret Thatcher, opposed the government at every step and shattered its twenty-one seat majority in the House of Commons (*The Economist*, 14 December 1991; *Financial Times*, 4 October 1992: 1). At the Maastricht summit in December 1991, Major negotiated three side clauses to the Maastricht Treaty because of this rebellion within his party; he obtained an exemption from the social charter on workers' rights, a clause preventing more power from being given to the EU, and an opt-out provision, giving parliament the right to vote on the move to monetary union before it was achieved (*The Economist*, 14 December 1991). After the Danish rejection, the Conservative rebels were emboldened and they forced Major to postpone the vote on the process of ratification until the autumn of 1992. At this point, Major was almost forced to call a vote of confidence just to obtain support for discussion of Maastricht. Supported by the opposition Liberal Democrats, the government won a small majority to move ahead with the ratification vote. The Labour and Conservative opponents of EMU also called for a referendum on the treaty, which Major rejected. Without the Liberal Democrats, however, the government would have failed (*Financial Times*, 5 November 1992:1). To get their support, Major promised no vote on the treaty until the Danes had passed it. Hence, the British were unable to ratify Maastricht until mid-1993, and then only after enduring a House of Lords challenge as well (*New York Times*, 21 May 1993). Both internal divisions and party competition delayed and encumbered the ratification process. By early 1997 Major had definitively lost his parliamentary majority and experienced a resounding defeat in the May elections. If Major had won against the odds, it is difficult to see how a Conservative-led government could successfully have pursued a policy of joining the single currency because of party divisions, even assuming an (unlikely) positive result in the referendum both Major and the Labour opposition now promised.

In France, the government also had much difficulty with the ratification process. Because it needed a constitutional amendment to implement Maastricht, the government had to obtain a majority in both houses and a three-fifths majority in a joint sitting of the parliament, but the Socialist government lacked an absolute majority in the National Assembly. To win the support of other parties, the government accepted four amendments to the agreement; the key one was a promise that the parliament would from then on have a greater role in debating EU legislation. In return, the centre-right UDF–UDC party backed the government, causing a split within the right since the Gaullist RPR party opposed it (*Financial Times*, 11 and 14 May 1992). Although the government won a three-fifths majority in parliament in June 1992, it decided that since elections were less than a year away a public referendum might be a good way for the government to gain public support and divide the right. The referendum, however, backfired on the government, as the public used it to register disapproval of the Socialists in general. None the less, in September 1992, the government obtained a tiny majority in favour of the treaty (*Wall Street Journal*, 21 September 1992). The French, who initiated the EMU process, ended up barely supporting it. Divided government and a change in the ratification process almost derailed ratification. Since ratification, opposition has hardly abated. Although the Gaullist party, which won the presidential elections and dominates the parliamentary majority, has accepted the idea of EMU as part of its policy, the process of meeting the convergence criteria imposed an economic squeeze which hardly helped the government's popularity. Serious strikes and opposition to the costs of economic austerity dogged the government at every turn. The game proved far from over when the Gaullist president called snap elections in Spring 1997, which resulted in the defeat of the governing coalition. The new Socialist government of Lionel Jospin has found life in the shadow of EMU little easier.

In Germany, political divisions also caused problems. As in France, the government had to amend the constitution to implement EMU and hence needed a two-thirds majority for the treaty. Because of this requirement, which the opposition parties forced on the government, in addition to its partners in the LDP the government had to obtain support from the SPD and the *Länder*, which also controlled the upper house, the Bundesrat. Kohl was thus forced to include certain amendments to the treaty to garner their support; the central ones were a pledge to give the *Länder* in the Bundesrat greater control over EU legislation and to give the parliament the final word on monetary union (*Financial Times*, 23 April 1992: 22, 8 May 1992: 8, 17 June 1992: 3). Thus Germany added an opt-out clause as well, solely as a consequence of the ratification process. In addition, as noted above, the government needed the support of the Bundesbank and this allowed it to impose important conditions on the treaty during its negotiation (*The Economist*, 22 September 1990). Other parties, who opposed EMU, called for a public referendum, since polls revealed that the public lacked enthusiasm for the treaty. When the government rejected this, these parties launched a Constitutional Court appeal. This further delayed ratification and imposed new conditions on the process. In October 1993, the Court ruled for the government, but forced it to consult more with parliament on future EU issues.

> The end result is that all agree that the Bundestag and the Bundesrat . . . should in the future exercise stronger democratic control over EC decision-making. In the future, German overseeing of Brussels legislation will be similar to that in Britain and Denmark . . . In a considerable tussle with the German government, the two chambers [of parliament] have wrestled constitutional powers to oversee all future Brussels legislation.
>
> (*Financial Times*, 13 October 1993)

The need for political support for ratification once again affected the treaty;

now no irreversible movement to EMU, as agreed in the treaty, would be possible. As with the other countries, controversy has not stopped with ratification; the implementation process continues to ignite ongoing debate, and opposition to the single currency may be firming up. As in the French case, German compliance with the convergence criteria (on which the German government after all insisted) has resulted in a squeeze on government expenditure at a time of rising unemployment, the highest since the 1930s. Whether the cause of these difficulties is the Maastricht criteria or not, Kohl faces direct criticism over his policies from within his own party (*Independent on Sunday*, 9 February 1997: 18).

The domestic politics model presented here highlights the process of ratification and its effects on international negotiations. Growing economic interdependence created incentives for leaders to initiate co-operative agreements. But the electoral concerns of political leaders and party competition also impeded domestic ratification. Divided government forced the leaders to attach new conditions to the EMU treaty in order to obtain ratification. Opponents tried to derail the process by altering the institutions of ratification, as evidenced in France, the UK and Germany. In the end, key elements of the treaty were altered because of these domestic concerns. The irreversibility of monetary union was rejected by Denmark, Britain and Germany; the process was slowed down to accommodate German concerns; and the role and status of the ECB changed to suit Bundesbank demands. Not only did ratification prove difficult politically, but it fundamentally affected the terms of EMU. The controversy has if anything intensified as the point of no return approaches in early 1998. Governments may insist on the irreversibility of the implementation process, but there is much which could yet derail the introduction of the single currency.

CONCLUSION

In this chapter a theory integrating domestic and international elements was proposed to explain the initiation, negotiation and ratification of the two co-operative regional agreements. Hypotheses from the theory were used to explore the NAFTA accord and the Maastricht Treaty on EMU. This conclusion discusses the contributions of the argument proposed.

Domestic politics proved useful in understanding many aspects of the cases. In each, national political leaders of highly interdependent countries initiated the accords. Crucial unilateral domestic decisions, which reflected the pressures of rising openness, preceded the initiation of negotiations. For NAFTA, Mexican trade liberalization was a necessary precondition; for EMU, French and Italian financial market liberalization were prerequisites. These unilateral decisions were made for domestic political reasons. Moreover, once they were undertaken the countries faced great pressure to seek co-operative solutions to their problems, since they no longer retained effective domestic control. Worries about the externalities imposed by unilateral

American or German policy choices motivated Canadian, Mexican and other European political leaders to search for co-operative measures. Heightened international economic openness meant that leaders were pushed to seek joint solutions to their economic problems in order to survive politically. Co-operation was intimately tied to the electoral calculus of political leaders.

The ratification process also cast a shadow over the international negotiations. Leaders knew that they had to find support internally for their agreements. The US had to protect its 'sensitive' sectors and to negotiate stronger environmental and labour standards to get Democratic support for NAFTA. Britain, France and Germany had to obtain the support of key political groups at home. Opt-out clauses and changes in the timing of EMU and role of the ECB were made to win domestic support. The model here focuses attention on the ratification process and the ongoing controversies which accompany the period after ratification is formally complete. It suggests the dual role that political leaders must play, negotiating internally and externally to reach agreement and see it through to implementation. It also links electoral competition, the problems of divided government and international negotiations. Domestic politics thus had important influences on these regional co-operative attempts, as did the globalization of markets in the countries involved.

NOTES

1 I would like to thank David Baldwin, William Coleman, Geoffrey Underhill and all the participants at the ECPR conference in Madrid, April 1994, for their helpful comments and advice.
2 But this need not be so, as the current situation in the British Conservative Party and in other parts of Europe amply demonstrates. The leader may be chosen in a non-representative (or non-democratic) way so that certain elements of the party are over-represented. The prime minister may be an outlier within his or her party.
3 It is interesting to note that had Bush remained president, divided government would have existed in the US; and, according to the argument here, this would have made ratification even more difficult, if not impossible. Bush would have had to obtain the support of many Democrats, who were under much pressure to reject the accord from their primary supporters. Clinton's election may have been necessary for ratification. Ironically, divided government soon intervened in the Clinton presidency as Newt Gingrich and his Republican colleagues overturned years of Democrat control of the Congress in the mid-term elections.
4 The aspect of the Maastricht Treaty with which this chapter is concerned is EMU; its other elements are not the subject of analysis.
5 Some, including Dyson *et al.* (Chapter 9 in this volume), have suggested that the government's interest in EMU which generated this report was propelled by the bad experience of the French government, which was forced to accept devaluation in difficult circumstances in 1987.

REFERENCES

Andrews, D. (1992) 'The structural roots of European monetary convergence', Manuscript, August.

Budge, I. and H. Keman (1990) *Parties and Democracy*, Oxford: Oxford University Press.

Calvijo, F. (1993) 'Discussion', in J. De Melo and A. Panagariya (eds) *New Dimensions in Regional Integration*, Cambridge: Cambridge University Press.

Cameron, D. (1993) 'British exit, German voice, and French loyalty', Manuscript.

Evans, P., H. Jacobsen and R. Putnam (eds) (1993) *Double-Edged Diplomacy*, Berkeley: University of California Press.

Frankel, J. (1988) 'Obstacles to international macroeconomic policy coordination', *Journal of Public Policy* 8: 353–74.

Frieden, J. (1991) 'Invested interests: the politics of national economic policies in a world of global finance', *International Organization* 45: 425–51.

Giavazzi, F. and A. Giovannini (eds) (1989) *Limiting Exchange Rate Flexibility*, Cambridge, Mass.: MIT Press.

Goodman, J. and L. Pauly (1993) 'The obsolescence of capital controls?', *World Politics* 46: 50–82.

Gourevitch, P. (1978) 'The second image reversed', *International Organization* 32: 881–912.

Gros, D. and N. Thygesen (1992) *European Monetary Integration*, New York: St Martin's Press.

Laver, M. and K. Shepsle (1991) 'Divided government', *Governance* 4: 250–69.

Loriaux, M. (1991) *France After Hegemony*, Ithaca, N.Y.: Cornell University Press.

Milner, H. (1988) *Resisting Protectionism*, Princeton: Princeton University Press.

Moravcsik, A. (1991) 'Negotiating the Single European Act', *International Organization* 45:19–56.

—— (1993) 'Preferences and power in the EC', *Journal of Common Market Studies* 31: 473–523.

Pastor M. and C. Wise (1994) 'The origins and sustainability of Mexico's free trade policy', *International Organization* 48: 459–89.

Putnam, R. (1988) 'Diplomacy and domestic politics', *International Organization* 42: 427–60.

Rogowski, R. (1990) *Commerce and Coalitions*, Princeton, N.J.: Princeton University Press.

Sandholtz, W. (1993) 'Choosing union: monetary politics and Maastricht', *International Organization* 47: 1–40.

Schott, J. (1989) *Free Trade Areas and US Trade Policy*, Washington, DC: Institute for International Economics.

Simon, H. (1955) 'A behavioral model of rational choice', *Quarterly Journal of Economics* 69: 99–118.

Strom, K. (1990) *Minority Government and Majority Rule*, New York: Cambridge University Press.

Tsoukalis, L. (1993) *The New European Economy*, (2nd edn), Oxford: Oxford University Press.

Tversky, A. and D. Kahneman (1981) 'The framing of decisions and the psychology of choice', *Science* 211: 453–8.

Webb, M. (1991) 'International economic structures, government interests, and international coordination of macroeconomic adjustment policies', *International Organization* 45: 309–42.

Whalley, J. (1993) 'Regional trade arrangements in North America', in J. De Melo and A. Panagariya (eds) *New Dimensions in Regional Integration*, Cambridge: Cambridge University Press.

2 The international political economy of regionalism
The Asia-Pacific and Europe compared*

Richard Higgott

INTRODUCTION

At a scholarly level, the study of comparative regionalism has been back in fashion for some time now – especially in the USA, where studies of NAFTA and the EU, and NAFTA and Asia-Pacific co-operation have emerged. A closer examination of the Asia-Pacific over the last few years suggests a potentially rich two-way vein of empirical and theoretical insight to be gained from comparison with Europe. Europe's present does not represent the Asia-Pacific's future but, as well as their obvious differences, there are striking parallels that might not seem evident at first but that do emerge via comparative analysis. The geographical, historical, political and cultural contexts are sufficiently different as to ensure different paths towards regional co-operation, but the context of managing regional economic policy co-ordination in an era of globalization is the same for both European and Asian actors.

For the student of international political economy, the comparative analysis of regionalism in the EU and Asia offers a chance to refine our theoretical knowledge in several broad areas of international relations and comparative political economy scholarship. First, at a 'mainstream level', it allows us to refine dominant neo-liberal institutionalist approaches to the understanding of economic co-operation. At a less mainstream level it allows us to see the utility of alternative 'constructivist' applications to the study of regionalism. Particularly, it shows that we must take 'ideas and ideational analysis' seriously. Questions that have not been on the research agenda of economic regionalism for quite a while – questions of identity – are now deemed to be salient.

In comparative analysis, economistic explanations of regionalism – especially of a neo-classical variety – are much more advanced than identity studies. This chapter attempts to redress this imbalance somewhat. Divided into three parts, section one attempts to provide an ideational, as opposed to a material, framework for the analysis of regionalism in an era of globalization. The relationship between ideas and interest still lies at the heart of the contemporary realist–liberal–institutionalist debate about how best to achieve international co-operation and/or policy co-ordination. We need to get beyond this debate. Consequently, section two offers a comparative analysis of the contemporary relationship between ideas and institutional development in Europe and Asia. Section three provides a more ideational analysis of regionalism in the Asia-Pacific than has been common in the literature to date.

IDEAS, IDENTITY AND REGIONALISM IN AN ERA OF GLOBALIZATION

For much of the post-Second World War period the realist assertion of the primacy of *interest* in a system of unconstrained anarchy passed largely unchallenged (see Waltz 1979). However, the last couple of decades, initially influenced by a recognition of the respective analytical importance of the growth of *interdependence* (see Keohane and Nye 1977) and *international society* (see Bull 1977) have seen a challenge to the realist orthodoxy. This challenge, or in some contexts reform (see Goldstein and Keohane 1993), has gained pace in the last decade with the growing recognition of the importance of ideas in the explanation of international co-operation. While a concern with the role of ideas in policy formulation, implementation and co-ordination is not new, the *explanatory importance* of ideas has gained currency with the passing of the Cold War and the loosening of the ideological strait-jacket that structured much post-Second World War foreign policy-making. This is not to suggest that the power of interests can be subsumed to the power of ideas. Rather, it is to suggest that for much of the post-Second World War era, the analytical and prescriptive strength of interests and power, embodied in a realist understanding, has minimized ideas as influential factors in the making of foreign policy.[1]

But we need to understand the impact of ideas on public policy and the manner in which ideas find their way into public policy. Policy is neither formulated nor implemented in the absence of ideas, knowledge and ideology. The difficulty, of course, is validating the causal relationship between a given policy and the ideational factors that inform it. None the less, an analysis of the impact of ideas must inform our understanding of region construction more than in the past. I wish to argue that over the last decade we have seen something of a convergence in the dominant ideas system underwriting policy change in *both* Europe and the Asia-Pacific.

The ideas that form the basis of policy-making on questions of regional co-operation are derived from, or draw their epistemological strength from, a converging form of neo-liberal (capitalist) ideology (Gill 1995). In policy terms in a European context, this is detailed in the development of the Single Market Programme. In an Asia-Pacific context it has led to the development of a policy commitment to *market-led open regionalism*. The source of these ideas, I want to argue, is to be found not simply in the *interests* identified by regional state policy-making elites, but also in the influence of emerging wider regional communities of like minded corporate sector actors, scholars, research brokers and practitioners (both public and private) engaged in the definition of regional identities, problems and putative policy proposals for the resolutions of these problems. For members of the Asia-Pacific policy-making elite, 'open regionalism' is a *normatively* good thing. APEC is a creature of the rise of economic liberalism (Biersteker 1992), and market-led integration is central to open regionalism, giving rise to the beginnings of what two of its protagonists call a 'General Theory of Integration for the Pacific' (Drysdale and Garnaut 1993).

Both substantively and procedurally, the similarities between the processes in Europe and the Asia-Pacific have more in common than the single region focused analyst might assume. From a rationalist perspective, the development of a 'regional' identity as an essential component of value change among the political communities of the member-states is understood to be self-regarding, particularist, and instrumental rather than other-regarding, universalist and cognitive. Thus there is in essence a very firm interest-driven, material basis to the analysis of ideas in explaining enhanced regional understanding across the spectrum, be it from the development of regional policy dialogues in the Asia-Pacific through to the creation of an integrated market in Western Europe.

This emphasis on the primacy of materialist factors in the explanation of integration in general and European integration in particular makes historical sense. But it is also sensible to be circumspect about their ability to be all-embracing in their explanation of the development of contemporary understandings of the processes of enhanced regional co-operation in train at various levels and in various contexts in the Asia-Pacific, and indeed Europe.

The implicit ideas underwriting the wider conception of regional economic co-operation in both Europe and the Asia-Pacific are neo-liberalism and rationalism. These ideas have gained force amongst policy-making elites in the context of the progressive globalization of the world economy. In their different ways and over different time-scales, both the EU and APEC are responses to three aspects of globalization:

1 the replacement of national markets by world markets;
2 the decline of geographical determinants of financial location and the internationalization of the division of labour;
3 the continued strengthening of multinational and private policy-making structures *vis-à-vis* the public authority of the state (Strange 1995).

Increased exposure to the effects of international markets, in both trade and investment, requires not only domestic policy adjustments but also generates an increased desire to address these problems collectively. Consequently, successful implementation of domestic policy adjustment increasingly requires interstate negotiated bargains. It is no coincidence that the more developed states, with accompanying significant intellectual-cum-policy-making communities, have recognized the political expedience of *externalizing* adjustment processes at a bilateral level where possible. This occurs most notably in the US determination to place the onus of change on Japan – but also via enhanced economic co-operation at the regional level, as in the EU since the mid-1980s and increasingly in the Asia-Pacific region in the 1990s. For the Newly Industrializing Economies (NIES) of the Asia-Pacific, this represents a new stage in their international economic understanding. Prior to 1997 they have been ruthlessly successful domestic adjusters, but slower than the USA and European states to recognize the international dimensions of adjustment via collective regional action. This understanding is now changing in the Asia-Pacific.

Within a general neo-liberal context, policy communities in all the major regions of the world are seeing a convergence of thinking about how to respond to globalization. Because globalization weakens the efficacy of national policy instruments, collective action approaches to problem solving with regard to issues demanding trans-national management solutions are probably easier at the regional level. At least, in theory this should be the case given an expectation of at least some shared regional political, economic and socio-cultural understandings. Region level problem solving may seem more politically manageable. Thus there would appear to be a greater consciousness of agency in regionalization than in globalization.

Policy elites have largely accepted 'new institutionalist' explanations as to why it is in the interest of actors to co-operate in regional contexts. In this approach, institutions are seen in the broad sense as organized rules, codes of conduct and structures that make gains from co-operation over time by solving collective action problems despite uncertainties present in mixed motive games. They do so not simply in a formal institutional way, but also by providing a kind of social cement that mitigates self-interest and opportunism (North 1981: 35–7). Interaction within the context of these institutional settings creates a path dependence and vested interest in these settings and arrangements, where priority is attached to process and social learning through iteration.

But this institutional rationalist approach to integration which sees regime building as the efficient response to fixed policy problems – important as it may be – is only part of the story. This theory, which draws primarily on revised neo-classical economic analysis and neo-liberal institutional scholarship in international relations, ignores the ideational dimensions of this process. As such, it misses alternative dynamics of regional co-operation and conflict that are of considerable significance in the closing stages of the twentieth-century. Ideational approaches allow us to see the extent to which regime building is influenced by ideology, beliefs and knowledge, and especially the evolution of consensual knowledge positions among crucial actors.

Knowledge and learning affect the nature of rules and co-operation in international relations. Perception and interpretative practices are also significant in shaping actor preferences. Interests can change as a result of learning, persuasion, knowledge and ideology,[2] a phenomenon that parsimonious rationalist assumptions about utility maximization cannot accommodate. States can still remain the dominant actors under this form of analysis, but the origins of policy are less structurally determined. Thus from a more sociological, constructivist position (see Wendt 1994; Hurrell 1995) national interest is the outcome of a combination of both power and values. Indeed, interests cannot be conceptualized outside the context of the ideas that constitute them. In a regional context, questions of regional awareness and regional identity become important factors.

In both the Asia-Pacific and Europe, the interplay between regional economic integration and identity is under researched, both theoretically and empirically. There are two research agendas of quite an old fashioned kind in political science that can be usefully reinstated and expanded in the comparative study of the international political economy of regionalism. These agendas would examine the interplay between power and purpose and between identity and interest. In such a context, the traditional focus of students of integration – be they realists or liberals – on states is simply insufficient.

In the discussion of the emergence of regionalism, there is often a failure to distinguish between cause and effect. In a European context, the development of inter-subjective understanding among 'region makers' is invariably seen as a *consequence* of the development of more traditional indicators of region (proximity, strengthened economic integration and the development of regional institutions). Some would argue that this is so because issues such as the development of inter-subjective understandings of region are secondary to traditional understandings based on rational utility maximizing understandings of interest, geography and gravity models of intra-regional trade. Even if we were to accept this point, such a position does not explain the new-found interest in enhanced regional dialogue, co-operation and nascent institutionalization in East Asia and the Pacific.

An examination of the activities of the trans-regional policy elites of the Asia-Pacific over the last decade can suggest that we should perhaps question the Eurocentric nature of these prevailing theoretical assumptions. The Asia-Pacific experience provides enough evidence to support posing the question whether the development of a regional 'identity' – or perhaps less contentiously 'a shared understanding of region' – amongst the international policy elites is developing alongside, or even prior to, the consolidation of the economic indicators of region. Indeed, is it not arising even in the absence of some geographical and historical indicators of expected 'regionness'? The question is posed in this way because all prior literature on the study of regional integration would find such a suggestion scarcely credible. It needs testing in the light of the behaviour of regional policy elites especially since the end of the Cold War, not only towards questions of economic co-operation, but also on political issues such as human rights and security.

IDEAS AND INSTITUTIONS IN REGIONALISM IN EUROPE AND ASIA

Do theoretical approaches to the study of regional integration, based on readings of the European experience, offer insight into the processes in the Asia-Pacific? The question posed here is not whether the Asia-Pacific is at the beginning of a process which, over time, will mirror the European experience. European observers invariably start from this question and, as one senior member of the Asia-Pacific policy community opines, see Asian approaches as 'mushy' and 'soft headed' (Sopiee 1994: 16). In so doing, Eurocentric analysis starts from a wrong assumption. Asian approaches to co-operation, rhetorically at least, reject the 'Cartesian' emphasis on legalism, formal agreements, contracts and institutions in favour of an emphasis on confidence building, 'hearts and minds' elite bonding, peer pressure and trust. They argue that the enterprises in the two regions are different. While this is a truism, I do argue that it masks a greater range of similarities – of normative aspirations, causal linkages and processes – in the respective histories of European and Asia-Pacific regionalisms, which can be revealed by comparative analysis.

The European experience

The Single European Act (SEA), the Single Integrated Market (SIM) and the 1991 Maastricht agreement to secure European Monetary Union by 1999 represent points of institutional departure for a comparison with the Asia-Pacific region. The SEA and SIM embody three major characteristics of co-operation currently absent in the Asia-Pacific:

1 the institutional removal of domestic regulations to achieve a common market guaranteeing the free movement of capital, goods, services and labour among member-states;
2 the development of supranational organs as vehicles for decision-making (qualified majority voting) on measures necessary to ensure the functioning of that market;
3 a commitment to develop policies to reduce regional imbalances and enhance socio-economic integration within and between members of the community.

To the extent that these processes have required a pooling of sovereignty, they are both qualitatively and quantitatively years ahead of Asia-Pacific economic co-operation as it has developed to date.[3]

These events of the second half of the 1980s also led to a growing dissatisfaction with traditional neo-functionalist approaches to explaining the evolution of the EU. Reformulations of neo-functionalism and the development of liberal intergovernmental regime analysis (Moravscik 1991, 1993, 1995) stressing the central role of the national state as the key decision-making actor and the mitigator of the integrationist impulse have come to rest centre stage in the theoretical literature in recent years. While they have provided sharper insights into the relationships between states and the wider European Union, they are still very much grounded in an instrumental rationality that treats ideas and ideational factors as secondary (Risse-Kappen 1996). Moravscik sees the European Union as an 'intergovernmental regime designed to manage economic interdependence through negotiated policy co-ordination (1993: 474). It is more efficient, he argues, to use the EU to manage economic policy co-ordination collectively than it is for states to manage it unilaterally. The development of the common market has come about through reciprocal market liberalization.

This analysis is consistent with the mainstream liberal institutionalist understanding of regime formation. Governments formulate policy in part as a response to the preferences and influences of the major actors in their domestic polities (Moravscik 1993: 487). State interests are defined and the bargaining process then runs its course. Of course, Moravcsik's reading of the decision-making processes in the European Community is not without challenge in the analytic community. While it is a robust and parsimonious analytic model, much scholarship (especially reformulated neo-functionalism) and most politicians (especially of the Eurosceptic persuasion) would argue that there has been a shift of control to Brussels in many areas of decision-making and that in any case, states are but one set of actors amongst many in the contemporary European polity. For contemporary neo-functionalists, the motor of the European movement in the late 1980s was an 'elite alliance' between the Commission and business (Sandholtz and Zysman 1989: 96–100).

Both liberal intergovernmental and neo-functionalist analyses of the process by which the EU arrived at its current destination offer useful insights into events in train in the Asia-Pacific in the closing stages of the twentieth-century. Differences notwithstanding, at the basis of economic co-ordination in both regions – and as quaint as it might seem to many post-modern members of the international relations community at the end of the twentieth-century – are states. To say so is not to privilege a traditional state-centric model of international relations. Regional economic co-operation needs to be located within a wider, multi-actor, multi-dimensional, globalized context. Neo-functionalist analysis does that, although governments remain the principal players. To date, although this could change, the development of the European Union has been a consensus-based negotiated process between states. There are a range of historical, strategic and economic factors that have driven and shaped this process, but states remain at its core.

Historical, strategic and political contingency also conditions the nature of economic co-operation in the Asia-Pacific in the contemporary era. As in the EU, institutionalization is formally determined in a system with states as the principal agents of agreement. In this regard, intergovernmental bargaining may be more of a model for APEC than many of the region's advocates of open regionalism might expect on the basis of their reading of the co-operative dialogue in the Asia-Pacific to date. If we resist the more mono-lithic image of government inherent in much state-centric analysis, the devel-opment of Asia-Pacific economic co-operation under the aegis of APEC appears to exhibit the characteristics of intergovernmental bargaining of a neo-liberal institutionalist kind. The importance of intergovernmentalism is that it privileges the state as gate-keeper against supranational legislation. In this sense, given the desire of East Asian states to enhance sovereignty, it may have more explanatory utility in the Asia-Pacific than in the European context.

In the Asia-Pacific context, liberal intergovernmental and neo-functionalist analysis need not be mutually exclusive. Under liberal intergov-ernmentalism, the nature of the bargaining process is determined by the principal players. To date APEC, especially prior to the advent of summitry in 1993, progressed by not threatening the perceived national interests of member elites – especially in those countries lukewarm on the project. But the asymmetries of wealth and power between the USA and Japan and some of the smaller states of the Association of South-East Asian Nations (ASEAN) are such that a range of negotiating alliances are forming as APEC develops. Indeed, the stated aim of the East Asian Economic Council (EAEC) is to offer smaller East Asian members of APEC the opportunity to establish unified positions within APEC. To date, relative gains issues have not been important. This may not always remain the case, especially if the US tries to use the organization as an instrument of extra-regional foreign policy (Nesadurai 1996).

Thus liberal intergovernmentalism offers potential insight into the evolu-tion of economic co-operation in the Asia-Pacific. In contrast to earlier neo-functional approaches, it places less emphasis on the role of supranational actors – of which there are none in the Asia-Pacific region – and more on the role of governments in interstate bargaining. APEC is not an exercise in integration but intergovernmental co-operation. Although concepts such as market-led integration and open regionalism may reject explicit institutional integration, they are replete with functionalist sentiment and flavour – espe-cially notions of market generated 'spill-over'. It is an approach based on the perceived self-evidence of 'comparative advantage'. In many ways, open regionalism approximates a cross between William Wallace's informal and formal processes of integration. Enhanced co-operation in the region is a product of market dynamics and technological change (Wallace 1990: 9). And while there is no *formal* shift of loyalty to a new political community and new jurisdictions, APEC is nevertheless a new stage in regional interaction in the Asia-Pacific.

Neo-functionalism's emphasis on elite alliances in the building of Europe 1992 is also a significant indicator of what is important in region building with parallels for the Asia-Pacific. Although the actors may be different – there is no equivalent strategically significant institution comparable to the Commission in the region – it is quite clear that pressures for enhanced policy co-ordination in the Asia-Pacific are elite-driven (Higgott 1993, 1994a, 1994b). They derive from a tripartite community made up of members from the corporate, research and government worlds.

Nevertheless, neither liberal intergovernmentalism nor neo-functionalism provide sufficient explanatory power for a complete understanding of enhanced co-operation in the Asia-Pacific. Both approaches are interest-driven, rational actor analyses of collective action. They *assume interests exist* rather than explain how interests occur, as was noted in the first section of this chapter. The development of new policy – be it in Europe or the Asia-Pacific – emerges out of the interaction of ideas and interests. The 'Single Market' programme of the 1980s and 1990s represented 'new thinking' in Europe just as much as the development of APEC since the end of the Cold War represents new thinking in the Asia-Pacific.

For some analysts in Europe, the evolution of the Single Market pro-gramme represented new thinking akin to a paradigm shift in the ideas that had underpinned European policy to that time. The initial Social Democratic/Keynesian/interventionist/welfare/statist consensus was under-cut by the growing influence of neo-liberal ideas that stressed the role of market liberalization and harmonization and a greater role for the private sector at the expense of the state sector. These ideas at the state level have found their way to the forefront of the policy process at the regional level (Wallace 1996a: 20–23). Wallace identifies the locus of these changing ideas in the existence of strong trans-regional policy networks and coalitions that developed around the Commission (Wallace 1996b: 57).

In effect, what Wallace would appear to be suggesting, if I read her cor-rectly, is that an epistemic-like community of technocratic and private sector elites that developed the 'initial idea of Europe' has given way to a newer group. This latter community has different normative visions and causal methodologies for how Europe should develop in a era of globalization char-acterized at that time by Eurosclerosis and the need to liberalize to improve competitiveness in the face of enhanced challenges from other regions (see Garrett and Weingast 1993). The Single Market programme and aspirations for a Monetary Union reflect the emergence of other sources of ideas in this period.

Various scholars have identified the European Round Table of Industrial-ists (ERT), and to a lesser extent the Union of Industrial and Employers' Confederations in Europe (UNICE), as being a major source of ideas – especially its *vision* for an open European market – within the European policy community from the second part of the 1980s (see Cowles 1995: 503–14). Moreover, it provided a forum within which the corporate sector, the Commission and the governments of the member-states could meet. Although exhibiting epistemic community-like properties – notably strong and shared normative and causal beliefs – these bodies are more akin to advocacy coalitions (Jenkins-Smith and Sabatier 1994: 178; Sabatier 1988). Although ideas are important to advocacy coalitions, they are accompanied by a more robust desire to influence public policy than the more 'scientific-ally' oriented epistemic communities.

East Asia and the Pacific

In trying to identify the importance of ideas and ideational factors in regional institutional development, three basic questions posed in a Euro-pean context (Rosamond 1996: 5) also assist in the build up of a picture of the emergence of an Asian policy-making space:

1 Can the existence of a series of regional as opposed to state policy prob-lems or challenges be recognized?
2 Are there sufficiently strong policy networks/communities that see the need to articulate policy responses to questions and problems in the context of a regional economic/corporate/political space?
3 Consequent on 1 and 2, does it therefore make sense to think in terms of the development of *regional arrangements*, in addition to existing national, arrangements, to enhance policy-making *vis-à-vis* these problems?

The discussion of the European Union in the previous section provides support in the identification of these three sets of circumstances. As I will try to demonstrate in this section, the recent history of both the *de facto* political economy and *de jure* institutional co-operation in East Asia and the Pacific over the last decade must also lead us (albeit qualified in ways to be outlined later) to answer yes to these questions.

In East Asia and the Pacific, transnational processes that mitigate some of the domestic-international separations that exist within liberal (and realist) explanations of decision-making have been constructed. The emergence of regional policy networks, in conjunction with an intergovernmentalist under-standing of decision-making, offers an analytical window into the possibilities and limits of the construction of collective identity in the region. Liberal intergovernmental bargains would appear to be developing out of the enhanced dialogue, trust and transparency engendered by the activities of the regional policy networks engaged in building institutional co-operation at a rate faster than often is appreciated. The principal characteristics of inter-governmental institutional change encapsulated in APEC are fourfold:

1 It is multi-dimensional, with economics and security as the principal policy domains on one axis, and state and non-state actors as principal partici-pants in these processes on the other.
2 Nascent informal arrangements, of greater or lesser strength, already exist at multiple different regional levels. We need to think of a set of at least four concentric or intersecting understandings of region – (1) South-East Asia (e.g. ASEAN, ASEAN Free Trade Area (AFTA), ASEAN Regional Forum (ARF)); (2) East Asia (eg. the EAEC, the Asia '10'); (3) the Asia-Pacific Level (principally APEC); (4) a number of Natural Economic

Territories (NETs or growth triangles). These different levels of under-standing region are 'contested' (Higgott and Stubbs 1995).

3 While APEC is a consensus based organization lacking any rules of enforcement, institutional development to date is rudimentary but not neg-ligible. From the initial ministerial meeting in Canberra in 1989, for example, APEC has seen the creation of a secretariat in Singapore, numer-ous active work groups and regular senior officials meetings (SOMs) and, since 1993, a regularized process of summitry.

4 Its activities are underwritten by a series of principles and norms distinctly neo-liberal in vein – notably, market-led growth, open regionalism, uni-lateral liberalization and a commitment (at the rhetorical level at least) to remaining WTO consistent (Higgott 1996b).

In short, APEC embodies a *de jure* approach towards co-operation which takes the form, to date, of semi-institutionally sanctioned trade commitments between states to enhance co-operation in a range of areas, and without a common external tariff. Thus, to explain efforts to reduce barriers to the continued development of intra-regional trade we also need to look to other factors. It is the interplay of 'politics' and 'economics' that determines the structure of the regional political economy. State policy elites are not *passive* actors. They have interests and will intervene to enhance regional processes when they serve the interests of their state or will mitigate them if they appear deleterious to state interests – however these interests may be constructed. As a consequence, and at different levels, ASEAN, the EAEC and APEC should be seen as a compromise product of the competing views of different groups of important regional policy actors. These views are encapsulated in Noordin Sopiee's (1994) distinction between Asian and European/Cartesian legalistic/ formalized approaches towards co-operation. At first this was largely a rhet-orical debate over styles and speed, but as APEC's agenda has begun to firm up it has taken a more concrete form.

Since the 1993 Seattle summit there has been an attempt to speed up the development of APEC, especially via the proposals of the Eminent Persons Group, the Bogor Declaration's commitment, rhetorical at least, to full liber-alization by 2020 and the Osaka Action Agenda (APEC 1993 1994, 1995; Yamazawa 1996). But if the aim of APEC has been to share information, enhance transparency, and build trust via regular interaction where it has not previously existed, this is not as unproblematic as it sounds. Most Asian members of APEC resist it becoming a formal negotiating body.

APEC and other regional interstate co-operation bodies such as ASEAN, and its ancillaries such as AFTA and the ARF in the security domain, are *statist* and are used to enhance regime legitimacy. In contrast to the EU, Asian regional organizations are geared to *sovereignty enhancement* not sovereignty pooling. Underpinning Asian and European approaches to the question of regionalism is a different approach to the relationship between sovereignty and territory, with Asian conceptions of sovereignty being much more territorially contingent. Consequently, regionalism becomes a tool for the consolidation of state power.

More generally, APEC is determined not to replicate the institutional structures of the EU (Higgott 1995). Open regionalism – *the progressive liberalization of trade within the Asia-Pacific region via concerted unilateral liberalization, but which is extended to non-APEC members on an MFN basis* – is invariably contrasted with the institutional-cum-discriminatory EU model (Drysdale and Garnaut 1993). But we must be careful not to overdraw the contrast. There is a process of 'enmeshment' taking place that alters the dynamics of interstate relations in the region. It is now apparent that there is a growing desire on the part of a wide range of policy actors in the Asia-Pacific and East Asia to establish a greater sense of regional cohesion. This cohesion will permit the given region (APEC, the EAEC, or ASEAN depending on the level) to have an impact on the conduct of interstate relations within the region and between the region and other international actors in a range of issue areas.

Moreover, the growth of APEC and its ancillary activities represent the culmination of longer processes of gestation in regional economic networking through organizations such as Pacific Trade and Development Conference (PAFTAD), Pacific Basin Economic Council (PBEC) and Pacific Economic Co-operation Council (PECC). Prior to the initial 1989 APEC Ministerial meeting, their early influence over the regional economic agenda setting process was central to the evolution of the co-operative dialogue. Indeed, based on these activities, a discourse of regionalisms has emerged.

The influence of the non-governmental bodies, however, seems to diminish as APEC becomes more politicized. As politicians and bureaucrats see APEC more as a vehicle for political gain rather than simply as a vehicle for the advancement of the normative goals of the epistemic community, then indicative agenda setting via epistemic politics will decline *vis-à-vis* deliberation in the context of intergovernmentalism. Non-governmental (corporate and academic) members of a policy community may be an important source of early ideas, but we should not underestimate the desire of governmental members of the community to resist intrusions into policy-making by non-governmental members.

The increased activity in APEC over the last few years has become more securely the preserve of senior officials than of the early advocates of the co-operative project from within the wider, but non-governmental, reaches of the policy community. In this context, while more senior non-government members of an epistemic community may take on the appearance of a court – ostensibly 'speaking truth to power' – in reality they are more like junior partners in a patron-client relationship. For example, national PECC committees are reliant on, and accountable to, government for much of their financial support and legitimacy. In the last instance it is governments (and especially political leaders in key positions) that negotiate co-operation.

A further difference in the manner in which ideas are insinuated into the policy process between Europe and the Asia-Pacific lies with the role of the European Commission. While APEC has a nascent Secretariat in Singapore, it has yet to develop a negotiating or brokering role. In contrast, if there is anything European that strikes both fear and scorn into the hearts of Asia-Pacific policy-makers, it is the thought of a giant regional bureaucracy like that in Brussels. There is a clear philosophical difference here. There is no place for an institution like the Commission and its role as a source of ideas (Sandholtz and Zysman 1989).

Beyond institutions, the major difference between the two regions is the more-settled understanding of the core of the region in Europe. The vision of a predominant and permanent role for APEC as the voice of the region is an ideas battle that is not as yet decisively won. It is tied closely to the question of the emerging 'identity' of the Asia-Pacific; how that identity is defined and by whom. By contrast, the core of the region is clearly delineated in the EU. The original six are embedded at the heart of its institutional framework. If we ignore Great Britain's two aborted efforts to accede to the Community, then the expansion to nine, twelve and now fifteen members has an orderly air to it. In the Asia-Pacific, the constitution of region remains a contested terrain. More than anything else it has been the desire of the 'non-Asian states' of the region to consolidate links with the 'open market oriented economies' of East Asia that has given APEC its definitional characteristic. But while the US, Japan and China are the major economic players in the region, they are not embedded at the centre of the decision-making process like France and Germany are at the core of the EU.

The contested nature of the region also limits the way in which we might consider APEC as an international actor in comparison with the EU. Notwithstanding public bickering over some issues and inertia over others, the EU exhibits 'actorness', as Hill (1994) would put it. Brussels conducted the Uruguay Round of MTNs on behalf of the members of the then EC. APEC may have demonstrated a developing presence in global economic relations, and East Asia (the Asia 10) may have convened the first formal meeting with European ministers in March 1996, but neither group can be said at this stage to demonstrate conclusively the existence of a collective will or institutional capability for regular, iterated unitary action. A final difference from Europe is the absence of a court of last instance anywhere at the regional level in the Pacific.

IDEAS AND IDENTITY IN THE DEVELOPMENT OF ASIAN REGIONALISM

The constitution of an Asia-Pacific identity is more problematic than that in the European Union. It needs to be understood not only as an evolving rationalistic process but also one that may defy the common rationalist logic that underpins both realist and liberal/institutionalist approaches to co-operation. Both realist and liberal understandings of the regional evolution in the Asia-Pacific are excessively economistic. They assume rational interest maximizing activity on the part of the states of the region. For liberal institutionalists this will, theoretically at least, lead to greater co-operation than for realists. But neither theoretical approach assumes that growing levels of systemic interaction at the regional level may be capable of transforming the nature of state interests, and that this process, in turn, is an essential element of any explanation of greater regional co-operation.

This is an omission within realist and liberal orthodoxies that has both theoretical and practical implications. In the latter parts of the twentieth-century we need to pay more attention to the theoretical impact of systemic interaction on the construction of identity in international relations in general and, in this instance, regional identity in the Asia-Pacific in particular. The question here is to what degree externalized systemic interaction in the form of collective responses to regional problem solving in the Asia-Pacific can be influential in creating new understandings of regional identity. This question represents an attempt to apply Wendt's (1994) important 'constructivist' insights on collective state identity formation to regionalist development in the Asia-Pacific.

It is in this theoretical context that the debates between APEC and EAEC in the Asia-Pacific are so interesting. They represent a range of alternative political-ideational constructs of region which their respective proponents hope will serve particular goals (Higgott and Stubbs 1995). They need to be analyzed not simply as rationalistic responses to a range of ideas and interests, but also as the development at the regional level of 'intersubjective structures' which, according to Wendt (1994: 389) are a set of 'shared understandings, expectations and social knowledge embedded in international institutions and threat complexes, in terms of which states define (some of) their identities and interests'.

Such structures obviously vary as to degree, kind and context. But their identification raises important questions that need to be addressed if we are to better understand the prospects for, and limits on, co-operation and policy co-ordination in the Asia-Pacific region. We need to ask if the material and ideational structures in the Asia-Pacific provide enhanced incentives for collective regional problem solving? Specifically in need of investigation are:

1 The degree to which the dynamic economic density and the more benign security environment that have developed in the last two decades provide a more positive context within which new discursive structures of regional economic and security co-operation might flourish.
2 The degree to which these enhanced economic interactions on the one hand, and a recognition of common security concerns on the other, strengthen the incentives of regional state policy-making elites to identify with one another in the interest of greater collective action and/or policy co-ordination.

These are important questions for policy and are complex to answer. It is not inevitable that states of the region will continue to consolidate collective interests. Indeed, historical experience does not provide us with firm ground on which to base any such claim for greater regional identification. In contrast to both realism's and liberal institutionalism's assertions that identity is endogenously given, a constructivist analysis alerts us to the possibility that systemic regional interaction may transform identity. As such it offers the prospect of explaining enhanced collective action in the Asia-Pacific. Systemic interaction in the Asia-Pacific may in itself be influencing the attitudes of state policy-makers to a series of important regional questions.

To state the position somewhat crudely – and notwithstanding the fact that the notion of Asia (let alone the notion of the Pacific) are clearly Western 'inventions' (see Dirlik 1993 and Leon 1995) – 'Asianness' is becoming a factor in inter-regional relations in particular and in international relations in general. This can be seen in the economic domain in the activities and effects of regional interstate bodies through AFTA, EAEC, APEC and the development of a range of NETS. It is also evident in the political/security domain in the activities of ASEAN and the development of the ARF, and in inter-regional relations via inauguration and development of formal ministerial meetings. These nascent institutional activities are in many ways secondary manifestations of regional activity that are accompanying the more strongly entrenched (and better understood) *de facto* processes of structural economic regionalization (Barnard and Ravenhill 1995).

There are critics of such a point of view – notably security specialists who focus on the seriousness of potential conflicts between the major players in the region on the Korean Peninsula, across the Taiwan straits and in the South China Sea (*pace* Buzan and Segal 1994). But many of the arguments advanced about the prospect of inter-regional conflict miss the point that in a post-Cold War context, the 'regionalization' of these conflicts is becoming one of their strongest characteristics. States may well behave badly, these conflicts may well have global implications, but they are looming consistently larger in regional discourse and taking on 'regional' characteristics.

The development of an 'imagined' or 'invented' understanding of region does not axiomatically imply a harmonious and consensual one. It simply implies that regions can be cognitively identified as much as they can be historically or geographically determined. Now I am not for one moment wishing to suggest that this is a deep process in East Asia at this stage, nor one equivalent to the EU. Moreover, the discussion is quite specifically restricted to those members of the burgeoning policy communities of East Asia and the Pacific – what we might call the 'stakeholders' or beneficiaries of economic globalization.

If the membership of the wider civil societies of the member-states of the European Union are tepid Europeans, then non-elite public opinion in most member-states of East Asia – even amongst the ASEAN states that do have some common historical, ethnic and linguistic commonalities – are even less accustomed to thinking in terms of 'Asianness'. There is still an absence in the region of anything other than an instrumental, or tactical, commitment to enhanced co-operation. As yet there is no collective (cognitive) objective comparable to the 'European Ideal' to which member-states can subscribe to ensure a 'deepening' of co-operation. 'Asianorms' do not have comparable support to 'Euronorms'. Notwithstanding the contemporary problems of the European movement, there exists in the minds of even the most sceptical Europeanists a conception of 'Europe'.[4] At this stage, the notion of Asia or the Asia-Pacific as a focal point for identity exists in the hearts and minds of only a very small number of the most devoted members of that trans-national community of Asia-Pacific scholars and practitioners. For most regional policy-makers APEC is seen in purely instrumental terms.

Such a broader regional identity, however, is not the point. The crucial question is whether there is developing amongst the policy communities, especially in the economic domain, an 'Asian regional approach' to problem solving? In the closing stages of the twentieth-century, the evidence is sufficiently strong to suggest that such a development is in train in the Asia-Pacific. Asian positions in many ways are beginning to mirror the questions dominating the policy agendas in Europe and North America. For example, if the US initially, and Europe secondly, have become concerned with how to contain competitiveness from Asia, then Asians too are coming to see that they need to respond to these issues in a collective rather than a national way. This realization is evident at a number of levels. The development of AFTA is spurred on by a need to enhance its attractiveness as a location for foreign direct investment in face of competition from other regions. Asian states see the need for a collective response to the challenges of US reciproctarianism (Bhagwati 1996), or what I call 'predatory liberalism' (Higgott 1996a). This US approach challenges their view of a beneficial multilateral trading regime (see Higgott 1996b) now that many of the states of the region recognize the need for the multilateral trade regime to continue to liberalize if they are to prosper. But perhaps the major example of a developing 'Asian' position is to be found in the resistance to US and European pressures for the reform of labour standards (and the adoption of more 'Western' positions on human rights in general). These efforts are coming to be viewed as a thinly veiled attack by the Europeans and the US on Asian competitiveness.

The development of 'Asian' positions on certain policy problems is a reactive process. It is the identification of European economic space and policy positions and American economic space and policy positions that is fostering the identification of (differing) Asian understandings of space and policy positions. For realist and liberal institutional sceptics of recent applications of post-modern theory to international relations, here we can actually see a classic illustration of the influence of particular 'discursive strategies' – the 'rhetoric of Europe', or the 'rhetoric of Asia' juxtaposed against the 'other' – on 'real' policy issues and processes. Rosamond (1996: 6) has demonstrated the manner in which the European Commission, via the Cecchini Report, developed a 'distinct discursive strategy ... to place the idea of

Europe as an economic entity on the agenda'. The regional and international diplomacy of Asia and the Pacific at present represents the development of similar discursive strategies by different groups of actors with multi-level regional agendas.

This argument then leads us to ask more searching questions about how interest is defined in an Asian context than can be addressed with the analytical tools of either rationalist-driven realism or even neo-liberal institutionalism (which does at least acknowledge the possibility of contextual influences on agent behaviour). Specifically, a reading of the development of Asian regional identities on various policy issues must lead us to resist the notion prevalent in realist and neo-liberal accounts that interest is formed prior to interaction. If we follow a more constructivist line of argument, then we can see that it is possible for understandings of interest to develop out of processes of interaction. Both interest and identity are emerging out of social and political practice. Indeed, 'Identities are the basis of interests. Actors do not have a portfolio of interests that they carry around independently of social context; instead they define their interests in the process of defining their situations' (Wendt 1992: 398).

For the comparative purposes of this chapter, we learn from Rosamond (1996) that

> the development of a sense of European identity was central to the unravelling of the policy programme which produced the project to complete the Community's internal market and generated spill-overs into the realm of deeper economic and institutional integration. The creation of a sense of European selfhood among key corporate and other non-state actors was ... bound up with the strategic interests of institutional actors such as the European Commission.
>
> (Rosamond 1996: 9)

We are seeing a similar pattern of interaction emerging within the tripartite Asia-Pacific regional policy communities. These consist of the key elite actors from the corporate, governmental/bureaucratic and research communities, which have been identified in the European context.

Clearly, these processes of interaction in Asia have not developed to as deep a level as those in Europe and are still at the instrumental/tactical end of an instrumental – cognitive spectrum of policy learning.[5] The instrumental end of the spectrum is one at which the desire for the institutionalization of social practices and relationships is still resisted. This resistance, however, is often stronger at the rhetorical level. Asian objections to 'Cartesian formalism' notwithstanding, *stronger institutions are playing a stronger role in the region*. The debate over regional economic co-operation in the Asia-Pacific poses a false dichotomy when it contrasts the consensus-based Asian approach and the supposed legal formal approach of the Europeans. It is false because the proposition resists the degree to which Asian states already adhere to institutional instrumental constraints in the practice of their trade policy (norms, principles and rules). These are greater than they either appreciate or are perhaps prepared to acknowledge publicly.

Institutions may be seen as organized rules, codes of conduct and structures that make gains from co-operation possible over time by solving collective action problems. Institutions in this sense are important to Asians as a kind of socio-political cement that mitigates self-interest and opportunism. Interaction within these institutions creates a path dependence and vested interest in these settings and arrangements where priority is attached to process and social learning through iteration (Axelrod and Keohane 1986). There is epistemic evidence in Asia that a cognitive adjustment to the principles of free trade and open regionalism in an era of regional growth is taking place in important quarters of the economic policy community (Higgott 1994a; Harris 1996). This is not a teleological process. Domestic political pressures – rent seeking or ideological – mean governmental responses will often be selective and tactical rather than cognitive and universalist.

The development of Asia-Pacific economic institutional structures is part of the re-ordering process accompanying the end of Cold War bi-polar political structure and the post-Second World War economic structures once underwritten by US hegemony. Institutional arrangements must now expect to be less coherent than in the era of these disciplines. Moreover, institutions can expect to have overlapping competencies in a post-modern, post-Westphalian context. Explaining this re-ordering process is not an exercise in economic theory, as much as one in international political theory. The world economy reflects the combined influences of twentieth-century technology, a nineteenth-century free trade ideology and the re-emergence of a polycentric alternative to the modern state system some call the 'new medievalism'.

We do not have to accept the cartography of Kenichi Ohmae's borderless world (1995) to recognize that we are entering an era of diminished state autonomy and sovereignty. The implications of these theoretical insights for the practice of the global trading system we are only just beginning to imagine. In an increasingly interlinked and globalized world the distinction between domestic and foreign economic policy is losing meaning and the presence of multiple identities, loyalties and conflicting sovereignties is more common. A globalized economy run by overlapping and interconnected networks of state and non-state actors in both public and private domains is mitigating the significance of space and territory. Symbolic understandings of space now exist side by side with geographical understandings of space. Such insights are not mere abstraction. They help unpack the multiple understandings of region currently 'alive' in East Asia and the Pacific.

Yet the (re)creation of an Asian identity is not a second wave of orientalism as seen by Westerners – exemplified by Huntington's (1993) populist attempt to 'create a clash of civilizations', or in more sophisticated and less polemical fashion in the World Bank's (1993) identification of an East Asian Miracle. It is much more an attempt by Asians to create a discernible Asian identity. Numerous prominent figures in the Asian policy community have recently made appeals to 'Asianness'. The significance of this for our understanding of region cannot be underestimated. Regions are not simply economic phenomena, they are cultural and ideational too. Several brief illustrations may serve to support this assertion:

1 Perhaps most notable is Malaysia's 'Look East' policy under Dr Mahathir, which is an attempt to draw on neo-Confucian behaviour patterns from Japan, Korea and Taiwan (Camroux 1994). Indeed, as one influential member of the Malaysian trans-regional policy elite tells us, the Malaysian programme of Looking East is an attempt to 'rediscover the value and the virtue of being Asian' (Sopiee 1994: 48). These influences lay at the core of the Malaysian insistence on the legitimate role for the East Asian Economic Caucus in any regional dialogue – especially in the APEC context (Higgott and Stubbs 1995).
2 Following from his nationalist polemic, *The Japan that Can Say No*, Shintaro Ishihara co-authored a similar work with Dr Mahathir entitled *The Voice of Asia,* but originally entitled *The Asia that Can Say No*. In the conclusion to the work, the point is made that 'As this century draws to a close we [the Japanese] should come home to Asia, our heritage and our future' (Mahathir and Ishihara 1995: 159). Similar culturalist appeals to the theme of an Asian identity are found in the works of other writers such as Anwar Ibrahim (1994), who asserts that 'the Asian renaissance is very much in progress. Although the economic dimension is the most visible aspect of the current revival, it is in fact more holistic than generally supposed.'
3 The Commission for a New Asia's report *Towards a New Asia* (1994: 57–8), while privileging the economic dynamism of the region, asserts the centrality of embedding this economic success within the broader context of Asian cultural values. The Japanese Report to the Commission, in decidedly post-modern vein, comments on how early, orientalist understandings of Asia emanating from the West defined Asia by what it was not rather than by what it was. It was not Europe in the context of the earlier understanding of Eurasia. In the end it remains vague about how to define Asia. But again, accentuating the negative seems to be the first stage. In the context of neo-liberal understandings of the modern, modernization is good in an Asian context. It is Westernization – notwithstanding the imprecision of what we might mean by it – that is being rejected. Efforts are being made throughout the region to harness modernity to indigenous forces.

In a regional context, it is possible to argue that the marriage of modernity with motifs and practices indigenous to the region is leading to the development of a system of regional interstate diplomacy. This system is attempting to provide a collective response to the individual state weakness in the international order that for so much of the early post-colonial period, indeed up to the end of the Cold War, characterized the foreign policy of many of the states of Asia. Indeed, it is possible to argue that 'the region' in Asia (in several of its multiple level definitions) provides a space, other than that of the nation-state, in which multiple loyalties – what Camroux (1996: 18) calls 'pan-nationalism' – might prove functionally useful. I would not, of course, wish to suggest that this process is at anything other than an embryonic stage and impute no teleological properties to it. But it allows for the articulation of policy positions the interest base of which can have a class, national and/or regional interest to them. The existence of multiple loyalties influencing the policy process might not lead to parsimonious political science, but it is surely not a very difficult concept to accept.

What is important about these examples is the 'Asianness' of them. They stand in sharp contrast to the 'Pacificness' of other mobilizing myths that currently permeate a wider region that includes the USA, Canada, Australia and New Zealand. Some see this effort as having an entirely different agenda – that of the incorporation of Asia into a global liberal discourse with the US at its centre. In an anti-colonial vein, the EAEC makes a great deal more sense in terms of shared attitudes and values than does a wider APEC. This point is forcibly made by one scholar-cum-activist, Chandra Muzaffar, who sees APEC as a vehicle for the US and other non-Asian countries of the Pacific to 'hitch a ride' with the more dynamic Asian economies. For him, the economic dynamism of the Asia-Pacific is in reality *Asian* dynamism:

> As a concept, 'Asia-Pacific' makes little sense. Unlike East Asia or South Asia or South-East Asia, it has no shared history or common cultural traits. Asia-Pacific is not even an accepted geographical entity. The US has vast economic ties with Europe but is not part of the European Community which jealously protects its own historical, cultural and political identity. Similarly, Japan is deeply involved in the US economy but it is not part of the North American Free Trade Agreement. It is only in the case of Asia, more specifically East Asia that there is a concerted attempt to suppress its collective identity and thwart its legitimate quest for a common identity.
>
> (Muzaffar 1993: 13)

The new Asian discourse resists the ideological hegemony of the USA within the context of an 'Asia-Pacific' discursive strategy of the USA and its acolytes such as Australia. This is not to suggest that what stands behind Asia-Pacific is incapable of co-existence with the ideas behind Asian thinking. Rather, there are different sets of interests at work with each myth. In some contexts, 'Western' writings are extremely influential with Asian policy elites – especially given that the audiences are limited by the fact that most publications are in English. For example, the works of populist management style 'gurus' such as Kenichi Ohmae (1990 and 1995), and Western interpreters of the Asian miracle such as John Naisbitt (1995) and Jim Rowher (1995), or at a more rigorous level the *East Asian Miracle*, are major vehicles for Asians wishing to imbibe a neo-liberal understanding of the inevitability and benefits of globalization.

This section of the chapter has not tried to rehearse the debate over what constitutes Asian values. Rather, by way of theoretical exposition, and a few examples, it has attempted to suggest that the debate forms part of a wider process in which ideational factors now demand significant attention in any explanation of the regional policy process. An 'Asian' identity is viewed in part as a reaction to the way in which the US treats the region (Mahbubani 1992). But the notion of an Asian identity is an exercise in invention, seen by leaders who advance such notions as a way of stemming the intrusion of Western moral value systems, without rejecting the dynamic aspects of economic-technological modernization. In the Asia-Pacific context this has significance to the extent that outsiders might come to feel increasingly obliged to define their policies towards individual states in regionalist terms.

In short, to the extent that the notion of an 'Asian Way' to diplomacy has any meaning, it is more in how it is received and responded to by actors *exogenous* to the region rather than how it affects the behaviour of actors within the region. This is not a process confined only to Asia. But the effect of the Singapore School arguments, if any, has been to shift the international discourse on a range of issues, such as human rights or economic relations, into a mode more amenable to Asian elite interest. Such socio-political aims may seem 'fuzzy' and difficult to define, but they are no less significant for the fact that they do not lend themselves to easy quantitative analysis. Cognition and ideas are important in the identification of regional communities.

CONCLUSION

The differences between the EU and the Asia-Pacific in both the levels of intent and capability in international economic policy co-ordination are stark. The EU is the most developed and most cohesive example of regional economic co-operation to date. Integration is a highly relevant concept. Indeed, there is a debate over whether a 'European State' is in the making. If we accept the most conservative position on this issue, then the EU is more than a regime but less than a federation and it has governmental features to be found in developed polities (Wallace 1996a: 17). A stronger position (Caporaso 1996: 45) argues that to the degree the EU political structures have policy competence, authority and autonomy from national political institutions, then an effective European state exists. By any judgement, the EU is the most institutionalized regional economic organization in the world.

On the basis of any of these readings, the contrast with any of the nascent exercises in regionalism in the Asia-Pacific is profound. In the Asia-Pacific we may talk tentatively about the beginning of economic co-operation, but some would even restrict this discussion to one of economic dialogue. Moreover, the EC has developed a common market, while APEC has not and has signalled it has no intention of doing so. Time will tell whether it will become a Free Trade Area.

At no regional level in the Asia-Pacific has there been any agreement to relinquish, or in Eurospeak, 'pool', aspects of the sovereignty of individual state economic policy-making procedures. While not unaware of the longer term economic welfare benefits of greater co-operation, regional leaders in Asia regularly demonstrate how they can easily be seduced by the short term political gains to be had from intransigence or non-co-operation at the regional level. Although this practice is no stranger to European politics, state and nation building in Asia, at this stage at least, take much more precedence over the idea of pooling sovereignty in the interests of enhanced policy co-ordination.

Whether the internalization of new regional understandings is in train or not in the Asia-Pacific can really only be determined on a state by state basis. But this is not a stark realist analysis of the prospects for greater co-operation. To the contrary, the evidence presented in this chapter, following Wendt (1992: 395), suggests that there is no 'logic of anarchy apart from the practices that create . . . one structure of identities and interests rather than another'. Future regional economic relations are not structurally predetermined. Notwithstanding regional heterogeneity and the rudimentary nature of the co-operation experience, stronger co-operation can be, indeed is, more than just a theoretical possibility. In periods of dramatic economic change – as in the Asia-Pacific in the 1990s – it is possible that the more optimistic advocates of APEC co-operation might have a point. Within this analytic framework, economistic conceptions of market-led integration and open regionalism have a secondary influence most economists would feel uncomfortable articulating. Exercises in institution building are not just the outcome of rational utility maximizing processes, as important as this theoretical insight may be. They can also, by their very act, be exercises in the internalization of 'new understandings and roles . . . [and] . . . shared commitments to social norms' (Wendt 1992: 417).

The approach that is emerging in the Asia-Pacific is less institutionalized than in Europe. This reflects different levels of development. It also represents a deliberate choice, based on Asian assumptions of greater flexibility in the relationship between the public and private sectors and of the importance of governments interacting with and coming to the help of business than is the case in many parts of Europe. It is a system in some ways alien to a Western cultural preference for arm's-length relationships between government and the corporate world – at least in the formal sense. In part this explains why there is a tendency in Europe to see the public-private interaction in East Asia as a form of cheating when compared to 'Western ways of doing things'. The economic policy-making communities of the Asia-Pacific operate with decidedly blurred lines of membership when compared with those in Europe. This, it was suggested, is explained by the existence of well identified policy networks with a neo-liberal vision of economic co-operation. Neat Weberian patterns of decision-making and opinion-forming are not easily identifiable in the Asia-Pacific. The degree of separation of government, the private sector, and even the academic community, existing in Europe is not so evident in Asia. Policy-making operates differently. The business sector, universities and think tanks, rather than government, supply much of the economic analysis that drives policy.

But it was also suggested that an explanation of enhanced economic co-operation in the Asia-Pacific in the 1990s needed to understand both ideational factors and material interests. This analysis was derived from the combined application of constructivist insights into some of the ideational aspects of policy analysis in the Asia-Pacific and a reading of Moravcsik's analysis of liberal intergovernmentalism in the EU and its relevance for Asia. Liberal intergovernmentalism, with its emphasis on interstate bargaining – and as the evidence of APEC activity since the Bogor Declaration might suggest – may well become more important to the understanding and evolution of the regional economic co-ordination process in the Pacific now that the rudimentary stages of epistemic community driven dialogue are receding.

NOTES

* An earlier, longer version of this paper originally appeared as 'Ideas, Identity and the International Political Economy of Regionalism: Asia and Europe Compared', in *Kokusai Seiji (International Relations* – Special Fortieth Anniversary Issue of the Journal of the Japanese Association of International Relations) 114, March 1997: 14–48. Research for this paper has been conducted with the support of the Economic and Social Research Council of the United Kingdom, Pacific Asia Programme Grant No. L324 25 3020. Special thanks go to Bill Coleman for his excellent editorial work on this version of the paper.

  This paper was finalised prior to the East Asian currency and Stock Market crises of late 1997. These events do not alter, in any fundamental way, the arguments advanced in this paper.
1 Not unusually, the scholarly interest of the international relations community in these, as in many other issues, lags somewhat behind that to be found in the wider social science community. See variously, Kingdon (1984), Hall (1989) and Gamble *et al.* (1989). Indeed, 'the knowledge utilization school' of public policy, with its emphasis on the importance of ideas, has its roots back in the 1970s. For a discussion see the essays in Weiss (1992). I would like to thank Diane Stone for bringing this point to my attention.
2 There is now a large body of literature on questions of learning and knowledge in international co-operation. It cannot be reviewed here. For a flavour see *inter alia*, Haggard and Simmons (1987), Adler and Crawford, (1991), Haas (1992).
3 See the essays in Keohane and Hoffmann (1991).
4 There are of course those, epitomized by Eurosceptics in all the major members of the EU, who think that the process has gone too far in Europe and that it might now be time to roll back some of the deeper aspects of integration. It is not coincidental that some of them – as for example some of the Eurosceptics of the British Conservative Party, with their focus purely on trade issues – see the looser non-institutional relationships developing in the Asia-Pacific as representing a preferable *modus operandi* for regional co-operation.
5 See Breslauer (1991) and Levy (1994) for discussions of cognitive and instrumental learning.

REFERENCES

Adler, E. and Crawford, B. (eds) (1991) *Progress in Post War International Relations*, New York: Columbia University Press.

APEC (1993) *A Vision for APEC: Towards an Asia Pacific Economic Community, Report of the APEC Eminent Persons Group to APEC Ministers*, Singapore: APEC Secretariat.

—— (1994) *Achieving the APEC Vision: Free and Open Trade in the Asia Pacific, Second Report of the Eminent Persons Group*, Singapore: APEC Secretariat.

—— (1995) *Implementing the APEC Vision: Third Report of the Eminent Persons Group*, Singapore: APEC Secretariat.

Axelrod, R. and Keohane, R.O. (1986) 'Achieving Cooperation under Anarchy: Strategies and Institutions', in Kenneth Oye (ed.) *Cooperation Under Anarchy*, Princeton: Princeton University Press.

Barnard, M. and Ravenhill, J. (1995) 'Beyond Product Cycles and Flying Geese: Regionalisation, Hierarchy and Industrialisation in East Asia', *World Politics*, 47 (2): 171–209.

Bhagwati, J.D. (1996) 'The US-Japan Car Dispute', *International Affairs*, 72 (2): 261–79.

Biersteker, T.J. (1992) 'The "Triumph" of Neo-classical economics in the Developing World: Policy Convergence and Bases of Governance in the International Economic Order', in James N. Rosenau and Ernst-Otto Czempiel (eds) *Governance without Government: Order and Change in World Politics*, Cambridge: Cambridge University Press.

Breslauer, G.W. (1991) 'What Have We Learned About Learning?', in G.W. Breslauer and P.W. Tetlock (eds) *Learning in US and Soviet Foreign Policy*, Boulder: Westview.

Bull, H. (1977) *The Anarchical Society*, London: Macmillan.

Buzan, B. and Segal, G. (1994) 'Rethinking East Asian Security', *Survival*, 36 (2): 3–21.

Camroux, D. (1994) *'Looking East'... and Inwards: Domestic Factors in Malaysian Foreign Relations during the Mahathir Era*, Brisbane: Centre for the Study of Australian Asian Relations, Griffith University.

—— (1996) 'Constructing Regional Identity in Asia: Beyond the End of Nationalism', Paris, Mimeo, 1–23.

Caporaso, J. (1996) 'The European Union and Forms of State: Westphalian, Regulatory or Post-Modern?, *Journal of Common Market Studies*, 34 (1): 29–52.

Commission for a New Asia (1994) *Towards a New Asia*, Kuala Lumpur.

Cowles, M.G. (1995) 'Setting the Agenda for the New Europe: The ERT and EC 1992', *Journal of Common Market Studies*, 33 (4): 501–26.

Dirlik, A. (1993) 'Introducing the Pacific', in Arif Dirlik (ed.) *What is in a Rim? Critical Perspectives on the Pacific Region Idea*. Boulder: Westview Press.

Drysdale, P. and Garnaut, R. (1993) 'The Pacific: A General Theory of Economic Integration', in Fred Bergsten and Marcus Nolan (eds) *Pacific Economic Dynamism and the International System*, Washington DC: Institute for International Economics.

Gamble, A. *et al.*, (1989) *Ideas, Interests and Consequences*, London: Institute of Economic Affairs.

Garrett, G. and Weingast, B.R. (1993) 'Ideas, Interests and Institutions: Constructing the European Community's Internal Market', in Judith Goldstein and Robert. O. Keohane, (eds) *Ideas and Foreign Policy : Beliefs, Institutions and Political Change*, Ithaca: Cornell University Press.

Gill, S. (1995) 'Globalisation, Market Civilisation and Disciplinary Neo-liberalism', *Millennium*, 24 (3): 399–424.

Goldstein, J. and Keohane, R.O. (eds) (1993) *Ideas and Foreign Policy: Beliefs, Institutions and Political Change*, Ithaca: Cornell University Press.

Haas, P. (ed.) (1992) 'Knowledge, Power and International Policy Coordination, Special Issue, *International Organization*, 46 (1).

Haggard, S. and Simmons, B. (1987) 'Theories of International Regimes'. *International Organization*, 41 (3): 491–517.

Hall P. (ed.) (1989) *The Political Power of Economic Ideas: Keynesianism Across Nations*, Princeton: Princeton University Press.

Harris, S. (1996) 'The WTO and APEC: What Role for China?', San Diego: IISS Conference, May 12–15.

Higgott, R.A. (1993) 'Asia Pacific Cooperation. Theoretical Opportunities, Political Constraints', *The Pacific Review* 6 (2): 103–17.

—— (1994a) 'Competing Theoretical Approaches to International Co-operation: Implications for the Asia Pacific', in Richard Higgott, Richard Leaver and John Ravenhill (eds) *Pacific Economic Relations in the 1990s: Cooperation or Conflict?*, Boulder: Lynne Reinner.

—— (1994b) 'Ideas Interests and Identity in the Asia Pacific', *The Pacific Review*, 7 (4): 367–80.

—— (1995) 'Economic Cooperation in the Asia Pacific: A Theoretical Comparison with the European Union', *Journal of European Public Policy*, 2 (3): 361–83.

—— (1996a) 'Beyond Embedded Liberalism: Governing the International Trade Regime in an Era of Economic Nationalism', in Philip Gummett (ed.) *Nationalism and Internationalism in Public Policy*, Aldershot: Edward Elgar.

—— (1996b) 'Libre-Échange et Régionalisme Asiatique', in Jean-Luc Domenach and David Camroux (eds) *Vers l'Invention de l'Asie*, Paris: Le Seuil.

Higgott, R.A. and Stubbs, R. (1995) 'Competing Conceptions of Economic Regionalism: APEC versus EAEC in the Asia-Pacific.' *The Review of International Political Economy*, 2(3): 516–35.

Hill, C. (1994) 'The Capability–Expectations Gap: Or Conceptualizing Europe's International Role', in Simon Bulmer and Andrew Scott (eds) *Economic and Political Integration in Europe*, Oxford: Blackwell.

Huntington, S. (1993) 'The Clash of Civilisations', *Foreign Affairs*, 72(3): 22–49.

Hurrell, A. (1995) 'Explaining the Resurgence of Regionalism in World Politics', *Review of International Studies*, 21 (4): 331–58.

Ibrahim, A. (1994) 'Asians Suddenly in the Spotlight, Will now have to do better', *International Herald Tribune*, January 31.

Jenkins-Smith, H.C. and Sabatier, P. (1994) 'Evaluating the Advocacy Coalition Framework', *Journal of Public Policy*, 14 (2): 175–203.

Keohane, R.O. and Hoffmann, S. (1991) 'Institutional Change in Europe in the 1980s', in R.O. Keohane and S. Hoffmann (eds) *The New European Community: Decisionmaking and Institutional Change*, Boulder: Westview.

Keohane, R.O. and Nye, J. (1977) *Power and Interdependence*, Boston: Little Brown.

Kingdon, J. (1984) *Agendas, Alternatives and Public Policy*, (Boston: Little Brown and Co.

Leon, C. (1995) 'Foundations of the American Image of the Pacific', in Rob Wilson and Arif Dirlik (eds) *Asia/Pacific as Space of Cultural Production*, Durham, N.C: Duke University Press.

Levy, J.S. (1994) 'Learning in Foreign Policy: Sweeping a Conceptual Minefield', *International Organization*, 48 (2): 279–312.

Mahathir, M. and Ishihara, S. (1995) *The Voice of Asia*, Tokyo: Kodansha International.

Mahbubani, K. (1992) 'The West and the Rest', *The National Interest*, 28, Summer: 3–12.

Moravscik, A. (1991) 'Negotiating the Single European Act: National Interests and

Conventional Statecraft in the European Community', *International Organization*, 45: 19–56.
—— (1993) 'Preferences and Power in the European Community: A Liberal Intergovernmental Approach', *Journal of Common Market Studies*, 31 (4): 473–524.
—— (1994) *Why the European Community Strengthens the State: Domestic Politics and International Cooperation*, Working Paper No. 52, Centre for European Studies, Harvard University.
——(1995) 'Liberal Intergovernmentalism and Integration: A Rejoinder', *Journal of Common Market Studies*, 33 (4): 611–28.
Muzaffar, Chandra (1993) 'APEC Serves Interests of the US More than Others.' *New Straits Times*, 21 July.
Naisbitt, J. (1995) *Megatrends Asia*, London: Nicholas Brealey.
Nesadurai, Helen (1996) 'APEC: A Tool for US Regional Domination?' *The Pacific Review*, Vol. 9: 31–57.
North, D. (1981) *Structure and Change in Economic History*, New York: Norton.
Ohmae, K. (1990) *The Borderless World*. New York: Fontana.
—— (1995) *The End of the Nation-State: Rise of Regional Economies*, New York: Free Press.
Oye, K. (ed.) (1986) *Co-operation Under Anarchy*, Princeton: Princeton University Press.
Risse-Kappen, T. (1996) 'Exploring the Nature of the Beast: International Relations Theory and Comparative Policy Analysis meet the European Union', *Journal of Common Market Studies*, 34 (1): 53–80.
Rosamond, B. (1996) 'European Regional Identity and International Political Economy of European Integration', Utrecht: Fifth Conference of the International Society for the Study of European Ideas, 19–24 August, mimeo, pp. 1–12.
Rowher, J. (1995) *Asia Rising*, Singapore: Butterworth–Heinemann.
Sabatier, P. (1988) 'An Advocacy Coalition Model of Policy Making and Change and the Role of Policy Oriented Learning Therein', *Policy Sciences*, 1 (2): 129–68.
Sandholtz, W. and Zysman, J. (1989) 'Recasting the European Bargain', *World Politics*, 42 (1): 95–128.
Sopiee, N. (1994) 'An Asian Way for APEC', *The Japan Times*, September 8.
Strange, S. (1995) 'The Defective State' in *What Future for the State: Daedalus*, 124 (2): 55–74.
Wallace, H. (1996a) 'Politics and Policy in the EU', in Helen Wallace and William Wallace (eds) *Policy Making in the European Union*, Oxford: Oxford University Press.
—— (1996b) 'The Institutions of the EU: Experience and Experiments', in Helen Wallace and William Wallace (eds) *Policy Making in the European Union*, Oxford: Oxford University Press.
Wallace, W. (1990) 'Introduction', in William Wallace (ed.) *The Dynamics of European Integration*, London: Pinter/RIIA).
Waltz, K. (1979) *Theory of International Politics*, Waltham, Mass.: Addison–Wesley.
Weiss, C.H. (ed.) (1992) *Organizations for Policy Analysis: Helping Governments Think*, London: Sage Publications.
Wendt, A. (1992) 'Anarchy is What States Make of It', *International Organization*, 46 (2): 395–421.
—— (1994) 'Collective Identity Formation and the International State', *American Political Science Review*, 88 (2): 384–96.
World Bank (1993) *The East Asian Miracle*, New York: Oxford University Press.
Yamazawa, I. (1996) 'The Osaka Action Agenda and Future Prospects of APEC', Mimeo.

3 Asia-Pacific regionalism versus globalization

Competing forms of capitalism[1]

Richard Stubbs

It is only recently that some of the countries within the Asia-Pacific – East and South-East Asia – have begun to think of themselves as forming a coherent region. There is a growing sense that while there are clearly differences among these countries there are also a number of important similarities which have produced an increasingly vigorous 'Asian consciousness and identity' (Funabashi 1993: 75). The notion that there is a shared set of values and attitudes with regard to economic and political issues which may be found within the Asia-Pacific region has variously been referred to as 'neo-Asianism', the 'Pacific Way' and the 'Asian view' (*Nikkei Weekly*, 17 January 1994; Mahbubani 1995: 100–11; Naya and Iboshi 1994). The prime minister of Malaysia, Dr Mahathir Mohamad, was even prompted into proposing the formation of an East Asian Economic Caucus (EAEC) to provide a forum for the governments of East and South-East Asia to discuss regionally significant issues (Low 1991; Higgott and Stubbs 1995: 522–6). And although the EAEC has not been fully developed, there are other signs that on particular issues an East and Southeast Asian grouping of states is emerging (Bowles 1997).

There are three reasons for this growing sense of an Asia-Pacific regionalism. First, foreign direct investment (FDI) and trade have become increasingly regionalized. The wave of Japanese FDI that swept through the region following the Plaza Accord of 1985 and the subsequent revaluation of the yen, when combined with the later wave of Taiwanese, South Korean and Singaporean FDI, have fostered the growth of a large number of production networks throughout the Asia-Pacific that have served to knit the region together (Bernard and Ravenhill 1995: 179–88). Similarly, while the US and, to a lesser extent, Europe remain major markets for goods produced in the Asia-Pacific, intra-regional trade is increasing rapidly (Asia Development Bank 1992: 61–3). Second, the advent of the North American Free Trade Agreement (NAFTA), which set the stage for a North American economic region, and the Single European Act (SEA) and the Maastricht Treaty, which created the Single European Market and European Union (EU), forced the Asia-Pacific region to think of itself as a region in contradistinction to North America and Europe.

Third, and the subject of discussion in this chapter, neo-liberalism associated with globalization and the resulting collapse of time and space in international economic transactions challenge many of the values and practices that are to be found throughout the Asia-Pacific region. As Suzanne Berger has noted, 'For many observing the globalization of international economic exchanges, the issue is not whether convergence of national regulatory regimes and production structures is taking place but only whether it is proceeding rapidly enough' (Berger 1996: 14). The result has been a coming together of Asian governments to try to forestall attempts by proselytizing Western government officials and academics to impose a neo-liberal version of globalization on the Asia-Pacific region.

Each of these three reasons for the development of a sense of Asia-Pacific regionalism underscores the more fundamental point that a distinctive form of capitalism is emerging in the Asia-Pacific which will not only encourage greater regional integration, but also may set the region apart from the other major economic regions of the world. The purpose of this chapter, then, is to set out the characteristics of this particular form of capitalism and to show how it differs not only from the neo-liberal model that has become increasingly associated with globalization, but also from the corporatist, social market form of capitalism to be found in some member-states of the EU.

Although the cultures of the region are in many ways diverse, they also have some common features. Perhaps most significantly they all tend to put a premium on family and community as well as on an acceptance of hierarchy and a respect for authority (Pye 1985). The centralization of power that these values have encouraged has been reinforced by recent history. Over the last half century, the region has been racked by the Second World War, the Korean War, the Vietnam War and the all-embracing Cold War. The need to mobilize resources and unite people in the effort to repel threats from Asian communism has meant that defence of the nation and the security of the general community have been reinforced as crucial ingredients in the thinking of the people of the region (Stubbs 1994: 366–71).

The associated distinctive nature of Asia-Pacific capitalism has been significantly highlighted as various East and Southeast Asian governments have fended off attempts by Western governments, most notably the United States, and international institutions, such as the General Agreement on Tariffs and Trade (GATT) – now the World Trade Organization (WTO) – the World Bank, and Asia-Pacific Economic Co-operation (APEC), to take advantage of the technologically induced globalization process to attempt to impose a Western, neo-liberal version of economic and political practices on members of the Asia-Pacific region. The key features of this Asia-Pacific capitalism can be summarized by looking at three phenomena: social relationships and economic theory, state–business relations, and business practices. This examination shows how this Asian model serves as a basis for regional economic co-operation and how it differs from the more neo-liberal model predominant in North America and supported by the more global of North American and European transnational corporations.

SOCIAL RELATIONS AND ECONOMIC THEORY

In the West, especially in North America and the United Kingdom, neo-liberalism, spurred on in good part by the process of globalization, has become an increasingly influential ideology in political decision-making circles and corporate boardrooms over the last two decades. This ideology emphasizes the maximization of individual economic welfare, the need for markets to operate without undue interference from governments, and the rule of law as the basis for economic transactions. The key, it is argued, is to open up the economy and establish competition across borders. Macro-economic policy should concentrate on setting the appropriate interest and exchange rates for price stability, and should forgo direct concern with collective goals such as full employment. Neo-liberals assume that as these relative prices are set through supply and demand, the market will operate efficiently to allocate resources and promote economic growth. In short, maximizing individual economic welfare under the watch of a minimalist state, it is believed, will benefit the largest number of citizens in the medium to long term.

In contrast, in many of the Asia-Pacific countries, culture and recent history have combined to promote a very different view of economic relations which emphasizes the community and a harmonious social order as well as a results-oriented approach to economic growth. As one analyst has noted 'The Chinese notion of Order positively excluded the [Anglo-American] notion of Law', indeed the 'Chinese world-view depended upon a totally different line of thought' which emphasized that the Chinese were 'all parts in a hierarchy of wholes forming a cosmic pattern, and what they obeyed were the internal dictates of their own nature' (Needham 1956: 582). After quoting this observation Hamilton underscores it by stating that 'Chinese organizational principles rest upon inviolate social relationships; people must obey the "internal dictates" of those relationships' (Hamilton 1991: 53). Consequently, in economic transactions, which are in many ways seen as social transactions, all individuals, their immediate and extended family and the group with which they are involved, are bound to the wider society by an 'expansive web of relations' which compels everyone 'to honour their obligations, remain loyal to their friends, and perform favours when asked' (Semkow 1995: 3).

This emphasis on social obligation rather than legal contracts and written regulations is common to most Asia-Pacific countries. For example, Orrù (1991: 263), quoting Dore (1987: 181–3), notes that 'Japanese relational contracting rests on the goodwill and benevolence of the parties involved'. The point being that it is not simply that 'benevolence is the best policy' but that 'benevolence is a duty', with most Japanese feeling 'more comfortable in high-trust relations of friendly give-and-take in which each side recognizes that he also has some stake in the satisfaction of the other'.

This argument should not be taken too far. The overall point is not that social relations as the basis of economic exchange is unknown in the other two major economic regions – clearly it plays a role in many European countries – or that law-based exchanges are not to be found in the Asia-Pacific region – Singapore obviously belies that notion. Rather it needs to be borne in mind that the prevailing ethos of economic exchanges in the Asia-Pacific is one which emphasizes the group or community and is rooted in social obligation. This emphasis stands in direct contrast to the neo-liberal approach so often associated, especially in the minds of North American economists and officials, with globalization. The general prevalence of this ethos also sets the Asia-Pacific region apart from the two other major economic regions of the world, where such a relational structure tends to be confined to particular regions or to some of the new sectors such as biotechnology.

This point is underscored by the general approach to economic development that has been adopted in most of the countries of the Asia-Pacific region. Rather than operating from theoretical first principles as many North American neo-liberal ideologues propose, the approach adopted in Japan, for example, 'places emphasis on the enhancement of productive capabilities of economic agents and the emergence and development of market relationships brought about through mutual interactions among agents in the process of economic development' (Yanagihara n.d.). In other words, the economic systems approach in Japan works in the opposite direction to Western orthodox economic theory in the sense that it recognizes what produces growth and builds on these aspects of the economy. This approach may mean, as Amsden has pointed out in her exhaustive study of South Korea's experience with late industrialization, deliberately getting 'the prices wrong' in order to stimulate the development of specific industries (Amsden 1989: 139–55).

This results-oriented approach eschews the individualism of neo-liberalism and emphasizes what has been called 'collective capitalism' (Bell 1995: 265–73). It highlights the synergy of business networks; the significance of strengthening industries, such as machine tools suppliers and semiconductor chip manufacturers, which help to build other industrial sectors (Thurow 1992: 146); and the importance of increasing production, 'not in order to consume more but to obtain leverage over other countries and to bolster their own national security and autonomy' (Johnson 1993: 52–3). Moreover, as a number of analysts have noted, the Asia-Pacific countries, especially Japan, are intent on generating 'producer economics' which stresses building up a business over the long term and capturing market share even at the expense of profits. This may be compared with Anglo-American 'individualistic consumer economics' which stresses the importance of consumption and the short-term maximization of profits so as to produce a return for shareholders (Thurow 1992: 117–42; Fallows 1994: 183–6).

The difference between the Anglo-American neo-liberal approach and that followed in Japan has recently become apparent in the debate that has taken place within the World Bank over its structural adjustment policies. The World Bank's uniform insistence on neo-liberal, market friendly policies which entrench competition and seek to get the prices right (World Bank 1991) has been criticized by the Japanese as ignoring the different requirements of developing countries as they move through the various stages of development (*Far Eastern Economic Review*, 12 March 1992: 49; Yanagihara n.d.). Prodded into action by the Japanese and others, the World Bank undertook a large-scale research project on economic development in East Asia. The resulting report (World Bank 1993) 'reflects the Bank's internal conflict' (Amsden 1994: 627) as the politically prescribed conclusion – 'that rapid growth in each economy was primarily due to the application of a set of common, market-friendly economic policies' (World Bank 1993: vi) – was contradicted by the point, also made in the report, that in 'most of these economies, in one form or another, the government intervened to foster development' and that 'these strategies of selective promotions were closely associated with high rates of private investment and, in the fastest growing economies, high rates of productivity growth' (World Bank 1993: 6–7). Hence, as the battle within the World Bank shows, there is an approach to economic development which is clearly associated with Japan and the wider Asia-Pacific region and which is quite distinct from the neo-liberal approach often associated with Anglo-American neo-liberals and their notions of globalization. It is an approach which is more interested in getting results than in adhering to a theoretical framework which Asians view to be of dubious practical value for the region's economies.

STATE-BUSINESS RELATIONS

One of the key ingredients in the Asia-Pacific approach to economic development is selective state intervention to give industrial sectors and even specific companies a comparative advantage in the domestic and international marketplace. This stands in direct contrast with the neo-liberal economic philosophy dominant in the United States and Canada and supported by Thatcherites in the UK where the state is expected to restrict itself to providing the public goods of law and order, economic infrastructure, sound money, a fair market, and national defence (Islam 1994: 95). If the state should intervene, in order to remove distortions in the market or to encourage fair competition for example, it is expected to withdraw as soon as possible so as to let market forces get the prices right. State intervention in order to 'govern the market' (Wade 1990) or to get 'the prices wrong' (Amsden 1989) is anathema to this Anglo-American way of thinking. Hence, the many forms of intervention practised in the Asia-Pacific region – 'targeting and subsidizing credit to selected industries, keeping deposit rates low and maintaining ceilings on borrowing rates to increase profits and retained earnings, protecting domestic import substitutes, subsidizing declining industries, establishing and financially supporting government banks' (World Bank 1993: 5) and so on – clearly set the form of capitalism practised in the Asia-Pacific region apart from the neo-liberalism that many in the US and UK assume should go along with globalization.[2]

The emergence of strong states in East and South-East Asia and their habit of intervening to promote particular industrial sectors and companies has been in good part the result of a unique sequence of events which combined the destructive effects of the Second World War with the formative influences of the United States' attempts to contain the spread of Asian communism. The Second World War, as well as events arising out of the post-war turmoil, undermined the social and political fabric of the old order in many countries of the region. The resulting social vacuum allowed for the rise of strong states with relatively little opposition from groups within society. The actual emergence of the strong states was, however, the product of the combination of the immediate threat of the spread of Asian communism; the massive funds made available by the US, as it sought to bolster its allies on the front line in the Cold War; and the general regional prosperity created by US spending on the Korean and Vietnam wars (Stubbs 1994).

The geopolitics of the region also supplied the incentive for states to intervene in their economies. The more robust the economy, the more resources each state was able to mobilize to defend its territory. The fact that the Cold War lasted from 1949 and the take over of China by the communists until 1989 and the withdrawal of Vietnamese forces from Cambodia in South-East Asia, and the fact that in many ways it still continues in North-East Asia, has meant that the habit of intervention has become well ingrained in the practices of Asian governments. In addition, state intervention in the economy has, of course, been associated with exceptional economic growth rates and is, therefore, unlikely to be abandoned just because Western advocates of neo-liberalism think Asian interventionism to be a theoretically flawed approach to economic development. As one analyst has noted, 'countries with improving living standards are apt to continue current policies rather than looking for new solutions' (Abegglen 1994: 241). Moreover, with the legitimacy of most Asia-Pacific states based on performance rather than on the Western notion of representation, governments in the region are likely to keep following policies which have both brought them rapid economic growth and solidified their political support.

Another significant consequence of the constant concern over security has been the links that the state has developed with the private sector. War and the threat of war have in the past brought government and business closer together and the experience of the Asia-Pacific countries over the last forty-five years is no exception. The private sector grew as states either dispensed US aid or manipulated the benefits from satisfying the burgeoning regional markets created by the Korean and Vietnam wars. Co-operation with the state was, therefore, often viewed as a necessary part of being a successful business in the region. The resulting policy networks that link the state to the business community mean that the autonomy of the state is 'embedded in a concrete set of social ties which bind the state to society and provide the institutional channels for the continual negotiation and renegotiation of goals and policies' (Evans 1992: 164). It is by this means that the state is able to shape the country's economy.

Just as importantly, it means that the clear division between the state on the one hand and the private sector on the other that is found in North America and the UK is not found in most Asia-Pacific economies. The close and harmonious relationship between the state and business has led some analysts to advance the inclusive label of 'Japan Inc.' and 'Korea Inc.' (Amsden 1989: 136; Kaplan 1972) when referring to state–business links and their impact on economic growth. While both Japan Inc. and Korea Inc. have become unbundled in the last decade and there is generally more competition among business networks than these labels might imply, none the less they give a good indication of the close ties between business and government. Similarly, in Malaysia, a Western commercial attaché has noted that, 'you cannot separate the corporate sector from the government sector; they work in partnership' (*Far Eastern Economic Review*, 10 March 1994). All of which serves to underscore the general point that the relationship between the state and business in the Asia-Pacific region is very different from that set out in the neoliberal orthodox economic theory that has been associated with American views of how the globalization process ought to proceed. Again, however, we must not draw this line too heavily because business–government relations in many continental European countries tend to be closer to the Asian model than that found in the US and the UK.

In addition, the close relationship between the state and business that characterizes the Asia-Pacific region excludes labour. In Asia, the traditional links between organized labour and left wing parties allied to the fear of the spread of communism and the perceived need to have a quiescent labour force in order to attract foreign investment led to the subjugation of virtually all labour organizations that were not controlled either by the state or by companies. In many of the countries of the region, the impressive coercive capabilities of the state, the latent communist threat, and the close ties binding the state and business interests led to labour being depoliticized as much as possible (Deyo 1989). Again this position of labour highlights the differences between the organization of Asia-Pacific capitalist states and Europe's social corporatist countries such as Austria, Norway and Sweden where there is a strong tradition of including labour in the development of economic policies (Katzenstein 1985). Overall, the combination of the strong embedded state and the exclusion of labour are characteristics of Asia-Pacific capitalism which are not duplicated in North America and most of the EU states.

BUSINESS PRACTICES

Although each of the countries of East and South-East Asia has developed major companies, Japanese, South Korean and ethnic Chinese businesses have come to dominate the regional economy. In doing so, they have nurtured networks of more local firms in ways not commonly found outside the region. Most importantly, as Japanese FDI has spread to various parts of the Asia-Pacific, so have Japanese business structures and practices come to permeate the region. During the 1970s, Japanese manufacturing companies began investing in South Korea, Taiwan, Hong Kong and Singapore, and in the early 1980s some Japanese manufacturing companies moved into Malaysia and Thailand. Beginning in 1986, however, the structural changes taking place in Japan combined with the rise in the value of the yen in the wake of the 1985 Plaza Accord to force a number of Japanese firms to relocate a significant part of their manufacturing production outside of Japan. Initially, these companies looked to South Korea and Taiwan but as the currencies of these countries also began to appreciate, many companies turned to the ASEAN region. As a result, from 1988 to 1994 Japanese FDI in the ASEAN economies totalled well over US$27 billion (ASEAN–Japan Centre 1995). Most of these investments were in the manufacturing sector, especially in electrical machinery, electrical components, precision machinery, and transportation equipment. The regional investments of Japanese manufacturing companies forced their competitors in the NICs to follow suit in order to establish low-cost export platforms of their own in South-East Asia. As a result, South Korean companies (which for historical reasons are patterned after Japanese companies), as well as ethnic Chinese companies from Taiwan, Hong Kong and Singapore, have also spread throughout the region.

Interestingly, Japanese and ethnic Chinese companies have increasingly developed links in their search for a competitive edge. These ties date back to the period after the Second World War when the Japanese were attempting to re-establish their presence in the Asia-Pacific region. They found that ethnic Chinese businesses provided them with invaluable information about local markets and major Western companies. For their part the ethnic Chinese companies were willing to take a chance on Japanese manufacturers in the hope of gaining on the local and Western competition (McVey 1992: 21; Kunio 1988: 49). By the 1970s the extent of these linkages was such that 'almost all Japanese joint ventures in Singapore and Malaysia were with local Chinese and about 90 percent of Japanese joint ventures in Indonesia and Thailand were made through Chinese middlemen' (Harianto 1993: 19–20). This trend continued in the post-Plaza wave of investment that swept over South-East Asia in the late 1980s and early 1990s.

The links between Japanese and ethnic Chinese companies are not really surprising given the similarity of approaches and practices they exhibit. Perhaps the most important feature of Asia-Pacific economies is the extent to which firms are organized into networks or business groups. Whereas in the North American economy (and to some extent in the European) individual companies are the main players, it is networks of companies that dominate the economy in the Asia-Pacific region. In Japan, networks may be based on ownership, financing, production, exchange or distribution. Most often, it is a combination of these factors, which means that the networks 'overlap and reinforce each other' (Orrù 1991: 245–6). Although ethnic Chinese networks are generally more fluid and are based on family and language links which may cross national boundaries, they are just as vital to the success of ethnic Chinese firms (Abegglen 1994: 204; Redding 1991). The most common pattern in ethnic Chinese business is the extensive networks of subcontracting relationships in a particular industry (Lam and Lee 1992).

Given the common emphasis on networks of firms, it is not surprising that Japanese multinationals and small and medium-sized Chinese family firms have combined to form country-specific and region-wide production networks. These regional networks have been especially effective in allowing for the integration of technology-intensive and labour-intensive production processes. For example, in Malaysia, a feature of the post-Plaza Accord wave of FDI has been the extent to which Japanese companies have become hubs in the establishment of networks, which include local and regional firms, for the manufacture of electronic goods such as videotape recorders. These networks make use of the increasing production in Malaysia of integrated circuits (ICs) and semiconductors. Importantly, this approach 'is in sharp contrast with U.S. multinationals in Malaysia, which do not form networks in spite of the fact that nearly all are producing ICs and semiconductors' (Aoki 1992: 91). This point is reinforced by Chen and Hamilton who note that, 'the network structure of Asian economies and the relative economic power of these networks make the patterns in Asian economies quite different from the patterns of competitive inter-firm relations that exist in Western economies' (Chen and Hamilton 1991: 5).

A further differentiating factor of the Asian model is that both Japanese and ethnic Chinese business networks have sought links to governments and quasi-governmental organizations when it has been in their interests to do so. In Japan, the general role of government in managing the economy has alerted Japanese networks to the benefits of working with governments, and the close links between Japanese firms and governments have been confirmed in Japan's aid programme in the Asia-Pacific region. Similarly, in a very pragmatic way, ethnic Chinese firms have cultivated good relations with governments, and when it has benefited them, 'coexisted and indeed developed a symbiotic relationship with public enterprises' (Clarke and Chan 1992: 207). Certainly, there are numerous instances in South-East Asia of Chinese businesses doing very well out of their links to government (Kunio 1988: 48–50).

Japanese networks tend to contain larger companies and to have had most success in developing heavy industries. In contrast, while there are some large ethnic Chinese conglomerates in South-East Asia, generally ethnic Chinese business networks are made up of small and medium-sized companies that have had most success in light industries. Despite these differences, both Japanese and Chinese networks are predisposed towards similar business philosophies. Chinese businesses are characterized by management's responsiveness to customer and market needs, mutually interlocking owner-ship of firms, and by a willingness to share information and resources among members of a business network (Lam and Lee 1992: 108). Although Japanese firms tend to be more bureaucratized, they echo many of these character-istics. Moreover, as Harianto has noted, among ethnic Chinese businesses the 'strategy of low margin, high-volume tight inventory and cash control, and the reliance on third party financing was manifest everywhere, even before the Japanese multinationals popularized the "market share" and "just-in-time" doctrines' (Harianto 1993: 19–20). Although there are clearly a number of important differences in the way Japanese and ethnic Chinese firms and networks operate, the similarities are striking. Their predisposition to use business networks and to work closely with governments certainly serves to reinforce the argument that Asia-Pacific capitalism is very different from the more neo-liberal form of capitalism often associated with globalization, and most commonly found in North America and the United Kingdom.

CONCLUSION

The emergence of a distinctive form of Asia-Pacific capitalism associated with an increasingly self-confident Asian consciousness has been one of the most important developments in the global political economy over the last decade. The characteristics of Asia-Pacific capitalism, which are the product of a very specific set of cultures and a unique set of historical events, clearly put it on a collision course with the neo-liberal economic orthodoxy which many Western-trained academic economists and a number of Western, espe-cially American, government officials argue goes along with the globalization process. The effects of the recent turmoil in Asian capital markets is as yet uncertain, but the crisis represents another intrusion of global pressures into a region of distinctive economic and political traditions.

Ironically, the forces of globalization can also bring about some levelling of long-standing intra-regional differences. This point is demonstrated by Coleman and Underhill in their examination of financial markets policies. Moreover, while Higgott (Chapter 2) cautions us that the institutionalization of economic co-operation in the Asia-Pacific is lower than in Europe and is likely to take quite a different form, it should be noted that the forces of convergence observed within the EU by Rhodes (Chapter 5), Moses (Chapter 6), and by Dyson, Featherstone and Michalopoulos (Chapter 9), would suggest that as supranational relations are institutionalized, formerly distinct national styles of capitalism become increasingly blurred. The European experience, then, appears to indicate that the embryonic regional capitalism of the Asia-Pacific will become more distinct and recognizable as the region becomes more integrated.

The development of an Asia-Pacific form of capitalism also means that both the NAFTA capitalism of North America and the SEA/Maastricht Treaty capitalism of Europe face competition from a third form of capitalism.

With no government or regional grouping wanting its form of capitalism undermined or another form privileged, it may be that in the future it will be increasingly difficult to reach agreements over the international rules governing economic relations. This problem may bedevil organizations such as the World Trade Organization and the Asia-Pacific Economic Co-operation forum, and even less institutionalized arrangements such as future Asia-European meetings.

NOTES

1 For their comments at various stages in the development of the central theme of this chapter I would like to thank Amitav Acharya, Mitchell Bernard, William Coleman, Michael Donnelly, Paul Evans, Farid Harianto, Eric Helleiner, Richard Higgott, Lou Pauly, Yoshi Kawasaki and Geoffrey Underhill. Although I have benefited from their advice, it needs to be emphasized that they would not necessarily wish to be associated with the argument that is made here.
2 Of course, many of these forms of intervention have been common in some European states, particularly France, where the state traditionally manipulated credit and other instruments in pursuit of an 'industrial strategy' (Zysman 1983; Loriaux 1991).

REFERENCES

Abegglen, J.C. (1994) *Sea Change: Pacific Asia as the New World Industrial Center*, New York: The Free Press.
Amsden, A.H. (1989) *Asia's Next Giant: South Korea and Late Industrialization*, New York: Oxford University Press.
—— (1994) 'Why isn't the whole world experimenting with the East Asian model to develop?: Review of *The East Asian Miracle*', *World Development* 22: 627–33.
Aoki, T. (1992) 'Japanese FDI and the forming of networks in the Asia-Pacific region: experience in Malaysia and its implications', in Shojiro Tokunaga (ed.) *Japan's Foreign Investment and Asian Economic Interdependence: Production, Trade and Financial Systems*, Tokyo: University of Tokyo Press.
ASEAN–Japan Centre (1995) *ASEAN–Japan Statistical Pocketbook*, Tokyo: ASEAN Promotion Centre on Trade, Investment and Tourism.
Asia Development Bank (1992) *Asia Development Outlook 1992*, Manila: Oxford University Press for the Asia Development Bank.
Bell, S. (1995) 'The collective capitalism of Northeast Asia and the limits of orthodox economics', *Australian Journal of Political Science* 30: 264–87.
Berger, S. (1996) 'Introduction', in S. Berger and R. Dore (eds) *National Diversity and Global Capitalism*, Ithaca: Cornell University Press, 1–25.
Bernard, M. and J. Ravenhill (1995) 'Beyond product cycles and flying geese: regionalization, hierarchy, and the industrialization of East Asia', *World Politics* 47: 171–209.
Bowles, P. (1997) 'ASEAN, NAFTA and the "New Regionalism"' *Pacific Affairs* 70: 219–33.
Chen, E. and G.G. Hamilton (1991) 'Introduction: business networks and economic development', in G. Hamilton (ed.) *Business Networks and Economic Development in East and Southeast Asia*, Hong Kong: University of Hong Kong, 3–10.
Clarke, C. and S. Chan (1992), 'Lessons from East Asia', in C. Clark and S. Chan

(eds) *The Evolving Pacific Basin in the Global Economy: Domestic and International Linkages*, Boulder: Lynn Reinner, 203–14.

Deyo, F.C. (1989) *Beneath the Economic Miracle: Labor Subordination in the New Asian Industrialism*, Berkeley: University of California Press.

Dore, R.P. (1987) *Taking Japan Seriously*, Stanford: Stanford University Press.

Evans, P. (1992) 'The state as problem and solution: predation, embedded autonomy, and structural change', in S. Haggard and R.R. Kaufman (eds) *The Politics of Economic Adjustment: International Constraints, Distributive Conflicts and the State*, Princeton: Princeton University Press, 139–81.

Fallows, J. (1994) *Looking at the Sun: The Rise of the New East Asian Economic and Political System*, New York: Pantheon Books.

Funabashi, Y. (1993) 'The Asianization of Asia', *Foreign Affairs* 72 (November/December): 75–85.

Hamilton, G.G. (1991) 'The organizational foundations of Western and Chinese commerce: a historical and comparative analysis', in G.G. Hamilton (ed.) *Business Networks and Economic Development in East and Southeast Asia*, Hong Kong: Centre of Asian Studies, University of Hong Kong, 48–65.

Harianto, F. (1993) *Oriental Capitalism*, Toronto: Centre for International Studies, University of Toronto.

Higgott, R. and R. Stubbs (1995) 'Competing conceptions of economic regionalism: APEC versus EAEC in the Asia Pacific', *Review of International Political Economy* 2: 516– 35.

Islam, I. (1994) 'Between the state and the market: the case of eclectic neoclassical political economy' in A. MacIntyre (ed.) *Business and Government in Industrialising Asia*, Ithaca: Cornell University Press, 91–112.

Johnson, C. (1993) 'Comparative capitalism: the Japanese difference', *California Management Review* 35: 51–67.

Kaplan, E. (1972) *Japan: The Government–Business Relationship*, Washington, DC: US Department of Commerce.

Katzenstein, P. (1985) *Small States in World Markets: Industrial Policy in Europe*, Ithaca: Cornell University Press.

Kunio, Y. (1988) *The Rise of Ersatz Capitalism in Southeast Asia*, Singapore: Oxford University Press.

Lam, D. Kin-Kong and I. Lee (1992) 'Guerrilla capitalism and the limits of statist theory' in C. Clark and S. Chan (eds) *The Evolving Pacific Basin in the Global Economy: Domestic and International Linkages*, Boulder: Lynn Reinner, 107–24.

Loriaux, M. (1991) *France After Hegemony: International Change and Financial Reform*, Ithaca: Cornell University Press.

Low, L. (1991), 'The East Asian economic grouping' *The Pacific Review* 4: 375–82.

McVey, R. (1992) 'The materialization of the Southeast Asian entrepreneur', in R. McVey (ed.) *Southeast Asian Capitalists*, Ithaca: Southeast Asian Program, Cornell University, 7–34.

Mahbubani, K. (1995) 'The Pacific Way', *Foreign Affairs* 74: 100–11.

Naya, S.F. and P.I. Iboshi (1994) 'A post-Uruguay Round agenda for APEC: promoting convergence of the North American and the Asian view' in Yue Chia Siow (ed.) *APEC: Challenges and Opportunities*, Singapore: Institute of Southeast Asian Studies.

Needham, J. (1956) *Science and Civilisation in China*, Vol. 2, Cambridge: Cambridge University Press.

Orrù, M. (1991) 'Practical and theoretical aspects of Japanese business networks', in G.G. Hamilton (ed.) *Business Networks and Economic Development in East and Southeast Asia*, Hong Kong: Centre of Asian Studies, University of Hong Kong, 244–71.

Pye, L.W. (1985) *Asian Power and Politics: The Cultural Dimensions of Authority*, Cambridge, Mass.: The Belknap Press of the Harvard University Press.

Redding, G.S. (1991) 'Weak organizations and strong linkages: managerial ideology and Chinese family business networks', in G.G. Hamilton (ed.) *Business Networks and Economic Development in East and Southeast Asia*, Hong Kong: Centre of Asian Studies, University of Hong Kong, 30–47.

Semkow, B.W. (1995) 'Chinese corporate governance and finance in the ASEAN countries: summary paper', Canada–Southeast Asia Policy Paper, Canada–ASEAN Centre, Singapore.

Stubbs, R. (1994) 'The political economy of the Asia-Pacific region', in R. Stubbs and G.R.D. Underhill (eds) *Political Economy and the Changing Global Order*, London: Macmillan, 366–77.

Thurow, L. (1992) *Head to Head: The Coming Economic Battle Among Japan, Europe, and America*, New York: Warner Books.

Wade, R. (1990) *Governing the Market: Economic Theory and the Role of Government in East Asian Industrialization*, Princeton: Princeton University Press.

World Bank (1991) *World Development Report*, New York: Oxford University Press.

—— (1993) *The East Asian Miracle: Economic Growth and Public Policy*, New York: Oxford University Press.

Yanagihara, T. (n.d.) 'The role of structural adjustment policy and remaining tasks: in search of a new approach to economic development', The 6th Economic Cooperation Symposium [Professor of the Economics Department, Hosei University, Japan].

Zysman, J. (1983) *Governments, Markets, and Growth: Financial Systems and the Politics of Industrial Change*, Ithaca: Cornell University Press.

4 In the whirlwind of globalization and multilateralism

The case of emerging regionalism in Latin America

Diana Tussie

The integration of a growing number of developing countries into world markets, most particularly those Latin American economies for a long time both forgotten and self-excluded, is a clear example of a transformation taking place in the global political economy. The new economic 'openness' across the globe should be seen as the heyday of liberalism, multiplying numbers of countries converting to open markets not by the force of empire but by the attraction of markets. For those influenced by liberal institutionalism, this environment should have been a conducive one for a re-invigorated multilateralism. Openness and multilateralism have traditionally been viewed as part and parcel of the same process. (Ruggie 1993)

If globalization is the precipitous convergence of world markets, increasingly incorporating countries formerly lying in the periphery, it should lead to a deepening and strengthening of multilateral trade relations. Since multilateralism also expresses an impulse and an aspiration to universality (Kahler 1993), globalization should naturally have come as the heyday of multilateralism. Yet multilateralism seems to have lost primacy precisely when more countries have become bound up with global trade relations. Advances in regional integration agreements are today considerably more pronounced than the successes of the multilateral system of the World Trade Organization (WTO). In practice, it may even be the case that globalization and multilateralism are diverging rather than reinforcing each other. It could be argued that, paradoxically, globalization has not accelerated but has actually slowed down the development of the multilateralist trading system over the last decade. An understanding of this paradox lies in the foundations of the multilateralist system, its fundamentals and assumptions, and on the challenges that the widespread adoption of liberal trade policies poses to its imagery.

This chapter is prompted by what I think is a paradox for institutionalist interpretations of international relations: why is the increasing openness and trade liberalization of developing countries not feeding into the accelerated development of the multilateral trade regime? Although the chapter is heavily inspired by the changes unfolding in Latin America, it also strives to attain a greater level of conceptual generality; it will attempt to resolve this paradox by arguing that the dynamics of globalization and multilateralism are not intrinsically related. They do not necessarily go hand in hand. Multilateralism was the province of deliberate decision-making by governments to manage their trade relations. In this sense state-driven multilateralism may or may not deepen economic integration and lead to a thorough-going globalization, which is a phenomenon based on the integration of markets.

One could even argue that multilateralism is a means of controlling and directing global economic integration. The GATT was singularly unsuccessful at integrating Japan, the East Asian NICs, and Latin America into global trade. In this sense the multilateralism as embodied in the GATT was in tension with further globalization, especially when viewed from Latin America. Barriers to trade with the North proliferated, and the accomplishments of even the Uruguay Round were more about imposing US conceptions of trade relations, through anti-dumping, safeguards, investment codes and intellectual property agreements, than about genuine globalization. By far the most dramatic progress in terms of market integration has been the result of the unilateral liberalization of economic policy in Latin America, including the regional process known as Mercosur. The question is, can the multilateral framework of the WTO catch up with this market-led process, or will multilateralism remain in tension with globalization?

The truth is that the multilateral trade regime of the post-war period, centred on the GATT, was born of American dominance. As an institution, the GATT developed as an extension of American, and over time transatlantic, rules of the game. As a framework created in the image of the US economy, it sought almost exclusively to cover barriers to trade at the border. It never sought to deal with internal impediments – institutions and practices – to free competition. It assumed a US model of domestic political economy, and when this was not the case the imperatives of the Cold War allowed impediments to co-exist in contradiction to the aspirations of multilateralism. In reality this situation undermined the sense of universality in the multilateral game. A renewed multilateralism will have to reflect the more dispersed configuration of power in global trade relations which follows from the end of the Cold War and the rapid development of Asia and Latin America.

The new regionalism in Latin America and elsewhere in the global economy may carry with it the solution to a reinvigorated and updated multilateralism. These regional arrangements are not associated with the aspirations of US-led multilateralism. The new regional deals are 'bottom up' integration processes based on the attraction of markets, not 'top down' government decisions. They are serving to integrate North and South in ways GATT never did, providing Latin America with the access to markets which the WTO was never built to guarantee. The new regionalism may yet hold the key to a multilateralism which will remain viable in the post-hegemonic era.

In this context the chapter will begin by highlighting the most important features of globalization. From there it will go on to clarify and to discuss some of the implications that follow from the unfolding of globalization. It will illustrate what challenges globalization poses for multilateral trading relations designed under the American post-war vision, and why as globalization advances it poses a source of tension to multilateralism as we know it; why globalization and multilateralism are not in fact converging. Path dependence (the notion that the logic of today can only be understood by tracing its development through time) plays a crucial role throughout the discussion. In the last section all the arguments are brought together for a general discussion of prospects.

THE PROCESS OF GLOBALIZATION

Certain conceptual boundaries need to be drawn to guide our interpretation and analysis. The concept of globalization does not refer merely to the fact that capitalism is now a world system. It involves more precisely a quantum leap in the transnationalization of production, distribution, and marketing of goods and services, and of financial flows. The organizational break-through that has made globalization possible is the ability to disperse economic activity geographically and bring it together electronically and vice versa.

The first outstanding feature of present globalization is the free and very rapid flow of tangible and intangible forms of capital – the most important link across national boundaries today. Foreign direct investment flows have increased almost fourfold since 1985 to their present $260 bn. To put this into perspective, these flows have grown twice as fast as world trade. Capital flows have a new magnitude and a new dynamism.

A second feature of globalization is that more countries than before are being integrated into the network of capital flows. The turning point is marked by the ebb and flow of capital to developing countries. Today 45 per cent of foreign investment flows goes to developing countries, as compared to one-fourth in the 1960s, the 'glorious' age of the post-war era. The explosive growth in capital flows has made governments in Latin America at large more responsive to international markets; they have made sweeping policy changes and become important magnets for the attraction of foreign direct investment. An economic policy revolution has taken place in all previously inward-oriented countries with the exception of Cuba – and even Cuba has begun a partial transformation.

Globalization has brought about particular growth dynamics. This new growth dynamic is the third feature of globalization, a feature that is in a way an extension of the preceding two. The flood of investments into peripheral areas of the world has led them to grow at rates above world averages. Between 1989 and 1996 Latin America, and also Eastern Europe and East Asia, grew quite vigorously despite the sluggish 2.5 per cent average annual growth in developed countries – an average which is forecast to remain at that mark for some time. In other words, to a large extent the rate of growth in these peripheral areas is decoupling from growth in the central economies. Engines of growth have multiplied. World economic relations have become relatively more decentralized.

Globalization has worked to overcome economic barriers but it does not overcome all. Global trade in goods has not followed the pace of capital mobility. Two indicators support this observation. First are the somewhat disappointing and rather erratic rates in the growth of global trade. True, over the last decade world trade has grown more rapidly than in the preceding decade from 1974 to 1984. But, despite the economic policy revolution in the communist and developing economies in the late 1980s, global trade in the 1990s has not returned to the steady annual 8 to 9 per cent of the 1960s. The second and third worlds by themselves do not muster enough weight to push global aggregates, even if their overall trade has been growing above average.

Another face of this divorce between globalization and trade in goods lies in the present sluggish pace of trade liberalization in developed countries. Trade liberalization among developed countries seems to have crested after the Tokyo Round. Between the end of the 1940s and the early 1980s average OECD tariff levels were reduced from 40 per cent to 5 per cent – they fell to barely one-eighth of their initial level. In contrast, since the mid-1980s barriers of various kinds have proliferated. Market access became increasingly unpredictable. The Uruguay Round, despite being proclaimed as a major accomplishment, has not yet improved market access to developed countries significantly. This is despite considerable promise in the services sector, but this is primarily of interest to developed countries anyway. The most important barrier-lowering process in the Uruguay Round was the one undertaken unilaterally by developing countries and bound in the GATT.[1] Such a move to free trade has led to an increase in exports as well as imports in developing countries. The move has not only increased trade with developed countries but also and very importantly among developing countries (Krugman 1995). Increasingly, they are becoming mutually important markets.

Together these characteristics mark an important trait of globalization: economic integration has slowed down among developed countries but, in contrast, it is accelerating in developing countries. This is the most striking feature of globalization. North–South and South–South links are developing relatively more vigorously than North–North links. Although these North–North links naturally still remain the core of world economic relations, there is an acceleration of transactions between North and South and within the South.

Viewed from Latin America, the globalization of markets has come with severe domestic costs of adjustment but the new international links being forged appear to be, if not fully auspicious, at least more permissive. And when it comes to development, as Peter Evans has pinpointed, 'transformation is inescapably defined in global terms' (1995: 6). Change hinges on the international division of labour.

Why is it that globalization has not provided revived impetus to multilateral trade liberalization? Why is it that globalization has emerged in a manner that seems to be estranged from multilateralism? Part of the explanation lies in definitions. Although both concepts express an impulse towards universality, globalization has to do with markets whereas multilateralism requires government purposiveness. Globalization, for better or for worse, is not necessarily a voluntaristic phenomenon; multilateralism in contrast is related to deliberate policy choices. Governments, both individually and collectively, provide the signals to underwrite the extent, speed and direction of the globalization process. Yet these signals do not appear to translate into negotiated changes in the multilateral framework to accommodate the pace and direction of globalizing markets. To address this paradox, which is not just a simple time-lag problem, the next section will take a step back to analyse the growth dynamics implied by globalization.

INTERNATIONAL IMPLICATIONS OF GLOBALIZATION

In the four decades running from 1945 to 1985 international economic integration (both productive and financial) grew more vigorously within the North. The first twenty years marked the North Atlantic era. The growth locomotive was primarily centred around that space. Subsequently the growth axis extended to a wider US–Japan area, and an intra-European area with spill-over effects on bordering regions. The centre of economic gravity started to expand (Mistry 1995). A great deal of this more complicated set of investment and trade relations has to do with the internationalization of the Japanese economy which accelerated very rapidly with the first revaluation of the yen after the breakdown of Bretton Woods and then after the Plaza Accord in 1985 which revalued the yen by another 40 per cent. Japanese foreign direct investment grew nearly five times in the five-year period after the Plaza Accord. Although the Japanese outflow subsequently slowed down, the overall surge continued, fuelled by lowering interest rates in the United States. International economic integration and the centre of economic gravity have continued to expand.

In the last ten years, between 1985 and 1995, international transactions have grown more rapidly in a North–South direction, and – even more recently – in a South–South direction. Trade and investment are growing at an unprecedented rate within Asia, especially between Japan and East Asia and between East Asia and South Asia. The Asian successes have been enthusiastically reported in both the press and the academic literature. In the Western Hemisphere a weaker surge, but no less a surge, is now evident between North and South and within South America, particularly among the countries at the tip, Argentina, Brazil, Chile, Paraguay and Uruguay – members of the customs union in the making, Mercosur. Intra-Mercosur exports have grown by an average of 24 per cent per year since 1990; from standing at less than 9 per cent of the overall trade of its members, the regional market now represents 20 per cent. In monetary terms intra-Mercosur trade has grown fourfold since the beginning of the 1990s. The regional market has become the main export destination for all its members, including Brazil, with Mercosur absorbing 15 per cent of its exports. The Mercosur process has produced a new and quite optimistic scenario for all countries in the region. Besides trade in goods, cross-border investments have expanded dramatically and with them trade in a number of services (Hirst 1996).

We do not have the tools or the knowledge to predict the future, so extrapolation is never safe. But in and of itself the exercise of extrapolation allows us to understand the magnitude of the change we are witnessing and to put it into context. If present trends were to continue, especially the rates of growth in heavily populated Brazil, China, India and Indonesia, the developing world, which accounted for one-fifth of real global production in 1950 and 40 per cent in 1980, will most probably account for over half of global production by 2005 (IMF 1995). East Asia and Latin America are likely to be the two fastest growing areas of the world economy over the coming decades. Asia as a whole is expected to contribute one-half of the growth in world trade in the period going up to the year 2000. True, this scenario could certainly slow down and even backlash without the maintenance of relatively peaceful relations and the acceptance of the benefits derived from economic interdependence. In any case, the unfolding of these trends augurs an exciting period of debate in academia, although less so in governments as policy adjusts, feeds or puts brakes on the process.

This is globalization in action. The changing investment strategies of multinational firms have shifted the ground rules. The increased complexity of the international division of labour represented by the incorporation of new countries is altering the structural context in which post-war international economic relations have been conducted. The growth of economic activity spans more and more regions and more and more countries. Although a new growth dynamic has made its appearance, the multilateral machinery to accommodate this change productively is lagging behind.

Institutions perpetuate themselves even as the structural conditions that initially gave rise to them no longer apply – by-products of past relations only gradually reflecting the present or providing a solution to the problems of today. In Gramscian terms, we are witnessing a crisis in the multilateral institutions of the trade regime. A crisis consists precisely in the fact that the old is dying and the new cannot be born.

MULTILATERALISM: A LOSS OF PRIMACY

In spite of the multiplying number of countries adopting trade liberalization and the growing globalization of markets, the 1990s saw a shift of emphasis away from global trade negotiations towards regional groupings. The weakening of multilateralism, or at least the emergence of competing modes of association, can be prima facie attributed to the metamorphosis of the United States. From being a brazen one track multilateralist to adopting regionalism as a second tier strategy, American policy has indeed made a U-turn. Starting with the negotiations for the Canada–US Free Trade Area (CUSFTA) and then the North American Free Trade Area (NAFTA), American policy has triggered reaccommodations elsewhere. It has left the breathing space that had often been lacking. It ought to be kept in mind that before this change of mood, regionalism and integration everywhere bar Europe were at best a dream in the face of overwhelming military and economic opposition from the United States. As the leader of multilateralism in the 1960s and 1970s, the United States worked assiduously to resist any efforts at closer regional ties, particularly in Latin America and Asia, which were seen as potential challenges to American predominance.[2]

But this transmutation of the United States is the last response to a chain of long-standing factors. Equally significant has been the growing appearance of new players in the world economy, above all Japan and subsequently the new industrializing countries at large which have redefined their interests in trade. Thus, one such explanation of the divorce between multilateralism and globalization is logically implied by the definition of multilateralism itself. Multilateralism is a deliberate pursuit; it has to do with the decisions of governments. It is an attempt at regulation. At its root, multilateralism is an institutional form whose breadth and diversity boomed after 1945 as a result of American hegemony. As put succinctly by Ruggie, 'it was less the fact of American *hegemony* that accounts for the explosion of multilateral arrangements than of *American* hegemony' (1993: 8). In a crucial sense, multilateralism has to do with a particular form of exercising power germane to American hegemony.[3] It has been American-centric.

Since the demise of the Bretton Woods arrangements, there have been attempts to build a new American understanding of the content of multi-lateralism in a now post-hegemonic world. Neo-liberal institutionalists created a renewed faith in international structures to evolve and mature 'beyond hegemony'. The dissipation of hegemony was perceived by liberal institutionalists as laying the ground for a new and perhaps even more conducive environment for the realization of genuine multilateralism – one under which smaller and weaker states could really hope to be awarded an antidote to the power of the mighty.

But this vision neglects the extent to which institutions can be used by powerful countries to create and enforce their values and norms. Moreover, the litmus test for the birth of such a world rests crucially on the disposition of the United States to follow the rule of law – a law that it cannot always control. If multilateralism is to be good for small countries, American attachment to it needs to be secured. The United States has to agree to take a dose of its own medicine. In these circumstances it becomes an onerous principle for the great power as well.

The United States is the only country that has an extensively developed body of doctrine and practice favouring the extraterritorial application of its laws, based on its strong sense of mission and manifest destiny. Traditionally,

US extraterritoriality involved matters relating to anti-trust cases and export controls in the context of national security. Additionally, however, it can also be used to obtain the intellectual property protection of its liking, by-passing multilaterally agreed-upon WTO standards and procedures. In effect, the US authorities still appear prepared to determine which are unlawful practices and which are outlaw countries (Hart 1994). For the United States a rule-based order has thus often meant the extension of American rules and procedures to the rest of the world. If this was a natural by-product of the hegemony enjoyed by the United States during the post-war years, then in a world where power is more widely dispersed unilateralism brings the whole system into question. The greatest potential for erosion of multilateralism lies here: the very real ability of the powerful to 'heavy-ride' and impose their preferences, rather than the problem of free-riding by the small and weak. 'Heavy-riding' breeds contempt and cynicism.

The continued decentralization of economic power and the dramatic rise of newly industrializing countries thus raises new questions. First, there is an arithmetical question. The conversion en masse to the market is happening with equal speed and fascination in a great number of countries. In 1950 there were about thirty members – 'contracting parties' – to the GATT, as they were called then. There are now four times as many. The line of entrants waiting at the door keeps growing. The dilemmas of large-number multi-lateralism have been described and analysed by Miles Kahler (1993). He has demonstrated how the system values a reduction in numbers and how it has groped towards minilateral devices to permit collective decision-making when influence is diffused. But the question is not just a mechanical one of quantities.

With the creation of an intensely competitive international trading system a need has now come for a more democratic, pluralistic and inclusive decision-making process for the first time since the Second World War. Inclu-siveness is a qualitatively new phenomenon and it faces major challenges. In the past, the dissatisfaction with international economic affairs was expressed first by withdrawing from active involvement, and then with obstructionist policies: de-linking, industrial planning, state trading, quasi-autarchy or heavy import substitution all expressed a discontent with the international order and a search for varying degrees of immunity from its effects. So long as they did not tilt the Cold War balance of power it was not something to worry about.

Later on, with the onset of the Uruguay Round when it was clear that immunity was no longer attainable, a loosely assorted coalition of developing countries led by Brazil and India reverted to a policy of obstructionism (Kumar 1993). The blurring of the North–South and the East–West divides has undercut this option and now active involvement for most of Latin America seems to be the preferred choice. Rather than push for utopia or obstruct the workings of the system, countries are now ready to uphold its principles and are thus placing new demands on it.

Philosophically, however, the multilateral system was created in the image of the United States policy process; organizationally, it was marked by two sets of dichotomies: the East–West confrontation and the North–South divide. It is not irrelevant that with the end of the Cold War, just as third worldism has lost ground, the national security argument for multilateral liberalization in the United States has lost legitimacy. With the bogey gone the image of a commonality of interests is less sustainable. Commonality of interests was at the base of trading relations, but the commonality of interests and a benign view of hegemony were restricted to the North Atlantic space.

Indeed, the trading system was never a genuinely global arena. The trade that was liberalized in the post-war period was largely two-way trade in goods where countries at both ends had production capacity and where there were possibilities for intra- rather than inter-industry specialization. By contrast one-way exports from North to South and South to North remained subject to high tariffs and non-tariff restrictions. The most highly restricted corridors of international trade were those that went from North to South and vice versa. Developing countries sought derogations from GATT rules to enforce import substitution or economic planning programmes; developed countries kept higher than average protection on goods in which developing countries were or could become competitive (Tussie 1987; de Castro 1989).

Economic multilateralism was shaped by these dichotomies. The communist world remained largely self-excluded; developing countries were only half-heartedly invited, not because their markets really mattered but because they were pawns in the Cold War strategic competition. Not even Japan ever became a full insider: its trade specialization more inter-industrial in nature; its philosophy (perceived or real) more grounded on interventionism and economic management than *laissez-faire*. Whatever the facts of the rivalry with Japan, the widespread perception is that the workings of the Japanese economy do not lend themselves easily to the GATT framework that, created in the image of the United States, was meant to negotiate over barriers at the borders but not over institutional structure. In terms of objective GATT measures Japan is among the most open markets. Yet the fact remains that business practices are a continued source of frustration to its trade partners. So far countries have had few beyond the border commitments: national treatment and mutual recognition seemed to suffice. They allowed members, once agreement on objectives was reached, to meet these through standards and procedures of their choosing. But because these principles do not touch institutional differences they are being called into question. As put rather starkly by Bagwhati, culture seems to be reduced into a (negotiable?) non-tariff barrier. Together these new players 'who are institutionally different enough from the original players to raise questions about what is being negotiated' (Krugman 1991: 18), undermine the meaning of the game as it has been played so far.

With the end of the Cold War, the premises on which the trading order rested for nearly half a century are in the process of being de-ideologized. The globalization of markets also exposes the extent up to which the North–

South and East–West dichotomies marked and fed the trading order. With the end of these collective organizing principles, the American visionary purpose has withered. The adhesion of small and weak countries in many instances has become necessary. The growing ambivalence of the United States vision is best exemplified by the tug of war between the Administration and Congress on issues that affect American relations with the rest of the world. The conflict causes havoc on international economic management. Witness the failure to renew fast track authority which was the prerequisite to the vision of a Free Trade Area of the Americas announced for the year 2005. If there is ambivalence about buying into the tiny Chilean market how will Brazil be accommodated? In the end, after the Miami Summit, the Latin Americans have opted to overcome American hesitations and push forward.

The United States no longer has the means to dominate world markets. It no longer has the power to bend every country to its will, particularly countries not belonging to the Western Hemisphere, perhaps the only area where US power still remains largely unchecked, and by some counts may even have become more prominent. But the US is still critical to the functioning of the global economy. The other major industrial actors have gained increasing power but they have been slow to accept global responsibility. The reluctance of the US to cede power is mirrored in the reluctance of Europe and Japan to assume a proper share in systemic efforts. Europe all in all, has not shown much ability or inclination either to provide direction or to set the agenda for the multilateral system. As the only trade bloc it has done much to teach others to emulate it. It seems to prefer a world in which inter-bloc bargaining prevails. Mercosur, for example, has been told time and again that negotiations would be eased if it changed its present intergovernmental mode of functioning to create a supranational machinery to resemble that of the European Union.

We thus have come to have a multilateralist system heavily biased towards the United States agenda in which Europe and Japan grudgingly follow from time to time but a large part of the rest of the world, although increasingly brought into the global web, remains largely unempowered. The present multilateral system has lost spirit. By and large, despite the successful ending of the Uruguay Round and the establishment of the WTO, the feeling is that multilateralism is pedalling very slowly against the backdrop of very rapid changes. There is one important exception to this slowdown and that is the frenzy with which countries have resorted to the new dispute settlement mechanism of the WTO. There are about sixty cases waiting in the pipeline, a third of which have been initiated by the small and weak. But to point to this growing credibility of the dispute settlement machinery is not inconsistent with my general argument. Despite such a 'leap to legalism' (Stiles 1996) the dispute settlement mechanism is a defensive mechanism, a mechanism of last resort. It does not by itself deepen economic integration. It only avoids a setback going unsanctioned.

Today many parts of the third and second worlds of yesterday are becoming increasingly active trade players. One of the more serious challenges waiting at our doorstep will be to engage China, a daunting puzzle; China is very much part of globalization, but is not even a member of the WTO. Globalization has thus fundamentally altered the context within which governments and institutions must function. It has forced us to focus on the squeaky wheels of multilateralism. How elastic is the multilateralism created under American hegemony to the decentralization of trade relations? How much institutional reorganization can it withstand? Can great power defection be discounted? Can new interested parties hijack the prevailing form of economic multilateralism and adapt it to their needs?

The slowdown of the machinery is a matter of concern for the economic policy revolution that has exploded in the former command economies and developing countries. The avalanche of trade liberalization that has occurred in these countries has neither been GATT-driven nor GATT-negotiated. It all proceeded unilaterally. But once through, expectations of what a properly functioning system must deliver have been raised. Expectations of smooth access to export markets have been raised. Here, more appropriate multilateral machinery is much needed to ensure that the North fulfils its obligations in terms of reciprocity.

Many of the newly converted countries no longer want, nor can they afford, to be silent bystanders; at the same time the original members can no longer afford to let them remain so. The rate of growth of imports into Latin America and East Asia, as a result of the trade policy revolution, has been a remarkable 12 per cent a year since 1990, doubling world averages.

Regional trading arrangements may step into the breach. There may indeed be a defensive component in regionalism as viewed from the United States. But viewed from countries previously excluded from the club, a regionalist-based order seems to be both more user-friendly and more forward-looking. Belonging to a regional grouping is for many of the developing countries an opportunity for the market access they always wished for but had never really extracted from negotiations in the GATT. Regional associations offer something in return for their trade policy revolution: their new belief in trade openness. The regional market is no substitute for the world market, but it has very dynamic effects in terms of the composition of exports. It is generally the case that trade with world markets tends to be made up of the traditional staples; whereas exports to regional markets tend to be non-traditional goods. Regionalism is being resorted to because the old multilateralism did not satisfy the expectations of many of its members. What may have been tolerated, or barely acceptable, because there was no other choice for some time, does not need to be so any longer.

MULTILATERALISM REINVENTED

The North Atlantic club has become archaic. The club does not even serve its founders very much, aware as they are of multiplying markets – multiplying

growth poles in the world economy. A growing number of developing countries have outgrown a policy of obstructionism and today feel the need to
uphold a rules-based order, making it tighter and less elusive. The search for
new roads towards a multilateralist system can take either a bottom-up or
top-down direction so as to accommodate the new regional units in the
making.

The top-down process builds on earlier ideas (cf. Curzon and Curzon Price
1986) and has been mooted by the Secretary-General of the WTO with the
help of other influential figures such as Fred Bergsten (1996) in the United
States. The proposal is to choose an ambitious objective and to push the
WTO towards it with a given time-frame: this is the creation of a global free
trade area that would remove all barriers at the border by possibly 2020, a
date chosen because it is the latest date in the calendar of regional pacts, the
time by when APEC expects to reach free trade among all its members. The
idea is that such a global free trade vision should be open-ended in coverage
and membership.

Ultimately, this open-ended free trade area would resemble the GATT as it
was originally conceived, but it would contain, in addition, the ultimate
objective of free trade among participating countries, which the initial GATT
never did. By proposing to meet this objective it would force all regional pacts
to grant most-favoured nation (MFN) treatment by a given date. Since East
Asia and Latin America are expected to be the two most rapidly growing
parts of the world economy in the near future, in essence a global free trade
area would rest on a 'grand bargain' between these two groups of countries
and North America, Western Europe and Japan which can offer full access to
their markets. But at present it is hard to foresee the realization of this grand
bargain as a natural consequence of the WTO's institutional development.
Again, it would require a dose of leadership and institutional energy that
seems to be lacking. At present, despite its 'leap to legalism' and the talk of a
new round for the year 2000, the WTO does not seem to have been granted
fuel for more than mediation services through its dispute resolution
mechanism.

In Latin America a more realistic scenario at present is the continuation of
the bottom-up process, with Mercosur gradually knitting a more or less loose
web of regional associations in the south of the Americas and thus gaining
some strength to prod the United States into making real its own promise of a
free trade area in the Western Hemisphere.

The point here is whether the new regionalism, including Latin America,
will be multilaterally friendly or unfriendly. 'Open regionalism' is the way that
Latin America has chosen to mark its path, regionalism in the context of the
trade policy revolution that has taken place. All countries today seem to be
more interested in the proper functioning of multilateralism. Most still carry
on an important and in many cases growing share of their trade with other
areas of the world. Japan has become the second market for both Chile and
Peru. Brazil's and Argentina's exports are still widely dispersed. All countries

want to keep their options open. Even the smallest, more heavily dependent on regional trade, would like to see a properly functioning multilateralism to counteract hegemonic 'heavy-riding' from the regional powers. Thus no country can afford to take regionalism as a sole alternative. Such a stance may not just be conducive to more effective future multilateralism, it may actually even be a prerequisite for building a new multilateralism, a multilateralism that more properly reflects multipolarity.

A benign view of regionalism is largely warranted for at least four reasons. First, the new brand of regionalism, the one growing out of Europe, is not merely old wine in new bottles. It is being driven more by markets and less by policy, or by fiat or even enlightened bureaucrats. Furthermore, few, if any, of the new regional associations could be considered a bloc. The new regionalism we are witnessing today is, in fact, a product of the globalization of economic activity – the production and marketing of goods and services. Regionalism is, in turn, feeding back to reinforce that same process of expansion.

Second, regional negotiations seem to be able to bridge the dichotomy that has existed in GATT between industrialized and developing countries. Large segments of international trade, particularly one-way exports in a North–South or South–North direction, had remained excluded from GATT negotiations and were even subject to proliferating barriers of all kinds. In a messy effort to compensate for the biased integration into world trade, developing countries were allowed 'special and differential treatment': they were not expected to provide fully reciprocal access to their markets and they were granted preferential access (albeit on paltry terms). Special and differential treatment proved to be no solution and turned to be a continuing cause of friction. On the one hand, developing countries remained dissatisfied with the market access they obtained; on the other, developed countries kept grumbling that they did not really make contributions to the system. In a latter-day twist of fate, preferential access has even been used as a form of conditionality: market access is granted on condition that certain policies, such as intellectual property protection up to required American standards, are in place.[4] Regional free trade agreements, in contrast, tend not to make a distinction between types of countries or levels of development. Within NAFTA, Mexico has eliminated virtually all border restrictions, in agriculture as well as in industry, from 70 per cent of its imports coming from the United States and Canada. The extension of NAFTA to Chile and the negotiations for the Free Trade Area of the Americas are expected to follow the same pattern – little if any special and differential treatment.

Third is the question of bargaining power. Bargaining power depends essentially on market size in the present multilateralist system. A regional trading unit will thus tend to have more market power than any of its members alone. By decentralizing decision-making and strengthening plurilateral processes in a framework which gives even the weaker countries some say, the new regionalism will lead to the kind of multilateralism in which regional units will have stronger bargaining power. A small number of units engaging in inter-bloc negotiations would tend to make co-operative solutions more likely. In the words of President Cardoso referring to Mercosur, 'in the end, if the name of the game is reciprocity, it is necessary to have something to offer, and market size is the first prize' (Hurrell 1996). Fourth is the question of the overstretching coverage of trade negotiations. Trade negotiations used to be limited to negotiations over products, not policies. The freeing of trade was pursued by dealing with measures as they were reflected at the border. In the course of the Uruguay Round the GATT was pushed to extend its domain beyond the border to include intellectual property, investment rules and a host of other issues. Now labour rights, tax and competition policies, and treatment of the environment are seen as legitimate trade issues. The trade door is being increasingly used to negotiate policies. This is the passage from shallow to deep integration (Lawrence 1993). Deep integration leads to or assumes the harmonization or convergence of policies. It requires that growing portions of sovereignty be surrendered – an exercise that cannot be tackled with 120 countries sitting at the table. Here lies another leading edge aspect of regional free trade agreements. Most now involve the integration or harmonization of a number of loosely assorted trade-related policies.

All this supports the 'building block' view in the debate over future consequences of current regionalism (Lawrence 1993). No regional unit seems to be inward looking; no regional unit can afford to be so for it would grow apart from others. Markets are so deeply intertwined through ongoing globalization that no unit can afford to sacrifice intra-regional trade at the expense of inter-regional trade. No unit has an interest in substituting regional for global trade. Countries are only choosing to forge ahead faster or further than the multilateral track affords. The result is that trade between the units may not grow as fast as within them, but it will not deteriorate.

A new multilateralism can emerge as the regional units become part of the collective decision-making process. Rather than being exposed directly to the multilateral level, as they are now, where power asymmetries are wide and affinities limited, countries will have a first direct say at the regional level instead. The new regional units will deal with each other on a more equal footing, thus replacing the workings of a multilateral system which is dominated by monopolistic behaviour: a power whose global significance is diminishing but which, nevertheless, can continue to dictate the rules of the game.

David Henderson (1994) has synthesized the dilemmas facing world trading relations. Will global economic integration increase? Will regional integration also continue to increase in scope and size? Contrary to what is often believed, these are not mutually exclusive paths. The future of the multilateral trade system, and of international economic integration, will depend not on the extent to which regional integration agreements in and of themselves multiply or become more deep-seated, but rather on how open they are.

Their openness rather than their mere existence will be the determining factor in shaping the course of global economic integration.

This is a world that is compatible with globalizing markets, a world in which regionalist groupings thrive and more players become committed to turn the flagging multilateralist imagery into contemporary reality. Because globalization entails a logic of multipolarity the leading edge of liberalization lies in regionalism. In the end the loss of American hegemony may not be such a bad thing and may even be good for the rest of the world.

NOTES

1 The major accomplishments of the Uruguay Round lie in the creation of an intellectual property regime (not genuinely a step towards freeing trade) and in the adoption of a new dispute resolution mechanism which, for one, does not allow the defendant to veto the process or the outcome and, for another, is expected to result in binding resolutions – indeed a triumph of multilateralism.
2 These regional efforts were indeed early signals of the discontent with a US-dominated 'multilateralist' world economy. For recent analyses for Latin America, see Bloomfield and Lowenthal (1990) and Hirst (1996); for Asia, see Pempel (1995).
3 In other words, multilateralism has had a cultural imprint. An indication of the cultural bias that surrounds both the practice and concept of multilateralism is the torrent of academic production that it has generated in the United States as opposed to other parts of the world. Neither European nor Japanese have ever worried as much about its meaning, while developing countries failed to be fascinated (see Escude 1995) by a principled concept so riddled with exceptions. Until recently multilateralism was a process they yearned for, but in actual practice had never been able to see the GATT as an institution over which entitlement was even conceivable. Witness the negligible resort by developing countries to its dispute resolution mechanism over the life of the GATT. Only after their conversion and the initiation of a less politically charged mechanism under the WTO is there an indication of a growth of faith in the process.
4 Argentine access to the United States market under the Generalized System of Preferences will be penalized because the United States remains dissatisfied with the law on intellectual property protection passed by Argentina's Congress in 1996. Because the law is widely regarded as compatible with Uruguay Round commitments, the United States does not want to risk taking Argentina to a dispute resolution panel under the WTO. Because preferences were never part of GATT commitments, Argentina cannot expect to have a positive hearing to any complaint in these circumstances.

REFERENCES

Bergsten, F. (1996) 'Globalizing free trade', *Foreign Affairs* 75 (May–June): 105–21.
Bloomfield, R. and A. Lowenthal, (1990) 'Inter-American institutions in a time of change', *International Journal*, 45 (Autumn): 867–88.
De Castro, J. (1989) 'Determinants of protection and evolving forms of North–South trade', *UNCTAD Discussion Papers No. 26*, Geneva, June.
Curzon, G. and V. Curzon-Price (1986) 'The GATT regime: issues and prospects', in R. Rode (ed.) *GATT and Conflict Management: A Transatlantic Strategy for a Stronger Regime*, Boulder: Westview Press.
Escude, C. (1995) *El realismo de los estados debiles*, Buenos Aires: GEL.

Evans, P. (1995) *Embedded Autonomy: States and Industrial Transformation*, Princeton: Princeton University Press.

Hart, M. (1994) 'Coercion or cooperation: social policy and future trade negotiations', *Canada–US Law Journal* 20: 351–90.

Henderson, D. (1994) 'Putting trade blocs into perspective', in V. Cable and D. Henderson (eds) *Trade Blocs? The Future of Regional Integration*, London: Royal Institute of International Affairs.

Hirst, M. (1996) *Democracia, Seguridad e Integracion: America Latina en un mundo en transicion*, Buenos Aires: Editorial Norma.

Hurrell, A. (1996) 'Progressive enmeshment, hegemonic imposition or coercive socialisation? Understanding policy change in Brazil', mimeo.

International Monetary Fund (IMF) (1995) *World Economic Outlook*, Washington, DC: IMF.

Kahler, M. (1993) 'Multilateralism with small and large numbers', in J. Ruggie, *Multilateralism Matters: The Theory and Practice of an Institutional Form*, New York: Columbia University Press.

Krugman, P. (1991) 'The move towards free trade zones', *Economic Review*, Federal Reserve Bank of Kansas City, November/December: 5–26.

—— (1995) 'Growing world trade: causes and consequences', *Brookings Papers on Economic Activity*, 1: 327–77.

Kumar, R. (1993) 'Developing country-coalitions in international trade negotiations', in D. Tussie and D. Glover (eds) *The Developing Countries in World Trade: Policies and Bargaining Strategies*, Boulder: Lynn Rienner.

Lawrence, R. (1993) 'Futures for the world trading system: implications for developing countries', in M. Agosin and D. Tussie, *Trade and Growth: New Dilemmas in Trade Policy*, London: Macmillan.

Mistry, P. (1995) 'Open regionalism: stepping stone or milestone toward an improved multilateral system?, in J.J. Teunissen, *Regionalism and the Global Economy: The Case of Latin America*, The Hague: FONDAD.

Pempel, T.J. (1995) 'Transpacific Torii: Japan and the emerging asian regionalism', Unpublished, Jackson School of International Studies, University of Washington, Seattle.

Ruggie, J. (1993) 'The anatomy of an institution' in J. Ruggie, *Multilateralism Matters: The Theory and Practice of an Institutional Form*, New York: Columbia University Press.

Stiles, K. (1996) 'Negotiating institutional reform: the Uruguay Round, the GATT and the WTO', *Global Governance* 2: 119–48.

Tussie, D. (1987) *Developing Countries and the World Trading System: A Challenge to the GATT*, London: Frances Pinter.

Part II

Public policy, globalization and regionalism

5 'Subversive liberalism'
Market integration, globalization and West European welfare states

Martin Rhodes

INTRODUCTION

This chapter considers the issue of European state autonomy in the social domain by examining the past, present and prospective influence of European integration and 'globalization' on national systems of social policy and welfare. The specific processes considered are the attempted creation of a European 'social' area; the completion of the internal market and, potentially, monetary union; the competitive effects of trade liberalization and the impact on policy autonomy of greater international capital mobility. If national social policies are being influenced increasingly by European Union (legislation, regulation and wider economic integration) and more constrained by the need to conform with the expectations and prejudices of international financial markets, then what are the implications for the dynamics of national welfare state development? The following analysis focuses on five major, interrelated questions: what is the relationship between regional economic integration and global trends, and between these two phenomena and domestic welfare state problems; do regional integration and globalization have independent effects; do they interact with one another to hasten convergence trends; are they strong enough to erode national specificities; and is there evidence of convergence on any particular model?

SUBVERSIVE LIBERALISM AND THE WELFARE STATE

Welfare states in Western Europe are extremely diverse and each is responding in its own way to the problems of cost-containment created by demographic pressures, life-cycle changes, fiscal strains and, arguably, by the transition from a Fordist to a post-Fordist economy. But at the same time, the scope for different responses to these problems is increasingly limited: by the need to avoid an excessive fiscal burden on the middle classes (a domestic constraint) and by increasing interdependence (an international constraint). This interdependence is the result less of new, pan-European structures than of the combined effects of regional economic integration (the creation of a single European market and the deflationary impact of moves towards monetary union) and globalization (competitive trade pressures and the liberalization of international financial flows).

Together, these forces are operating what one can call a 'subversive liberalism'. Although not creating a full-blown 'crisis' of the welfare state, 'subversive liberalism' is eroding the principles of universalism and solidarity in welfare provision and subjugating social progress to the exigencies of economic competition. In the early 1990s, an analysis by Garret and Lange that asked 'What's "left" for the Left?' concluded that 'governments of the Left – in alliance with powerful labour movements – have been able to maintain their traditional goals of redistribution, welfarism and full employment while simultaneously adjusting to the new exigencies of international economic competition' (1991: 564). This may have been true before the mid-1980s. But the 'new exigencies' of the 1990s derive not only from market interpenetration. They are also the product of an internal deregulatory agenda – backed by powerful neo-liberal arguments (often presented as 'economic necessity') – coupled with external pressures in the global economy. Perhaps most importantly, Ruggie's international regime of 'embedded liberalism' – in which capital controls still figured prominently – has witnessed (as Ruggie himself forecast) a loss of control by governments over financial transactions and international and domestic liquidity creation as credit and exchange controls have been abandoned (Ruggie 1982: 414–15). In consequence, the domestic economy – which has to come to terms with *internally* generated welfare state problems – must also cope with greater external pressures. It must shoulder the burden of adjustment in restraining the expansion of credit and money stock effected by international markets, defend the external balance of trade and payments and control inflation. Under these circumstances, innovation, change and material progress have emerged as pre-eminent (Mishra 1993); and social progress is slowly becoming subservient to the perceived needs of the market economy.

The following discussion briefly outlines Europe's different welfare models (as a prelude to considering the issue of convergence) as well as their internally generated pressures for change. It then analyses the importance of regional integration and the role of the European Community (now Union), before considering the influence of global forces on welfare state developments. The concluding section examines the independent and interactive effect of regional economic integration and global trends on welfare states and asks whether they are strong enough to break down national particularities.

WELFARE STATE MODELS AND INTERNAL PRESSURES FOR CHANGE

In recent years there has been a proliferation of comparative social policy studies which have developed typologies of welfare state regimes, inspired largely by the seminal work of Esping-Andersen (1990). Esping-Andersen argues that welfare states cluster into three regime-types:

1 The Scandinavian regime-type has a high degree of universality, institutionalization, and 'de-commodification' (i.e., the distancing of the individual from the market via social citizenship). This model 'crowds out the market' and creates a cross-class solidarity in favour of an extensive system of welfare provision.
2 The liberal, Anglo-Saxon model emphasizes publicly organized and financed social insurance (the Beveridge approach) with low flat rate provision in combination with private charity. Solidarity and de-commodification are minimized and weaknesses derive from growing gaps in the safety net and the creation of poverty-traps by means testing.
3 The corporate, 'Bismarckian' model of the central European countries (and Italy) includes strong elements of de-commodification but is most distinctive for its 'status' differentiating welfare programmes, where income maintenance and health care are strongly related to employment and family status.

A fourth regime – the 'Latin Rim' or southern model – added by Leibfried (1992) and developed by Ferrera (1996) has four main traits which, arguably, distinguish it from Esping-Andersen's 'corporate' model: a high level of dualism in income maintenance and pensions; the establishment of national health services; a special welfare mix (including the family, church and charity); and extensive clientelism. Katrougalos (1996) argues that such characteristics make the 'southern' model a 'sub-variety' rather than a distinctive regime-type. Nevertheless, as in the case of the other 'models', the special traits of the southern variant conditions its response to contemporary challenges.

Regardless of their membership of different welfare families, all European countries have in the past experienced common *internally* generated pressures for change which are important to consider in any discussion of convergence. Two sets of pressures have produced and are producing a certain degree of convergence: the first – from the era of welfare state expansion – stemmed from attempts to bolster legitimacy and social cohesion and redistribute costs, while the second relates to the problems of restructuring the welfare state after the end of 'the golden age'.

Legitimacy and cost-shifting games

During the expansionary phase of the European welfare state, there was already a degree of convergence between the two broad types of welfare state in Europe: those which sprang from the Bismarckian tradition (relating welfare rights to wage-earners' and employers' contributions) and those inspired by the Beveridgean concept of general insurance. In the Bismarckian countries social insurance was supplemented by measures to allow the payment of benefits to non-wage-earners and to the whole population (e.g. family allowances and medical care), pension schemes were set up for non-wage earners and a right to a guaranteed minimum was recognized. In the Beveridgean countries, an opposite evolution has led to a guarantee in the case of average or above average salaries of a higher rate of replacement income in the event of unemployment (through supplementary schemes) (Chassard and Quintin 1992). This process of 'convergence' was driven largely by the search for legitimacy by political actors in the face of interest group lobbying and electoral pressures.

One consequence of these changes, according to Overbye (1993), is that there has been a parallel convergence on a more *dualized*, 'middle-class oriented' welfare model. The competition among elites for votes is the driving mechanism, generating 'cost-shifting' games in which the relationship between forms of social security spending and types of benefits have been modified over time in accordance with voter preferences, producing a convergence in social policy *outcomes*. Focusing on pensions politics, Overbye (1993) argues that the European countries have traditionally been divided into two main groups – 'assistance' countries (the Nordic countries and Britain) and 'insurance' countries (Germany, Belgium, France, Italy and Spain) – but that they have gradually converged on a dual pension structure in which the whole working population receives earnings-related pensions while the non-working population relies on different tax-financed, means-tested benefits. In the case of the *'assistance group'*, the Nordic countries increasingly emphasized income maintenance alongside minimum protection, and, financing such schemes through 'contributions' rather than general revenues, they have moved progressively towards an 'insurance approach' to old-age pensions. The Anglo-Saxon countries have also made similar movements, producing a common trend towards giving the whole population access to public superannuation and/or compulsory occupational pension coverage, while marginal groups are dependent to a growing extent on various types of tax-financed, means-tested pension supplements. In the case of the *'insurance group'*, there has been a general tendency in countries which began with contribution-based, income maintenance schemes for the industrial working class either to extend coverage to other groups or to introduce parallel schemes for various occupational groups. This type of change has occurred in those countries like Germany and France where pension schemes were originally targeted on industrial workers as well as in those countries which started out with subsidized voluntary schemes. To some extent, therefore, national particularities were beginning to break down even during the welfare state's 'golden age'.

The welfare state after the 'golden age'

As the Western economies went into recession in the 1970s, a first set of internally generated problems appeared with a loss of welfare state legitimacy. Jallade (1992) argues that, although the fiscal crisis identified in welfare state management may well have been exaggerated (e.g. O'Connor 1973;

Gough 1979), there was, none the less, a legitimacy problem owing to the poor redistributive performance of welfare systems and managerial difficulties. In addition to an apparent loss of capacity on the part of central governments in delivering social services, this caused a decline in support for egalitarian policies and centralized provision among policy-makers and public opinion. The legitimacy problem was subsequently corrected by shifting the emphasis in welfare provision towards income maintenance and protection against risk. Delivery problems were addressed by a greater diversification and decentralization of some services and a greater reliance on new 'solidarity networks' (including the voluntary sector) even if the major maintenance programmes (pensions, sick pay, unemployment compensation) remained centralized.

A different set of problems, manifest since the 1980s and much less easily dealt with, is linked to fiscal and demographic necessities (the rising number of elderly has created greater demand for pensions, health services and social care); changes in the structure of the family (which have produced new pressures for financial assistance); and the perverse effects of programme design (forcing up the costs of unskilled or semi-skilled employment through higher social charges – especially in the service sector – and creating poverty traps and enforced dependency) (Gilbert 1992; Lindbeck 1993). The common response across Europe has been to tinker with provisions: changing the rules for eligibility for pensions (increasing the age of entitlement, making conditions more stringent), finding a new balance between statutory and supplementary protection, and integrating social protection into programmes of employment promotion (Chassard and Quintin 1992; European Commission 1995).

But critics of the welfare state from both left and right think that tinkering may not be enough. From the left, commentators like Jessop and Esping-Andersen argue that there is now a clear incompatibility between the welfare state and the emergence of a post-Fordist economic order. In tones reminiscent of a neo-liberal critic, Jessop (1993) argues that the conditions favouring 'Fordist accumulation' have been eroded by the expansionary dynamic of a welfare state built on bureaucracy, centralization, clientelism and the construction of political empires, creating personal dependence, poverty and unemployment traps. The necessary response is a shift from the Keynesian welfare state to the 'Schumpeterian welfare state' in which, as is already increasingly the case, welfare provision is used to stimulate economic adjustment. In similar fashion, Esping-Andersen (1994) argues that the postwar welfare state is integral to Fordism: the risks it addresses, the ideals of equality and social citizenship it promotes, and its basic assumptions relate to the family, life-cycle and work of the prototypical Fordist (male) industrial production worker. It has therefore become an obstacle to a successful adjustment to the post-industrial era since this type of worker and (his) life-cycle are becoming increasingly atypical.

The most serious adjustment constraint derives from employment rigidities: the average male earner is 'trapped' in guarantees of stable job and high earnings, while increasing numbers of younger workers are excluded from the workforce by high labour costs. The solution is a removal of the rigidities that prevent the creation in Europe of a large number of low-paid service-sector 'McJobs' – the US solution to employment creation. The increase in inequality this would otherwise produce could be combated by a radical change in the nature of welfare provision, extending a citizen's guarantee of skill acquisition and social servicing at any point during the life-cycle, especially through education and training. Lindbeck (1993, 1994) places much greater 'neo-liberal' emphasis on 'moral hazard' (the exploit-ation of welfare state benefits and the inevitable increase in beneficiaries in line with programme expansion) as *the* basic dilemma of the welfare state. But he also recommends a radical (Schumpeterian) redesign of income pro-tection to avoid poverty traps and economic disincentives and to provide the sort of flexibility required by Esping-Andersen's post-industrial life-cycle. Apart from a removal of insurance systems from the public sector, the three basic elements would be a common safety net for well-defined contingencies; additional benefits based on a compulsory, strongly actuarial pay-as-you go system (i.e., benefits that rise strictly with previous income); and substantial scope for voluntary saving and insurance on top of the compulsory system. To increase demands for flexibility during the life-cycle, Lindbeck makes the case for allowing the individual to draw on his/her pension benefits in advance (in an actuarial) fashion for studies, leisure periods or early retirement.

Thus, after a phase of convergence during the golden age in terms of the spread of welfare cover, more recently internally generated problems have triggered not just a common response across the various models of European welfare in terms of market or growth-conforming policies, but also a certain degree of intellectual convergence: there is now broad agreement – even out-side the neo-liberal camp which has launched its own high profile assault – that the welfare state has been responsible for many of its own problems and may have become a major obstacle to employment-creating growth. Objective reality and subjective evaluation are difficult to disentangle. In sum, this is the internal agenda of 'subversive liberalism'. We now turn to its external dimension.

EUROPEAN REGIONAL INTEGRATION AND WELFARE STATES

Will regional economic integration in Europe strengthen or weaken welfare states? Will it promote convergence, and if so in what direction? As Chassard and Quintin (1992: 107) point out, one of the objectives of European social policy has been to overcome traditional rivalries among the various phil-osophies of social protection, especially between the Bismarckian and Beveridgean schools, and promote a 'European model' based on three fundamental aims of social protection: a guarantee of a living standard consistent with human dignity and access to health care; social and economic integration; and the maintenance of a reasonable standard of living for those no longer able to work. But it is evident that, despite the convergence trends mentioned above, the diversity of different welfare regimes does not lend itself to a spontaneous 'bottom up' strategy of social integration. To quote Leibfried (1992: 253), these regimes 'start from rather different, sometimes contradictory, goals and are built on quite disparate intervention structures; and they do not share a common policy – and politics – tradition that could serve as a centripetal force'. Moreover, in terms of traditional definitions of social policies – actions by a state to counteract the market, distribute resources and benefits to the disadvantaged and promote social citizenship rights – the role of European policy has been minimal. Thus, a set of European welfare state arrangements to compensate for the erosion of national provision is unlikely to emerge. Indeed, many of the developments within Europe conform with rather than contest the thrust of 'subversive liberalism'.

Thus, most direct European intervention in the social domain, either through regulation or legislation, has been of the 'market-making' rather than 'market-breaking' variety, and rights to a European social citizenship are virtually non-existent (Kenis 1991). In the post-Single European Act (SEA) era, this pattern conforms to the predominantly market-based, deregulatory character of the internal market project, for the treaty base changes introduced by the SEA provided little in the way of additional competence for supranational activity in this arena. It is clear, therefore, that nothing resembling a European 'welfare state' currently exists and few social risks are dealt with at the European level, except for some experimental projects linked to the structural funds (Leibfried 1993). Moreover, given the European Union's budgetary constraints, there seems little likelihood of its acquiring the resources required to provide itself with a supranational, redistributive welfare state role. There are several proposals as to how this could be achieved – including the adaptation of the existing structural fund system (and its transformation into a distributive regime), the establishment of the EU as an 'extraterritorial' state with its own rights and entitlements and the creation of a European Social Policy Band, emulating the structure of the European Monetary System. However, thus far, the Commission has restricted itself to more limited forms of social regulation.

The impediments to a regional welfare state

How can this limited role in institution-building ('positive integration') be explained, by contrast with the much greater role of European policy in developing the single market ('negative integration')? A major point is that the political structures of the EU prevent the transfer of major welfare/ distributive resources to the European level. First there is the issue of the societal prerequisites of welfare state construction. In individual member-states, corporatist policy-making systems have been dependent on left incumbency, high union membership density, and union as well as employer centralization. None of these factors exist or are likely to emerge within a Europe of fifteen and more member-states, although the presence of Sweden may help tilt the social policy agenda towards distributive concerns. Second, the creation of a redistributive welfare state has been dependent on a political coalition supportive of such a project. The best case scenario for a welfare state coalition at the European level would involve an alliance of social democratic and Christian democratic forces, but the importance of the latter would militate against the development of a redistributive welfare state project in favour of one based at most on transfer payments (Huber and Stephens 1993: 13–15). Third, the establishment of any form of European welfare state would require political structures whereby majority decisions can be translated into policy. However, under even the most optimistic projections concerning the creation of 'sovereign-state' European structures under the Treaty on European Union, the political institutions of the EU will continue to fragment power and the structure of decision-making will remain multi-tiered.

As Pierson and Leibfried (1995) point out, some of the most important impediments to a European welfare regime stem precisely from the EU's multi-tiered structure. Indeed, the presence of multiple, potentially competing jurisdictions creates new strategic opportunities for those opposed to extensive, highly redistributive social policies. At the very least, they create the conditions for 'joint decision-making traps' (Scharpf 1988) in which policy innovations are hedged by accommodation and procedural guarantees. Streeck and Schmitter (1991: 142) suggest that it is partly this fragmentation of power which has allowed the emergence of a 'centripetal centre' in the EU, in which the opponents of centralized regulation occupy the high ground of policy-making influence. Within such structures, the existence of territorially dispersed authority over social policy creates the possibility of *competitive deregulation* (of which the British have been accused as a result of their opt-out from the Maastricht social policy arrangements) as well as 'regime shopping' by firms. The latter may have an important impact on national regulatory systems by forcing the renegotiation of local or national bargains with unions and governments, placing growing pressure on welfare state regimes. Hence the German debate on *Standort Deutschland* and the preservation of the German model (see Streeck 1995). The restrictions on currency devaluation created by membership of the ERM (and its future impossibility under monetary union) could encourage the use of 'social devaluation' – the reduction of wage costs by a reduction in the level of social charges and social cover for employees (Chassard and Quentin 1992). More immediately, constraints on welfare state policies may also stem from the harmonization of VAT, especially in countries like Denmark where generous welfare provision has been funded by indirect taxes (Kosonen 1994).

At the same time, the strong links between social policy development and political legitimacy mean that multi-tiered systems are vulnerable to the dynamics of *competitive state building* – the competition between tiers of authority for credit for social provision. Member-states will resist a significant transfer of fiscal capacity to the European level and be protective of their social policy authority (Pierson and Leibfried 1995). This 'pre-emption of policy space' is a major obstacle to Europeanization beyond a loosely organized system of multi-tiered policy development with a 'hollow core' of limited supranational authority. For the diversity of European national welfare regimes is reflected not only in large differences in social expenditure but also in embedded and historically shaped national principles of organization. Policy space, as well as administrative/organizational and fiscal space, is therefore occupied by nation-states, among which integration in the core areas of welfare state regimes – education, health care and retirement security, not to mention forms of labour market organization – is highly unlikely.

While these institutional features rule out a process of 'top-down' harmonization, chances for a 'bottom-up' construction of a European 'social dimension' are also slim without a common labour market (Leibfried 1994). Indirectly, the Commission's social action programme measures proposed since 1990, and inspired by the 1989 Social Charter, have begun to have an impact on *workers'* rights and entitlements across the Community. Thus, European working hours' legislation – with its minimum requirements for daily and weekly rest periods and rules on night and shift work, and the directive on pregnant women in the work place – has forced even the recalcitrant British government to compromise its position of outright opposition to European labour market regulation beyond the confines of health and safety legislation. A long-awaited European directive on workers' participation in multinational companies has been achieved, albeit in heavily diluted form, under the Maastricht Social Protocol and Agreement (Rhodes 1992, 1995). Nevertheless, a *European* industrial relations system based on an elevation of neo-corporatist principles to the supranational level is extremely unlikely. Such structures have already been eroded at the national level and their replacement by functionally equivalent European institutions is ruled out by problems of diversity and the interdependence of national economies. Attempts to build a European system are being counteracted by what Wolfgang Streeck (1992) has called a European *neo-voluntarism*, in which decentralized market forces and enterprise level-bargaining feature prominently.

Social policy, market-building and spill-over

It has been argued that the European Union already operates a *de facto* social policy through its various interventions. Montanari (1995) identifies four areas of European intervention which could broadly be conceived as 'social policy': the Common Agricultural Policy (CAP); funds created for transfers – the regional fund, the social fund and the new cohesion fund created at Maastricht; labour legislation (protection, health and safety, equal pay, social security for migrant workers); and regulatory policies regarding the environment, product safety policy and consumer protection. But do these amount to a European system of welfare provision? Social policy within European welfare state systems is traditionally conceived as redistributive of benefits and resources, 'breaking the market's monopoly of reward' (Montanari 1995). Arguably, the CAP does just this, for it contains a strong, redistributive element. But it operates in a strongly distorted fashion, subsidizing producers in wealthy regions to the expense of others, and constrains other areas of spending by absorbing a vast proportion of the European budget. As for the regional funds, these too are redistributive to a degree and are inspired by the principle of European solidarity. They could conceivably provide the basis for a pan-European system of compensatory social transfers and risk insurance. However, for them to do so, they would have to be expanded and address issues of social inequality and deprivation in addition to their present concern with regional disparities. As for regulatory policies, whether they concern the harmonization of certain health and safety standards and directives on equal pay, health and safety in general, or environmental and consumer protection, they are generally intended to *secure* or *clear* the market (i.e. removing for European companies the need and cost of dealing with multiple regulatory systems) rather than attenuate or interfere with market outcomes. Social policy which might either change the course of the economy or promote social citizenship rights has largely been absent.

Indeed, some of the most important social policy developments in Europe have been linked to the process of *market*-building. As Leibfried and Pierson (1995) point out, regardless of the limited extent of welfare state construction at the European level, member-states are increasingly constrained 'by Community-wide social policy innovation: as part of the market-building process which is central to that of integration, national courts and the European Court of Justice (ECJ) have produced an impressive corpus of national and supranational adjudication eroding national sovereignty and autonomy in the interest of labour market and consumer mobility, in line with the co-ordination requirements introduced with the Treaty of Rome in 1958. This they see as operating via a moderate neo-functionalism since it has less to do with grand welfare state policy initiatives than with an incremental process of spill-over from single *market* policies. Thus, a national welfare regime may not target its benefits at its citizens only but also at all member-state foreigners employed on its territory, and national benefits should be portable across all of EU Europe. And member-states can no longer exclusively decide who may provide social services or benefits on their territory; the mutual recognition of degrees and licences from other member-states increasingly intervenes.

More generally, the completion of the single market means that, in principle, there should be some attempt to lower the barriers to mobility created by the lack of co-ordination of social security regimes. The evidence of recent migration flows suggests that transnational labour movements are likely to be limited to corporate executives, on the one hand, and low-skilled, low-paid migrant workers, on the other. If intra-European mobility remains low, there will consequently be little requirement for welfare regimes to undergo reorganization and convergence. Hagen (1992: 278–9) counters, however, that irrespective of the desirability of eliminating the barriers to labour mobility (as well as the need to prevent 'welfare tourism' and a drain on generous national welfare schemes from new residents) the demand for a system of social insurance in which rights are more generalized throughout the EU is likely to increase. However, this demand is unlikely to provoke the emergence of a complicated and costly system of mutual recognition of rights. Rather, it is likely to spawn the creation of a form of citizenship linked to the individual rather than to legal citizenship, specific employers, family status or country of residence (Hagen 1992: 279) in which mobile workers would enjoy portable rights linked to labour-market based schemes. This would conform with those trends – to be discussed below – that have appeared in all European welfare states and that relate benefits more closely to occupational status.

GLOBALIZATION AND THE LOSS OF NATIONAL POLICY-MAKING AUTONOMY

Moving beyond the European region itself, there is a further set of pressures on welfare states deriving from the international environment. Although an imprecise and over-used term, 'globalization' encapsulates several developments which have important consequences for traditional welfare state arrangements: international competition (between welfare regimes as well as firms), and international interdependence.

Competition between regimes

As argued above, with the more acute competition in goods and services stemming from the creation of the single market and the lowering of international trade barriers, there may be a growing degree of competition among regimes due to their variable social costs. This could conceivably produce 'social dumping', 'regime shopping' by footloose firms and 'social devaluation' by member-state governments. It is frequently pointed out that competition between regimes ('competitive deregulation') is likely to be limited due to the lack of any clear relationship between high welfare state spending and competitive decline (Pfaller *et al.* 1991). Among the various arguments put forward to counter what Korpi (1993) calls 'the Welfare State Jeopardy Hypothesis', are the lack of any clear connection between welfare spending and economic performance; the coincidence of international trade success and high labour costs (in Germany and the Netherlands, for example); and the arguably positive effects of high costs for industrial modernization: high costs force employers to produce higher productivity from capital investment and social security systems employ a large number of people, redistribute income and sustain levels of demand (e.g. Jallade 1992: 42–3). Similarly, 'social dumping' and 'regime shopping' by firms in tightly regulated labour markets with high social expenses will also be mitigated by the importance of a whole range of factors other than simply basic or indirect labour costs in the location decisions of firms. These include unit labour costs, production organization, skills and education provision, quality, marketing, market-proximity and after-sales service as well as the 'constructive flexibility' that derives from productive forms of labour market regulation and industrial relations arrangements (Rhodes 1992, 1993).

Nevertheless, under certain circumstances, new competitive pressures, exacerbated in Europe by the single market programme, could have important consequences for the welfare states. The critical questions are therefore: how will Europe deal with growing unemployment without permitting greater dualism; and how will it respond to the relocation of firms and its impact on the domestic status quo of social rights and entitlements? This is where the domestically generated problems of the welfare state are exposed by globalization. For globalization, industrial decline, and increased competition from lower-cost countries are driving forward the revolution in manufactured products, technology and work organization that is both marginalizing the standard manual worker (Esping-Andersen 1994) and making standard, Fordist, welfare state arrangements expensive and inappropriate. To deal with this, traditional methods of ensuring cost discipline (a wages policy and tight monetary and fiscal controls) may well prove insufficient. A restructuring of the welfare state, as recommended, for example, by Lindbeck and Esping-Andersen may be necessary.

International interdependence

The argument that the internationalization of economies has led to a dramatic narrowing of policy options may well have been exaggerated (see, e.g., Hirst and Thompson 1995). For the surrender of national policy autonomy is not the inevitable consequence of a process of globalization. In the first place, globalization in the full sense of the word – the 'subsuming and rearticulation of individual national economies within a global system by international processes and transactions' – does not at present exist, even if a number of its features (the organization of the international division of labour within transnational companies) are being established (Kosonen 1993). Second, countries are not forced to liberalize exchange controls by anonymous international forces. For as Notermans (1993) points out, the recently increased vulnerability of the Scandinavian countries (particularly Norway and Sweden) to international capital flows has been the result of consciously taken policy choices, designed to provide a nominal anchor for the price system given the problems in delivering lower inflation through domestic institutional arrangements. Their liberalization of exchange controls and the *de facto* pegging of their national currencies to the Deutschemark has as much to do with national political and ideological developments than with 'globalization' *per se*.

But whatever the primary cause of increased vulnerability, it is apparent that the loss or surrender of national policy autonomy is creating problems for previously well-entrenched national welfare state regimes. 'Subversive liberalism' – operating via the effects of increased capital mobility – favours owners of capital over other groups (as argued by Frieden 1991) and, as discussed by Moses (Chapter 6 in this volume), undermines one of the key characteristics of social democratic governance: the relative immobility of capital. In essence, this result derives from the abolition of exchange controls and requires a subordination of domestic policy priorities to the defence of the external balance. The shift from the 'embedded liberalism' era to an era of 'subversive liberalism' has forced the redirection of traditional monetary and fiscal tools away from full employment towards defending the balance of payments. This has profound consequences for political and economic autonomy, especially in the smaller social democratic countries (Moses, Chapter 6, this volume).

Kosonen (1993) argues that, in the past, the European Free Trade Association (EFTA) countries enjoyed much greater policy autonomy (allowing the preservation of comprehensive welfare state provision) than the European Community (EC) member-states. He demonstrates that a first group of countries (Austria, Denmark, Finland, Norway and Sweden) were open but economically relatively autonomous (in terms of inward and outward investment and the share of foreign trade in GDP). They were therefore better able to make their own economic–political decisions than a second – more internationalized group – comprising Belgium, Ireland, the Netherlands and Switzerland. The main welfare distinction is that the 'economically relatively autonomous countries' have higher social insurance coverage and replacement rates, and a higher proportion of public employment (implying an effort to create a net of public services targeting all citizens).

In the 1970s and 1980s, these extensive welfare states were also able to maintain satisfactory growth figures. While there was a weakening of the stability of the other group (especially Belgium and the Netherlands) which, integrated into international markets much earlier, experienced low growth, high unemployment and fiscal strains, the more autonomous countries preserved an independence in monetary and fiscal policy and intervened actively to modernize industry and combat unemployment (see Kurzer 1991). However, everything changed after the mid-1980s with 'Europeanization' and the deregulation of currency and monetary markets. In the early 1990s, Finland, Norway and Sweden all experienced substantial declines in GDP growth linked to financial instability (caused by deregulation, overheating and banking crises) and are now suffering from high long-term interest rates, the emergence of larger public debts and soaring unemployment. Domestic demand has been depressed and public expenditure cuts and a process of welfare state dismantling has been proposed, bolstered by an increasingly widespread political acceptance of 'the Welfare State Jeopardy Hypothesis' – the incompatibility, that is, of large welfare states and economic growth.

We can conclude that the capacity of these welfare states to 'mediate' the impact of international developments has been substantially eroded since the late 1980s. Independent monetary policy has lost its role and rising deficits and debts are constraining fiscal policy options as well. As the Swedish example shows, the freeing of capital movements greatly increases the risk of speculative panic and can make economic policies a hostage to international financial opinion. This will lead to cutbacks in employment and welfare state spending, including a reversal of traditional welfare policies. Compensation levels of pensions, unemployment and sickness benefits will be reduced and public services such as health care and day care will be curtailed; income inequalities will widen (Gould 1996).

IS THERE CONVERGENCE?: COMMON TRENDS IN WELFARE STATES

Given the limited extent of either European welfare state building or significant spill-over effects from regional integration (apart from the web of rules linked to labour mobility), it is hardly surprising that analyses of welfare state development in the EC since its foundation have found little evidence of harmonization. In a recent study, Montanari (1995) addressed the issue of *indirect* harmonization (the result of 'planned consistencies' as well as other economic, political and social forces) in three core social policy areas – old age pensions, sickness benefit and unemployment compensation. Three dimensions of possible convergence are examined: coverage, the net replacement rate and financing mechanisms. The analysis distinguishes between the EC 5 (the original six member-states minus Luxemburg), the post-1972 EC 8 and the EFTA countries. It shows that the latter (spanning the Scandinavian and 'Bismarckian' models) rather than either the EC 5 or EC 8 experienced a degree of harmonization. As pointed out above, they also achieved a higher average level of replacement rates and coverage in the three social insurance areas than the EC member-states. This convergence has not been the consequence of political design across the EFTA group. Rather it has arisen from the relatively similar constellations of power to be found in these countries – by contrast with the political diversity of the EC member-states – creating similar interplays of social, political and economic forces under social democratic hegemony. Thus politics triumphs over markets in determining the evolution of welfare state structures.

However, while Montanari's analysis may present an accurate picture of the pre-1985 period – especially for the EFTA countries – the more recent developments analysed above are now exerting greater pressure for change (a form of 'global over-determination') in which markets triumph over politics. But what are the independent and interactive effects of these pressures?

The pressures for change

The first set of interactions is between 'Europeanization' and trends in domestic policy design. As noted by Jallade (1992) and Overbye (1993), during the 'crisis years' the continental welfare states have restricted their redistributive role in order to retain political acceptance (legitimacy) among the dominant middle classes. As a result, there has been a common shift from flat-rate to earnings-related benefits, initially in pension systems but also now in other areas as well (including sickness, accident and unemployment compensation in the four Scandinavian countries); and a creeping 'privatization' of welfare provision through the proliferation of occupational, company-based pensions or private life insurance contracts (Jallade 1992: 50–2). Abrahamson makes a similar point, although his conclusions are more boldly stated, suggesting that the different European welfare states are converging towards the corporate, Bismarckian model. This process, he argues,

> implies a strengthening of the trend towards dualization of the welfare state, i.e. a bifurcation of the welfare system whereby the [labour] market takes care of the well-to-do workers through various corporate arrangements leaving the less privileged to mainly local institutions – either in the form of municipalities or local charities.
>
> (Abrahamson 1992: 10)

The result will be the generalization of a new 'welfare pluralism' in which it is accepted that market, state and civil society will all play a role in social provision.

From this perspective, an EU social policy linked largely to labour market participation will sustain present trends in the member-states towards differentiation, segregation and polarization, preventing member-states from determining their own policy mix. One way in which this will be encouraged will be via the effects of accommodating the EU's co-ordination doctrine. As Leibfried and Pierson (1995) point out, welfare state provision that can be construed as an 'earned' individual right can be more easily co-ordinated without the risk of massive leakage of benefits from one country to another, a clear risk of extending provision to all EU citizens and making benefits portable: thus, policy-makers are encouraged to follow the programme designs of Bismarck not Beveridge. Non-contribution based national income transfer programmes (child allowances, minimum pension benefits) are likely to lose favour, and this will reduce the possibility of policies to combat low incomes, adding to the problem of increasing dualism in welfare provision which is already evident in housing and poverty policy.

Second, there is the interaction between one of the most important problems facing the European welfare states – unemployment – and globalization. A common source of pressure on social policy across the EU member-states derives from the persistence of high levels of unemployment – the most important source of fiscal strains during the 1970s and, to cite Jallade

(1992: 45) 'the Achilles' heel of the European welfare states'. In the past, an increased burden of social contributions on labour costs in the continental European welfare states has been alleviated by striking a new balance between direct salaries and social contributions. But in the 1990s, European countries are experiencing new increases in unemployment, placing new strains on budget deficits and producing new demands for wage cost containment (achieved, if possible through consensual 'social pacts') and calls for a reduction in employers' social contributions in the interests of competitiveness. Under the new European employment agenda developed in 1993–4, the European Commission has sought ways of reducing employers' social costs without under-cutting social security budgets by raising revenue via taxes on energy consumption for example (Rhodes 1993). However, ready solutions are not available (such taxes on a sufficient scale risk depressing demand) and only a return to employment-creating growth will produce a durable remedy. For if the ratio of employed persons to social security beneficiaries declines further, social security benefits will have to be reduced, especially in the health and retirement area.

This, in fact, has already occurred with the postponement of the retirement age in a number of European countries, an indexation of pensions to prices rather than salaries, and increased users' charges. Although the basic institutional features of the welfare states are being maintained, significant reductions in replacement rates in one or more of these programmes has occurred in the Netherlands, Germany, Denmark, France and more recently in Finland and Sweden (European Commission 1995). The Netherlands and Germany also reduced real benefits through their social assistance programmes and social services targeted at particular categories of needy people (Stephens *et al.* 1994: 15–17). In all of these countries there is a growing problem of welfare 'disentitlement' – the result either of explicit policies (limiting access to unemployment benefits or social assistance) or changes in the labour market (as higher unemployment and more 'atypical' jobs render individuals less eligible for welfare cover, especially in the 'insurance' countries) (see Standing 1995).

The dimensions of change

Returning to the four models of welfare introduced in the first section, we can see how different types of regime are responding to the combination of domestic and external challenges.

The most dramatic example of how changes in the international environment have interacted with domestic policies can be found in the high-spending *Scandinavian welfare states* (Stephens 1996; Stephens *et al.* 1994). Sweden, Finland (now members of the EU) and Norway experienced dramatic increases in unemployment in the late 1980s and early 1990s, triggered by a simultaneous rise in international interest rates and an internationalization of financial markets. This made it impossible for them to maintain low interest rates and to privilege borrowing by industry over consumers of credit – a key element of these countries' supply-side growth/employment models. As discussed above, governments in all three countries made an identical series of decisions on the timing of financial deregulation, income tax changes and exchange rate policy which had strong pro-cyclical effects, contributing to an overheating of their economies in the late 1980s and aggravating the crash of the 1990s. The rise in unemployment meant rising demands on the welfare state and a decline in social security contributions and taxes. This exposed a key weakness in these high-spending welfare states: for while a full-employment commitment has been critical to maintaining their core, legitimizing ideal of solidarity, sustaining such a system is highly costly, requiring that revenue is maximized and social problems minimized (Esping-Andersen 1990). Henceforth, replacement rates were cut, waiting days introduced, qualifying conditions increased and services cut. In Denmark, international vulnerability and a rise in unemployment (exacerbated by its lack of an active labour market policy and concentration on consumer exports) have produced similar measures, including increases in the selectivity of benefits, the introduction of income testing, modifications of indexing, and temporary de-indexation (Stephens 1996: 23–4). In the process, decommodification is being reversed (Gould 1996: 91).

A number of analysts detect further evidence of 'Bismarckian convergence' in these high-spending welfare states under stress. Kuhnle (1993) reports that, in Scandinavia, growing numbers receive welfare via fiscal benefits (tax privileges and deductions) and occupational welfare. He forecasts that a diminishing number will receive full assistance transfers, creating new social inequalities, undermining the bases of organized solidarity and producing a welfare state with schemes strictly tied to employment and position in the labour market, based on premiums paid by individuals rather than on financing via general taxation. In an analysis of Finland and Sweden, Kangas (1994) comes to a similar conclusion, arguing that the German insurance model is becoming more generally diffused at the expense of many of the traditional features of the Scandinavian model. More generally, Ferrera (1993: 12–13) expects the influence of the Bismarckian model to spread, due to the success and weight of the model in the European political economy (which has increased since unification), its flexibility (the readiness with which basic protection can be supplemented by company-based or private insurance) and the absence of attractive alternatives.

In the *Anglo-Saxon group*, Ireland and the United Kingdom are responding rather differently, although a change of government in the latter may herald a shift away from neo-liberalism. Ireland, which has an extensive range of social citizenship rights and a predilection for corporatism but only a limited commitment to universalism and egalitarianism, may adapt quite readily to an employment-based European welfare system (see Cochrane and Doogan 1993). As for the United Kingdom, integration could bring dramatic change and turbulence since it faces a declining resource base, increased demands as a result of economic restructuring in the single market, a new set of demands from the growth of the elderly population and a growing problem of poverty (see Benington and Taylor 1993). The 'pay-related' social security system which is likely to be generalized at the EU level may even threaten the universalistic aspects of the present system. Moreover, it is unlikely that the shift in policy priorities in the UK since 1987 away from its Beveridgean origins – towards a low-cost, minimal system of welfare, with benefits targeted on the 'deserving' and an unfettered labour market generating low-wage jobs – will be counteracted by EU developments, given the more general trend towards dualization (Deakin and Jones Finer 1993). Moreover, if competitive deregulation does occur, the UK could conceivably attract continental imitators as EU countries seek an additional competitive edge by trimming their generous social provisions.

In the *corporate, 'Bismarckian' group*, the current weaknesses lie in the high incidence of social charges (non-wage labour costs) on employers, a spending bias towards pensions (a phenomenon even more marked in the southern welfare states) and an apparent inability to respond to growing levels of unemployment. Labour costs rule out an expansion of lower-paid, service sector jobs as a solution to unemployment, while the creation of their high-technology, highly paid equivalents on a substantial scale is ruled out by a low presence and lack of competitiveness in high-technology, as opposed to medium-technology, sectors. Even in the strongest of these economies, unemployment – at over 8 per cent in western Germany and higher in the east – will lead to new cuts in welfare provision if these levels do not abate. Given the occupational insurance basis of the system, higher unemployment means that fewer people meet the criteria for employment-linked benefits and the number with 'insufficient claims' on the system is increasing, exposing them to greater risks of poverty, especially in old age.

At the same time, while there remains a consensus on the desirability of extensive welfare provision, this is coming under attack from certain employer groups (e.g. small and medium-sized firms) who are campaigning for a curtailment of provision in the interests of lower social charges. This is where the vexed issue of competitiveness becomes important. For while the traditional strengths of the German system have enabled it to remain competitive regardless of high social costs, the standardization of production processes means that they can be duplicated elsewhere at lower cost – not just in the Third World, or newly industrialized countries, but in Western Europe (the UK is an increasingly favoured site for relocation) and the former Eastern bloc countries. Rising unemployment and a lack of technological dynamism means that, more generally, the German system of knowledge production and diffusion may have lost touch with changing markets, and that its past virtues – the training system, cost structure and pattern of product and process innovation that helped sustain a comprehensive, and expensive, welfare system – are becoming liabilities in a globalized economy (Streeck 1995).

In the *southern welfare states*, global pressures (competition and financial market influence) will combine with those coming from EU co-ordination requirements and EMU convergence criteria and reduce provision in systems where there are already serious inadequacies in both organization and provision, potentially creating problems of social unrest (Ayala 1994; Saraceno and Negri 1994). Spain, Italy and Greece all suffer from acute labour market difficulties, especially among younger workers and women, revealing major adjustment problems in the more traditional sectors of the economy. High rates of unemployment also signal increasing polarization in terms of income maintenance and pensions between 'hyper-protected' groups (public employees, white collar workers and full-time, permanent employees in medium-sized and large-scale firms) and the 'under-protected' (the unemployed and workers in weak sectors or the extensive informal economy).

While high unemployment levels do not herald a crisis for these countries' social assistance regimes (for the simple reason that their social safety nets are absent or minimal) (Gough 1996), they do have implications for revenue and the funding of other welfare programmes, especially health and pensions regimes which are heavily in deficit. Intensified competition can only exacerbate the unemployment problems facing these countries as they face a difficult task of adjustment, both to the single market and trade liberalization after the Uruguay Round (which is undermining their strengths in traditional, labour-intensive sectors). At the same time, large public deficits mean that these countries are paying a high cost for convergence in line with the timetable for participation in EMU. While the expanded structural funds and the new 'Cohesion Fund' will supposedly provide some compensation for the 'costs of Europe', austerity and budget cuts at a time of growing demand for social support can only compound the problems facing these incompletely institutionalized welfare states.

CONCLUSIONS

It is clear from the above analysis that, although the role played by the EU in social policy has not acquired the dimensions of a state, and while traditional welfare state models in Europe retain their distinctive characters, state autonomy is being progressively eroded in a number of ways. But beyond a limited encroachment on national policy autonomy through the EU's regulatory role along the social dimension, this has little to do with the legislative or regulatory role of the EU or a 'Europeanization' of decision-making. Rather it is related to common trends in policy outcomes (creating a certain 'dualization' of welfare state provision and a shift towards a 'Bismarckian' form of social welfare provision) and a reduction of national policy autonomy linked to economic integration, competitive pressures and the liberalization of capital controls and financial markets.

The future for the European welfare states is unclear, but recent developments suggest that the turbulence they have experienced since the late 1980s is set to increase. At the European level, the concept of social citizenship is likely to remain subordinate to that of economic citizenship, even if the full realization of the latter in an open internal market will require some modification and 'Europeanization' of national social security regimes. In the worst case scenario, at least for those who advocate a strengthened social dimension, 'unity in such a restrictive frame would turn into a unity of "possessive individualism", a unity of markets only' (Leibfried 1992: 261). This impression is reinforced by recent documents from the European Commission which recommend the reduction of social charges, more private cover and a 'new' welfare mix, involving a transfer of certain services for which the state was previously responsible to the market (Kuper 1994).

Given the unlikely constitution of a European welfare state, the alternative is to preserve the welfare state project at the national level by successfully reconciling growth and high (if not full) employment and by preserving the legitimacy of redistributive systems among a disenchanted middle class and against the onslaught of the 'New Right'. This is a tall order and may well require the sort of extensive modification of welfare state arrangements advocated by Esping-Andersen (1994) and Lindbeck (1994) to render them more flexible. For despite their diversity, the central problem facing European countries is the same – maintaining the legitimacy of the welfare state by adjusting political expectations and reshaping the domestic coalitions on which they are based. This poses a difficult dilemma, because, as Sigg *et al.* (1996) point out, in doing so they have to strike a balance between the three goals of any social welfare system – insurance against risk, the welfare safety net and income redistribution. By prioritizing the insurance function (as would occur if countries converge on the 'Bismarckian' model), the poorer and inactive members of society will be penalized and 'social citizenship' undermined. If, on the other hand, they prioritize the assistance objective or income redistribution, they risk losing the support of the middle classes and business for expensive welfare programmes. Ultimately, this too would seriously damage the ideal of social solidarity which is still central (although increasingly under threat) in all except the Anglo-Saxon variety of welfare. Defending the essence of the European welfare model requires navigating a difficult course between these two scenarios, while also withstanding pressures from the global economy.

REFERENCES

Abrahamson, P. (1992) 'Welfare pluralism: towards a new consensus for a European social policy?', in L. Hantrais, S. Mangen and M. O'Brien (eds) *The Mixed Economy of Welfare*, European Research Centre, Loughborough University.

Ayala, L. (1994) 'Social needs, inequality and the welfare state in Spain: trends and prospects', *Journal of European Social Policy* 4 (2): 159–79.

Benington, J. and M. Taylor (1993) 'Changes and challenges facing the UK welfare state in the Europe of the 1990s', *Policy and Politics* 21 (2): 121–34.

Chassard, Y. and O. Quintin (1992) 'Social protection in the European Community:

towards a convergence of policies', *International Social Security Review* 45, (1–2): 91–108.

Cochrane, A. and K. Doogan (1993) 'Welfare policy: the dynamics of European integration', *Policy and Politics* 21 (2): 85–95.

Deakin, N. and C. Jones Finer (1993) ' "This halo business": the British welfare state in European perspective', Paper presented at the International Sociological Association's Research Committee on Comparative Research on Welfare States in Transition, Oxford, 9–12 September.

Esping-Andersen, G. (1990) *The Three Worlds of Welfare Capitalism*, Cambridge: Polity Press.

—— (1994) 'Equality and work in the post-industrial life cycle', in D. Miliband (ed.) *Reinventing the Left*, Cambridge: Polity Press.

European Commission (DGV) (1995) *Social Protection in Europe 1995*, Brussels.

Ferrera, M. (1993) 'Dinamiche di globalizzazione e stato sociale: un introduzione', in M. Ferrera (ed.) *Stato sociale e mercato: Il welfare state europeo sopravviverà alla globalizzazione dell'economia?*, Turin: Edizione della Fondazione Giovanni Agnelli.

—— (1996), 'The "southern model" of welfare in social Europe', *Journal of European Social Policy* 6 (1): 17–37.

Frieden, J.A. (1991) 'Invested interests: the politics of national economic policies in a world of global finance', *International Organization* 45 (4): 425–51.

Garrett, G. and P. Lange (1991) 'Political responses to interdependence: what's left for the Left?', *International Organization* 45 (4): 539–64.

Gilbert, N. (1992) 'From entitlements to incentives: the changing philosophy of social protection', *International Social Security Review*, 45 (3): 5–17.

Gough, I. (1979) *The Political Economy of the Welfare State*, London: Macmillan.

—— (1996) 'Social assistance in southern Europe', *South European Society and Politics* 1 (1): 1–23.

Gould, A. (1996) 'Sweden: the last bastion of social democracy', in V. George and P. Taylor-Gooby (eds) *European Welfare Policy: Squaring the Welfare Circle*, London: Macmillan.

Hagen, K. (1992) 'The social dimension: a quest for a European welfare state', in Z. Ferge and J.E. Kolberg (eds) *Social Policies in a Changing Europe*, Frankfurt: Campus Verlag and Boulder, Colo.: Westview Press.

Hirst, P. and G. Thompson (1995) 'Globalization and the future of the nation state', *Economy and Society* 24 (3): 408–42.

Huber, E. and J.D. Stephens (1993) 'The future of the social democratic welfare state: options in the face of economic internationalization and European integration', Paper presented at the International Sociological Association's Research Committee on Comparative Research on Welfare States in Transition, Oxford, 9–12 September.

Jallade, J.-P. (1992) 'Is the crisis behind us? Issues facing social security systems in Western Europe', in Z. Ferge and J.E. Kolberg (eds) *Social Policies in a Changing Europe*, Frankfurt: Campus Verlag and Boulder, Colo.: Westview Press.

Jessop, R. (1993) 'Le transizione al postfordismo e il welfare state postkeynesiano', in M. Ferrera (ed.) *Stato sociale e mercato: Il welfare state europeo sopravviverà alla globalizzazione dell'economia?*, Turin: Edizione della Fondazione Giovanni Agnelli.

Kangas, O. (1994) 'The merging of welfare state models? Past and present trends in Finnish and Swedish social policy' *Journal of European Social Policy*, 4 (2): 79–94.

Katrougalos, G.S. (1996) 'The south European welfare model: the Greek welfare state in search of an identity', *Journal of European Social Policy* 6 (1): 39–60.

Kenis, P. (1991) 'Social Europe in the 1990s: beyond an adjunct to achieving a common market', *Futures* 23 (7): 724–38.

Korpi, W. (1993) 'Economists as policy experts and policy advocates: on problems of values and objectivity in the welfare state-economic growth debate', Paper presented at the International Sociological Association's Research Committee on Comparative Research on Welfare States in Transition, Oxford, 9–12 September.

Kosonen, P. (1993) 'Europeanization, globalization and the lost stability of national welfare states', Paper presented at the International Sociological Association's Research Committee on Comparative Research on Welfare States in Transition, Oxford, 9–12 September.

—— (1994) 'National welfare states and economic integration in Europe', Paper presented at the COST A7 Workshop, Convergence or Divergence? Welfare States in the Face of European Integration, 9–11 June, Sorø, Denmark.

Kuhnle, S. (1993) 'Il modello scandinavo nell'era dell'integrazione europea: spinte al cambiamento interne ed esterne', in M. Ferrera (ed.) *Stato sociale e mercato: Il welfare state europeo sopravviverà alla globalizzazione dell'economia?*, Turin: Edizione della Fondazione Giovanni Agnelli.

Kuper, B.-O. (1994) 'The green and white papers of the European Union: the apparent goal of reduced social benefits', *Journal of European Social Policy* 4 (2): 129–37.

Kurzer, P. (1991) 'The internationalization of business and domestic class compromises', *West European Politics* 14 (4): 1–24.

Leibfried, S. (1992) 'Towards a European welfare state? On integrating poverty regimes into the European Community', in Z. Ferge and J.E. Kolberg (eds) *Social Policies in a Changing Europe*, Frankfurt: Campus Verlag and Boulder, Colo.: Westview Press.

—— (1993) 'Conceptualising European social policy: the EC as social actor', in L. Hantrais and S. Mangen (eds) *The Policy Making Process and the Social Actors*, European Research Centre, Loughborough University.

—— (1994) 'The social dimension of the European Union: en route to positive joint sovereignty?', *Journal of European Social Policy* 4 (4): 239–62.

Leibfried, S. and P. Pierson (1995) 'Semi-sovereign welfare sates: social policy in a multi-tiered Europe', in S. Leibfried and P. Pierson (eds) *Fragmented Social Policy: The European Union's Social Dimension in Comparative Perspective*, Washington, DC: Brookings Institution.

Lindbeck, A. (1993) *Overshooting, Reform and Retreat of the Welfare State*, Institute for International Economic Studies, Seminar Paper No. 552, Stockholm.

—— (1994) *Uncertainty Under the Welfare State: Policy Induced Risk*, Institute for International Economic Studies, Seminar Paper No. 576, Stockholm.

Mishra, R. (1993) 'Social policy in the postmodern world: the welfare state in Europe by comparison with North America', in C. Jones (ed.) *New Perspectives on the Welfare State in Europe*, Routledge: London and New York.

Montanari, B. (1995) 'Harmonization of social policies and social regulation in the European Community', *European Journal of Political Research* 27 (1): 21–45.

Notermans, T. (1993) 'The abdication of national policy autonomy: why the macro-economic policy regime has become so unfavourable to labour', *Politics and Society* 21 (2): 133–67.

O'Connor, J. (1973) *The Fiscal Crisis of the State*, New York: St James Press.

Overbye, E.G. (1993) 'Convergence in policy outcomes? The development of social security in European and Anglo-Saxon countries', Paper presented at the International Sociological Association's Research Committee on Comparative Research on Welfare States in Transition, Oxford, 9–12 September.

Pfaller, A., I. Gough and G. Therborn (1991) *Can the Welfare State Compete? A Comparative Study of Five Advanced Capitalist Countries*, London: Macmillan.

Pierson, P. and S. Leibfried (1995) 'Introduction: the dynamics of social policy integration', in S. Leibfried and P. Pierson (eds) *Fragmented Social Policy: The European Union's Social Dimension in Comparative Perspective*, Washington, DC: Brookings Institution.

Rhodes, M. (1992) 'The future of the social dimension: labour market regulation in post-1992 Europe', *Journal of Common Market Studies* 30 (1): 23–51.

—— (1993) 'The social dimension after Maastricht: setting a new agenda for the labour market', *International Journal of Comparative Labour Law and Industrial Relations* 9 (4): 297–325.

—— (1995) 'A regulatory conundrum: industrial relations and the "social dimension"', in S. Leibfried and P. Pierson (eds) *Fragmented Social Policy: The European Union's Social Dimension in Comparative Perspective*, Washington, DC: Brookings Institution.

Ruggie, J.G. (1982), 'International regimes, transactions and change: embedded liberalism in the postwar economic order', *International Organization* 36 (2): 379–415.

Saraceno, C. and N. Negri (1994) 'The changing Italian welfare state', *Journal of European Social Policy* 4 (1): 19–34.

Scharpf, F. (1988) ' "The joint-decision trap": lessons from German federalism and European integration', *Public Administration* 66 (3): 239–78.

Sigg, R., I. Zeitzer, X. Scheil-Adlung, C. Kuptsch and M. Tracy (1996) 'Developments and trends in social security 1993–1995', *International Social Security Review* 49 (2): 5–126.

Standing, G. (1995), 'Labor insecurity through market regulation: legacy of the 1980s, challenge for the 1990s', in K. McFate, R. Lawson and W.J. Wilson (eds) *Poverty, Inequality and the Future of Social Policy: Western States in the New World Order*, New York: Russell Sage Foundation.

Stephens, J.D. (1996) 'The Scandinavian welfare states: achievements, crisis and prospects', in G. Esping-Andersen (ed.) *Welfare States in Transition: National Adaptations in the Global Economy*, London: Sage Publications.

Stephens, J.D., E. Huber and L. Ray (1994) 'The welfare state in hard times', Paper presented at the American Political Science Association, New York, 1–4 September.

Streeck, W. (1992) 'National diversity, regime competition and institutional deadlock: problems in forming a European industrial relations system', *Journal of Public Policy* 12 (4): 301–30.

—— (1995) 'German capitalism: does it exist, can it survive?', in C. Crouch and W. Streeck (eds) *Modern Capitalism or Modern Capitalisms?* , London: Frances Pinter.

Streeck, W. and P.C. Schmitter (1991) 'From national corporatism to transnational pluralism: organized interests in the Single European Market', *Politics and Society* 19 (2): 133–64.

6 The social democratic predicament and global economic integration
A capital dilemma*

Jonathon W. Moses

Whereas there is much agreement among economists and political scientists about the efficiency-gains associated with a unified market in tangible goods, the internationalization of capital markets has received fewer words of praise. Recent tensions within the European Monetary System (EMS) might even suggest that capital market integration has brought with it a new international economic regime which governs by an iron law of policy. This chapter addresses the constraints placed by this particular aspect of global and regional economic integration (financial capital mobility) on a particular regional form of capitalist development (northern European social democracies). This problem of the Nordic countries carries with it considerable implications for welfare state arrangements in a number of European countries (see Chapter 5 by Rhodes in this volume).

The social democracies of northern Europe, until recently, were able and willing to pursue relative policy autonomy, maintaining full employment as a primary objective of economic policy. For these countries, at this time, the distinction between national and international concerns was clear-cut. Today, Nordic unemployment rates and policy objectives are approaching those on the rest of the continent. Efforts to maintain national policy objectives are being challenged by forces at two overlapping levels: one global, the other regional. As a result, solutions to once national dilemmas are now being sought at both of these levels.

The most important global factor, financial capital mobility (henceforth, just capital mobility), is challenging national policy autonomy in all of its variants. To the extent that Nordic social democracies had a distinct policy line that varied from other developed nations, their conformity under global pressure is an interesting subject of study. This chapter argues that social democratic governments want to maintain full employment, but are handicapped by changes in the international economy. Its intent is to ask whether the traditional policy mixes of these countries can be maintained in the new international economic environment, and if so – how? In this way, the story told here is similar to those told in other areas (e.g., Japan): global capital mobility challenges heretofore unique regional modes of development (cf. Chapter 3 by Stubbs in this volume).

In addition to these global forces, however, there are pressures for change (and potential solutions) circulating at the regional level. European attempts at solving the dilemmas that arise from global capital mobility present themselves as alternative regime options for the Nordic social democracies. Joining the European single market and the prospect of a single currency represent potential solutions to the problems arising from international capital mobility. At the same time, however, European regime decisions represent yet another challenge to (neighbouring) national policy autonomy. Finland and Sweden's decision to join, and Norway's taxing decision to opt out of, the European Union should be read in this light.[1] This chapter aims to understand the relationship between regional and global factors – between the pressures from European integration and an increasingly global financial market – by looking at the effect that they both have had on social democratic policies. The Nordic social democracies, as neighbouring states to the European Union, were under unique pressure from both regional and global factors.

The argument which follows offers a parsimonious explanation of the way in which increased capital mobility affects the traditional policy matrix of social democratic regimes. While many authors have alluded to the nature of the problem, there has been no explicit detailing of the mechanisms by which small state autonomy is being undermined by international (and regional) economic (and political) integration. It is my hope that the formalization in the first part of the chapter, in a closed-capital economy context, will shine light on the nature of the problems that accompanied the increased international mobility of capital.

Generally, my intent is to provide a framework for understanding the social democratic predicament (in all of its variants) in terms of a policy dilemma brought about by regional integration and the development of global capital markets. Although my focus is on the Nordic countries, the lessons are intended to be generalizable. Small, porous, social democracies have represented one of the most autonomous economic policy regimes in the post-war era. In that role, they represent a good test on the bounds of autonomy in relation to increased capital mobility. As the Nordic social democracies are smaller and more porous than most, they should feel the impact of this integration earlier and hardest. In this respect, Nordic adjustment might be seen as a bell-wether for the larger economies.

The chapter is divided into three parts. The first part looks at traditional models of social democracy in terms of an internal (full employment) balance encouraged by active government intervention. The social democratic compromise is modelled in terms similar to a simple iterative prisoners' dilemma, where organized capital and labour are encouraged to achieve co-operative, Pareto efficient, outcomes through government transfers, information and guarantees. The specific nature of government intervention is assumed to be primarily fiscal or monetary in nature.

The advent of unprecedented levels of capital mobility has made this domestic level game obsolete. The second part of the chapter shows how governments face policy dilemmas when capital is fully mobile. Because governments, under conditions where there are policy dilemmas, are unable to provide the incentives required to overcome the prisoners' dilemma in section one, the social democratic compromise might break down.

The third section offers an explanation for the lag between the advent of increased international capital mobility and the increased rates of unemployment in the Nordic social democracies. Using the model from the second section, I suggest that exchange rate adjustments could be (and were) used to overcome the policy dilemma. De/revaluations were used as a means to defend the external balance so that traditional policy instruments could remain focused on the full employment objective.

The conclusion sums up this deductive argument and suggests some avenues for future empirical research with which to test the hypotheses presented.

A SOCIAL DEMOCRATIC MODEL

Quite possibly there are more definitions of social democracy than there are social democracies to be defined. Whereas it may be more common for political scientists to point to the electoral hegemony of a Social Democratic Party, I intend to use a broader definition which emphasizes the economic and social aspects of the political movement. In particular, social democracy can be understood as a corporatist-based[2] institutional- and policy-mix aimed at full employment. Full employment growth policies can be seen as the result of a bargained outcome between peak, hierarchical, organizations representing capital and labour, combined with government policies aimed at complementing those national bargaining outcomes.

The disadvantages of such a general definition are clear and many, such that little reflection on them is required. To its advantage, the model presented below can be used as a surrogate for political autonomy in the international economy. The lessons learnt from the theoretical section are those for social democracies with centralized peak bargaining organizations in a world with managed capital flows. Along with others, I assume that these institutions make the full employment outcome more likely than in less centralized systems (e.g., Lange and Garrett 1985; Garrett and Lange 1986, 1989; Alvarez *et al.* 1991; Moene and Wallerstein 1993).

It is accepted academic wisdom that the benefits of social democracy in the post-war era can be explained in terms of these small countries' dependence on, and access to, international markets (e.g., Katzenstein 1985). It is my contention that it is this very dependence and access which is the primary impetus for the fall of social democracy. The difference between the traditional explanation and the one that follows is the difference between free trade in tangible goods and free trade in capital.

Earlier definitions of social democracy have emphasized the openness of markets for tangible goods, but failed to note explicitly the necessity of having closed capital markets. This is quite peculiar as the socialist objective, if often only in rhetoric, was social ownership of the means of production (i.e., capital). By assuming that the international context was fixed, and by concentrating on the internal determinants of policy, these authors are unable to explain adequately (or anticipate) the crisis in social democracy. Without belittling explanations based on the contradictions of the welfare state (Offe 1984), the deradicalization effects of industrialization (Kerr *et al.*, 1964) and a growing middle class (Parkin 1972), class divisions (Abrahamson 1971; Esping-Andersen 1985; Swenson 1989), the demographic retreat of the working class, or the shifting priorities of policy-makers (Notermans 1993), I wish to argue that the roots of the current dilemma grow beyond the domestic realm and are part of a wider process of global economic integration which is increasingly interdependent with domestic/regional arrangements.

The defining characteristic of social democratic governance is not solely the relative strength (weakness) of labour (capital); it must also be defined by the relative immobility of capital. Social democracy was a prisoner of its period; as an autonomous economic regime, its traditional policy mixes worked well as long as the free trade rhetoric did not extend beyond tangible goods. Thus, references to social democracy – as is the case below – should assume a condition of managed capital flows.

THE CLOSED-CAPITAL ECONOMY MODEL: A PRISONERS' DILEMMA

Traditionally, social democracy has been characterized mostly in class-theoretical terms. Full employment and solidaristic wage policies are explained in terms of the institutions and norms that sprouted from the relative strength of domestic labour (e.g., Korpi 1983; Esping-Andersen 1985) or the relative weakness of domestic capital (e.g., Castles 1978; Baldwin 1990). This balance of class power crystallized in highly organized class-based institutions (and parties) which minimized conflict between capital and labour. In Scandinavia, Norway's (1935) Basic Agreement and Sweden's (1938) Saltsjöbaden Agreement constituted 'historic compromises', establishing the foundations of effective social democratic rule (Korpi 1983).

It can be argued that corporatist style agreements were able to minimize political confrontation, offer a stable business and bargaining atmosphere, and avoid the pitfalls of both unemployment and inflation.[3] This is a common explanation for the fact that the social democracies have been so successful at maintaining economic growth at full employment levels. Some have even suggested that concerted bargaining and centralization promote 'virtuous circles' that benefit capital, labour *and* governments together (Castles 1978; Przeworski and Wallerstein 1982).

The logic of these arguments is best captured in simple game terms. With highly centralized collective bargaining arrangements, successful policy outcomes can be understood as solutions to something akin to a prisoners' dilemma problem (Maital and Benjamini 1980; Crouch 1985; Lange 1984; Scharpf 1987; Hedström 1986). This is the framework which I intend to use for understanding the current policy dilemmas facing social democracies.

We begin by assuming that a capital-closed economy is organized along class lines in two encompassing (and equally powerful)[4] peak organizations (one representing labour, the other capital). The assumption of power symmetry shared by labour and capital is important for the game's outcome.[5] Wages and prices are determined at regular intervals as a result of bargaining between the two groups.[6]

Government, in the model below, plays a guarantor's role in the capital-closed economy game.[7] Thus, it matters little whether a government is 'left' or 'right' in orientation: its preference is for low inflation, full employment outcomes. Indeed, any government mindful of re-election can be assumed to have these preferences (a formal ranking of the government's preferences is found below). This assumption is all the more reasonable in the Scandinavian context where (a) one can speak of a post-war Social Democratic Party electoral hegemony and (b) where government change has meant little in terms of actual policy outcome.

Following Hedström (1986), this game begins by assuming that a Peak Centralized Labour Organization begins each bargaining round with the following preference ranking: $\beta > \alpha > \delta > \gamma$ (see Figure 6.1). In other words, organized labour would prefer real-wage increases (β); over a low inflationary outcome with no real-wage change (α); over a high inflationary outcome with no real-wage change (δ); over real-wage losses (γ). It is assumed that there is a direct trade-off between wages and profits such that real-wage loss implies increased profits for employers. This helps to explain why the Central Employer Organization prefers the following ranking: $\gamma > \alpha > \delta > \beta$.

In the non-interactive outcome, both organizations find it 'individually' rational to choose δ: increased prices/wages, no real-wage change, outcome (i.e., both a unique Nash and a dominant strategy equilibrium). This equilibrium is not only Pareto Sub-optimal for both negotiating actors, it is also undesirable for a sitting government considering re-election: it is inflationary. This provides an incentive for the government to intervene in the negotiations and attempt to bring about a solution which is consistent with its own preference ranking: $\alpha > \beta > \gamma > \delta$.[8]

In theory, then, governments can be expected to intervene to bring about Pareto efficient outcomes: shifting the corporatist bargaining outcome between labour and capital from δ to α (i.e., to a less inflationary, full employment outcome). The government can, and has the incentive to, encourage co-operative solutions along several lines: by providing information,[9] guarantees,[10] transfers and contemporaneous economic policies (i.e., monetary and fiscal policy mixes).

Government interventions, in particular the latter type (transfers and economic policies), assume an important role in the second part of my argument.

	Central Labour Organization	
	Moderate wage increases	Maximum wage increases
Central employer organization — Moderate price increases	α	β
Central employer organization — Maximum price increases	γ	δ

Rankings	Outcomes
Trade Unions β, α, δ, γ	**Non-Co-operative.** Likely outcome δ: maximum price, maximum wage increase. Not Pareto efficient (α, for example, is preferred by both)
Employers γ, α, δ, β	
Government α, β, γ, δ	**Induced Co-operative Equilibrium.** Government provides guarantees, information and transfers to reach Pareto efficient α solution.

Figure 6.1 The corporatist game

Therefore, before moving on, it may be worth while to explain their relationship to bargaining outcomes in more detail. The general idea is to integrate traditional economic policies (i.e., monetary and fiscal policies) as part of a government strategy of providing incentives for negotiating partners to obtain co-operative outcomes. Oftentimes this linkage is made explicit, especially in connection with incomes policy and/or price freeze agreements. (For example, a price and/or wage freeze is accompanied by an explicit promise by the government to pursue a restrictive economic policy during the agreement's lifetime.)

Indeed, examples of this type are numerous in Scandinavia. A Norwegian Labour Party government in 1973, and again in the period 1975–80, offered tax cuts for wage moderation; and from 1978–9 the central wage agreement was complemented by a mandatory wage freeze. In Sweden, explicit linkage is less frequent, but in the Haga Agreements (1974–6) the wage-earner organizations promised to moderate their wage claims in return for increased payroll taxes. In the period 1983–4 there was also some adjustment of the Swedish tax schedules in connection with the upcoming bargaining round. Thus, it was not uncommon for governments to intervene and induce a co-operative equilibrium.

But traditional policy mixes can be important influences even when they are only implicitly part of the negotiations. Consider two cases. First, the likelihood of encouraging both organizations to move from δ (a high inflationary outcome with no real-wage change) to α (a low inflationary outcome with no real-wage change) surely increases during periods when the government pursues a restrictive policy mix (or when both actors anticipate such a move in the near future). Alternatively, in the aftermath of a devaluation (or under expectations of a government's future devaluation), it may prove very difficult to get labour market partners to agree to make the move from δ to α. The importance of such government 'background' policy was seen in the wake of the recent (1993) Swedish devaluation. Leif Blomberg, the Swedish Metal Industry Workers' Union (Metall) spokesman, publicly demanded (for his industry) wage increases that would shadow competitiveness improvements in the immediate aftermath of the devaluation.[11] Thus, it was the government's prior policy which set the context for subsequent corporatist bargaining rounds.

In these closed-capital models, monetary and fiscal policies can be applied in traditional fashion, according to simple IS/LM[12] logic. During the pre-stagflationary period, counter-cyclical demand management could be efficiently directed at the full employment internal balance. Supply-side measures were more easily funded, facilitating the co-operative solutions outlined above. Under conditions of stagflation, fiscal and monetary policies became less effective at addressing so-called cost-push inflation and demand-gap unemployment, but these policies could be (and were) fortified with effective wage policies (Scharpf 1987: 232; Weintraub 1978), and exchange rate changes (see below, section three).

If this is an accurate, albeit amorphous, depiction of the social democratic compromise, the nature of its recent collapse might be said to have come from one of three directions. First, a relative shift in the power of one organization would make the compromise unlikely and problematic. Should the power of capital (*labour*) grow relative to labour (*capital*) it would be less inclined to enter into such a co-operative arrangement, and might try to secure its preference, γ (β), in the open market. The relative bargaining strength between the two organizations would approach levels found in the rest of the developed world, and less co-operative solutions might be expected. In a similar vein, changing perceptions of relative strength might also encourage one of the organizations to jettison corporatist solutions in the hopes of achieving better outcomes in the open market.

The co-operative solution might also be problematic if fragmentation undermines the encompassing nature of the two organizations. Fragmentation might occur, as Høgsnes and Hanisch (1988) have shown, when peak bargaining organizations pursue solidaristic wage policies and/or allow wage drift. The game theoretic framework is useful only in so far as the peak bargaining institutions remain highly centralized and encompassing. The recent breakdown of collective bargaining in Sweden, along sectoral lines, is indicative of the problem. The causes of fragmentation may be manifold, but increased international capital mobility might be responsible for significant sectoral divisions (Frieden 1991).

Another, non-exclusionary, explanation for the collapse of the model might be found in the weakening of the government's position to offer feasible transfers, information and/or guarantees to cement Pareto efficient outcomes. Without devaluing the importance of the other two government instruments (information and guarantees), or suggesting that the other variables do not offer significant explanations for the breakdown of collective bargaining, it is the remainder of my argument that the government's ability to wield the third instrument (domestic economic policy and transfers) has been undermined by changes in the international economy.

While there are many explanations of the collapse of social democracy that emphasize the internal dynamic of class and organization strength, the fact that the model has been undermined in several countries simultaneously suggests an additional reason to search for an explanation beyond the domestic realm. Thus, a comparative analysis would suggest that an external variable may be responsible for effecting changes in one of the three ways mentioned above.[13]

INTERNAL AND EXTERNAL BALANCES: THE POLICY DILEMMA

This second section adds another layer to the bargaining model outlined above. The first section assumed a closed economy with effective fiscal and monetary tools at the disposal of government officials. These tools, along with other government incentives, helped move collective bargaining rounds to co-operative solutions. In this depiction, policy effectiveness may be understood in simple IS/LM terms.

Governments in this model wielded monetary and fiscal policy in textbook style, providing both counter-cyclical impetuses to smooth economic expansions (retractions) and supply-side measures to encourage even growth and distribution (Stephens 1994). Regular collective bargaining rounds are both affected by, and made within the context of, government economic policy in 'virtuous circle' fashion. In this way, social democracies were able to maintain some of the world's lowest unemployment rates combined with egalitarian income distributions.

Recently, the social democratic model (as well as much of its collective bargaining core) has collapsed. The hardest evidence of this can be found in Figure 6.2, where Swedish and Norwegian unemployment levels are shown to have skyrocketed in recent years. I propose that the reason for this breakdown can be found in the fact that increased capital mobility has undermined the effectiveness of traditional monetary and fiscal policies, making the induced co-operative solutions more difficult to attain. In a world with increased capital mobility and fixed exchange rates, it is quite difficult to pursue an independent policy mix.

Traditionally, social democratic models have focused only on the internal

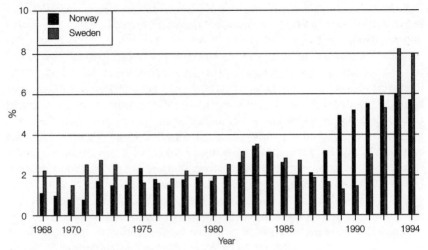

Figure 6.2 Unemployment (percentage of total labour force)
Sources: OECD (1983, 1993); *Nordic Economic Outlook*, 14 February 1994

balance (full employment); the external balance (of trade and payments) is assumed to be of marginal interest.[14] This is largely an artefact of an international regime characterized by Ruggie as 'embedded liberalism': external balances never become threatening as payment flows were largely restrained by exchange controls (Ruggie 1982). Erik Lundberg has juxtaposed the Swedish post-war experience with that of the United Kingdom. His prominence as a leading Swedish economist, and the relevance of his juxtaposition for our current purposes, justifies the following, lengthy citation:

> The most important difference from the United Kingdom developments is the absence of disturbing balance of payments difficulties. Since 1947 and up to 1965 foreign exchange conditions have not – or at most only to a negligible extent as a potential factor – worked as a restriction on demand and costs, and have therefore not necessitated restraining policies. It is in fact quite remarkable both in the shorter and longer run how parallel export and import volume as well as value indices have been moving ... After the liberalization of imports in 1950 (more or less completely effectuated by 1954), there have been no controls of any relevance on imports, and Swedish tariffs have been kept on a relatively low level ... The regular long-term capital import and export movements are controlled by the government and are of small importance ... It should be emphasized that Sweden has during the whole period kept a certain amount of exchange regulation, mainly implying control of long-term capital movements, thereby also giving more free space for independent monetary policy than is possible in countries with internationally highly integrated money markets.
>
> (Lundberg 1968: 206–8)

The removal of these capital controls has led to an erosion of the independent monetary policy to which Lundberg refers.[15] In order to understand the impact of increased capital mobility on the social democratic policy mix, it is necessary to extend the game framework of the first section to another level.

The problem can be captured visually by using a two by two box matrix drawn for internal and external balances. Whereas the closed economy model might be presented in two by one terms (where the government responds to a recession with expansionary policies, and to a boom with restrictive policies), increased capital mobility requires that another dimension be added to the model. Both the closed- and open-capital economy models, for the time being, assume fixed exchange rates. That assumption is briefly relaxed in section three. Both dimensions (internal and external) are captured in Figure 6.3.

Generally, small open economies trading in the world market are faced with two policy objectives (internal and external balances), leading to four possible outcomes. These economies face the following four quadrants:

1 a domestic boom with an external surplus;
2 a domestic recession and an external surplus;
3 a domestic boom with an external deficit; or
4 a domestic recession and an external deficit.

In this characterization, both internal and external balances are at equilibrium at the intersection of the four quadrants. The unshaded quadrants (two and three), though complicated by the addition of an external imbalance, can be resolved using traditional economic policy tools. In quadrant two, for example, an expansionary economic policy will correct both internal and external imbalances. In the closed-capital economy, countercyclical spending is straightforward. Thus, by lowering interest rates, the domestic recession *and* the external surplus are solved concomitantly. On the fiscal side, an external surplus can be corrected by borrowing abroad. The money borrowed can be spent at home to spark output, bettering the internal balance. The same, though reversed, is true for quadrant three. Foreshadowing

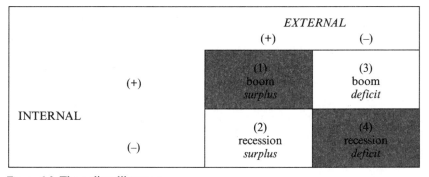

Figure 6.3 The policy dilemmas

the next stage of the argument, contrast the situation in the open-capital economy: an expansionary domestic policy might spur growth internally by lowering the interest rates. However, lower domestic interest rates will provoke capital flight in search of higher returns abroad, nullifying the effects of the policy.

Returning to the assumption of a closed-capital economy, the shaded quadrants (one and four), however, represent policy dilemmas in that pursuing a solution to one balance worsens the other (given traditional policy instruments). Consider the following examples. In the fourth quadrant, expansionary policies to achieve full employment work against the restrictive policies required of a foreign deficit. The same conflict is evident in the first quadrant: restrictive domestic policies would exacerbate the external surplus by restricting import demand. The dilemma is not hopeless, as we shall see below, but its solution requires an additional policy instrument.

However, a switch to free capital mobility severely exacerbates this dilemma. Increased capital mobility undermines the effectiveness of government policy when it is reliant on traditional policy mixes of either the monetary or fiscal type. This, in turn, undermines the induced co-operative outcomes to the model outlined in section one. Under these new conditions, fiscal and monetary policies must be redirected to defend the external balance; no longer can they be reserved for effecting an internal, full employment, balance. Domestic interest rates are severely constrained by the rates on foreign currencies to which the home currency is fixed. Budget deficits and fiscal policies are also constrained by creditworthiness constraints, real appreciations (fed by debt-financed fiscal expansions), and the loss of seignorage and surprise-inflation revenues (Moses 1994, 1995).

Thus, in order to return to the full employment equilibrium of social democratic bargaining outcomes, and in order to restore confidence in the possibility of achieving Pareto efficient outcomes in the corporatist game modelled in section one, monetary and fiscal policies need to be effectively redirected to the internal balance. This can only be achieved by once again securing the external balance. The lifting of capital controls in these countries has meant that the external balance demands more attention, at the expense of the internal balance. Monetary and fiscal policy in these countries must now be diverted *away* from securing the internal balance *to* defending the external balance. In effect these countries are suffering from a classical policy dilemma: too many policy targets and not enough instruments.

In the post-war era, the external balance has traditionally been maintained by the widespread resort to exchange controls. This is not the only possible instrument; earlier periods of capital mobility (and the instability associated with it) were met and managed by government implementation of both exchange and trade constraints. In the inter-war period, for example, tariffs were used within the framework of bilateral trade agreements.[16] Under Bretton Woods, foreign exchange controls dominated. During both of these periods, an internal balance – one more favourable to labour – could be obtained with traditional monetary and fiscal policies *because* the external balance was secured with another, independent, instrument.

Indeed, during the formative inter-war period of social democracy in Sweden, the autonomy issue became dominant in the policy debate:

> The regimes of fixed versus free exchange rates were compared. The economists used the conception of 'international space' as a reminder, rather than a measure, of the limited latitude the country might have for independent expansionary policies. They paid attention to import leakages when discussing multiplier processes; they considered international capital flows when studying what scope there was for expansive monetary policies, not least as to their effects on interest rates.
>
> (Lundberg 1985: 9)

In 1931 that 'international space' was provided for by large devaluations which significantly undervalued the krona throughout most of the following decade (Lundberg 1983: chs 2–4). It is the same sort of space that was utilized by the social democracies in the 1970s as a means of extending autonomy and policy effectiveness in a world economy more and more characterized by international capital flows.

With the advent of increased capital mobility from the 1970s onwards, the social democratic model, as depicted in the first section, was severely undermined. Policy-makers had to redirect their policy instruments to manage problems with the external balance, at the expense of the internal balance. In short, price stability came to replace full employment as the major objective of policy.

THE DEVALUATION DECADE

What remains to be explained is the decade-long lag between the rise of capital mobility and the rise of unemployment. After all, social democracies were able to maintain high employment levels throughout the 1970s and early 1980s – when most of the other industrialized economies were suffering from serious adjustment difficulties. One simple explanation for this difference may be that capital mobility develops over time. While the process itself may have begun in the late 1960s and early 1970s, the policy constraints were only beginning to be felt in the 1980s. A second explanation may be the judicious use of exchange rate adjustments.

During much of the 1970s social democracies used re/devaluations as a means of dividing the two balances, before conquering them both (Lybeck 1985). Exchange rate adjustments allowed the social democracies to maintain their full employment equilibrium while other economies fell prey to external disequilibria. The model in the second section suggests how exchange rate adjustments might have supplemented the traditional economic policy mix as a means of defending the external balance, leaving the monetary and fiscal policies free to promote employment.

If we return to the shaded policy dilemmas in quadrants one and four of Figure 6.3, we can see how flexible exchange rates might liberate policy-makers from their external constraint. By adjusting the exchange rate, policy-makers can manipulate the internal/external price mix to isolate the internal and external effects of a given policy.[17] An example may prove illustrative. If we assume fixed exchange rates and free capital mobility with the domestic economy in quadrant four (i.e., a domestic recession and an external deficit), the government is one tool short of recovery. This is the point of the previous section. Now, assume that the government devalues its currency. A devalu-ation will immediately shift domestic demand away from imports, and increase the export of its products by lowering their production costs relative to competing countries.[18] Thus, a devaluation will address the problem of the trade deficit in quadrant four. The domestic recession could then be alleviated by the new demand in both exposed and sheltered sectors.

Similarly, the dilemma in quadrant one can be solved by a revaluation. In this case there was a boom in the domestic economy, and a trade surplus with the rest of the world. Revaluing the currency will shift demand from domestically produced goods to those imported from abroad. It will also undermine international demand for its exported goods, as their production costs will become relatively expensive. This will lighten the trade surplus burden. At the same time, the reduced demand for goods in both sectors will dampen the overheated domestic economy.

Thus, the devaluations of the 1970s seem to support the hypotheses pur-ported by the analytical framework above: de/revaluations can be used as a means to free up traditional policy tools in the face of increasingly burden-some external imbalances. Obviously, exchange rate adjustments are not the only tool available for defending the external balance, but they do help to shine some light on the nature of the current dilemma.

CONCLUDING REMARKS

I have tried to provide a parsimonious analytical model which explains and contextualizes social democratic full-employment policy outcomes. Full employment outcomes were explained in terms of a simple model in the context of embedded liberalism dominated by relatively fixed exchange rates. Government intervention is non-partisan and is directed at securing Pareto efficient outcomes for the negotiating parties, and society in general. The main government tools for assisting and securing those outcomes are assumed to be autonomous monetary and fiscal policies.

In effect, the capital dilemma facing social democracies is twofold. As others have shown, global capital mobility increases the relative strength of capital in corporatist bargaining environments, offering it an effective 'exit option' (Gill and Law 1989; Martin 1994). Capital, now liberated, can cir-cumvent traditional fiscal and monetary policies, exacerbating the external balance problem. In addition, however, I have argued that increased capital mobility also places constraints on traditional government policy instruments. With fixed exchange rates, traditional monetary and fiscal tools must be redirected away from full employment to defending the balance of payments. This leaves the government without adequate tools for maintaining the domestic balance. Unless a new tool is devoted to securing the external balance, traditional policy tools will not be able to eke out the political and economic autonomy traditionally associated with small social democratic regimes.

Nordic desires for EU membership are a reflection of these problems. For Sweden and Finland, the hope is that the European Union will be able to implement traditionally national policy instruments at the regional level. This may be optimistic in that it will require the development of new capital controls, as well as fiscal and monetary policies, at the regional level. Furthermore, the EU appears to be moving in the opposite direction as its capital markets have become increasingly integrated with global markets. Norway will need to decide whether to pursue the exchange rate adjustment option as outlined in section three, or follow in the shadow of European regime decisions. At any rate, Norway's options for autonomous policy – as a non-EU member – are more numerous.

The investigatory nature of this argument has required that it be balanced on two related fulcrums. Future work might be aimed at more explicitly grounding the assumptions that underlie these pivotal points. The first assumption regards the nature of the connection between collective bargaining institutions, outcomes, and government policy. Were social democratic policies really utilized as incentives to secure co-operative outcomes in the centralized bargaining rounds?

The second pivotal assumption of this chapter is the linkage of increased capital mobility with an effective external constraint on domestic economic policy. Mainstream macroeconomic theory would recognize the argument in terms of the constraint placed on monetary policy, but would suggest that fiscal policy should only increase in effectiveness with free capital mobility. Why, and if, fiscal policy is no longer an effective instrument for encouraging collective agreements needs to be examined more closely.

Casual observation suggests that both of these assumptions are consistent with the empirical record, but further empirical investigation can and should be followed up to provide firmer grounding for the central hypothesis posited herein. After all, the models provided are not meant as definitive explanations for the fall of social democracy. Obviously, the nature of the problem is much more complex than could be provided for by this simple framework. My intent is to try and formalize the relationship between internal and external balances as a means for generating both counter-intuitive and future empirical findings in the field and to suggest why this regional variant of economic development is under threat from global economic integration. The models do, however, clearly show the nature of the problems facing economies that wish to pursue full-employment policies in an increasingly integrated regional and global context. As exchange controls have become increasingly difficult to maintain, and traditional policy weapons have become increasingly unwieldy and ineffective, regional and global integration has effectively imposed upon states an iron law of policy.

NOTES

* An earlier version of this chapter was presented to the 22nd Annual European Consortium for Political Research (ECPR) Joint Sessions of Workshops, Madrid, Spain, April 17–22 1994. I would like to thank Jeffry Frieden, Scott Gates, Torbjørn Knutsen, Geoffrey Underhill, and the Madrid workshop participants for their useful comments and suggestions. No responsibility on their part is implied.

1 For a more detailed analysis of the Nordic EU referendums, see Moses and Jenssen (1996).

2 Obviously, social democracy can be defined as being more than highly centralized, encompassing bargaining institutions. European history also teaches us that the existence of these institutions does not in itself guarantee social democratic outcomes. In other words, these institutions represent a necessary but not sufficient part of the social democratic definition. Still, they are an essential part of the policy mix, and concentration on them for purposes of analytical parsimony is justified.

3 This view is not universal. Several observers have held that either capital (Hibbs 1977; Korpi 1983; Korpi and Shalev 1980; Stephens 1980) or labour (Offe 1981; Panitch 1977, 1980) loses from centralized bargaining arrangements.

4 The assumption of symmetry is important. If organized capital thinks itself stronger than organized labour (or vice versa) it will be inclined to try and achieve its objectives in a more suitable forum (e.g., the open marketplace).

5 Obviously, this depends heavily on how the game is structured.

6 In the model, wages and prices are determined contemporaneously. Generally, however, prices are determined after wages are set (Maital and Benjamini 1980: 465). Although the decisions involved are more complex than a prisoners' dilemma game, because wage and price decisions are more complex than a simple moderate/maximum dichotomy, the situation is 'strategically in a class with' prisoners' dilemma games (Kreps 1990: 38).

7 The iterated nature of a wage bargaining game might suggest that the role of a government guarantor is not all that large. Iteration, in itself, is said to encourage co-operative outcomes, as players pursue strategies over time which signal preferences (Oye 1986). Iteration alone, however, is not enough to bring about collectively optimal solutions as countless examples from international relations show us. Indeed, iteration is a highly fragile means of effecting co-operation (Conybeare 1986: 150).

Iteration alone may not affect co-operation as the perceived payoffs of the game may change over time and obscure the interactiveness of the game. In addition, punishing defection with direct and proper retaliation is often crucial for the success of contingent strategies in iterated games. State intervention in both these realms, as well as providing the over-arching context (favourable or not) of the negotiations is important for inducing co-operative outcomes. Essentially, it is the government's role in this context which ensures that perceived payoffs remain unchanged over time, and that penalties are swift, so that iteration is an effective incentive for co-operative solutions.

8 We can assume that this is the preference ranking of a traditional Social Democratic Party. Conservative parties may prefer $\alpha > \gamma > \beta > \delta$. The difference is

unimportant, however, in that both governments prefer the low inflation/Pareto Optimal outcome.

9 Technically, in terms of game theory, the actors are moving simultaneously and therefore play with imperfect information. Informally, however, the centralized bargaining institutions outlined in so-called Basic Agreements can be understood in informational terms, as information is shared by all three actors (labour, capital and government) at each bargaining round. In Scandinavia, for example, it is commonplace that bargaining organizations share economic data and projections from which their individual strategies are planned.

10 Guarantees in this context might be understood as legislated income policy solutions, price and/or wage freezes, or even government sponsorship of dispute settlement commissions/courts.

11 For a description and interview, see 'Ett genomruttet lönesystem' in *Dagens Nyheter*, 28 April 1993.

12 The IS/LM model represents the core of modern macroeconomics. The IS schedule represents a goods market equilibrium, while the LM schedule represents the money market equilibrium. See Dornbusch and Fischer (1994) for a description.

13 It might also be the case that integration itself raises uncertainty in that information-gathering costs rise along with the likelihood of cheating by partners (i.e., increased difficulty of detection).

14 That full employment is desirable is fairly obvious, but the desirability of an external balance may be less clear. The simplest answer is that (with fixed exchange rates) a current account deficit requires borrowing. See Moses (1994).

15 For an explanation of the impetus for their removal, see Goodman and Pauly (1993), Tranøy (1993), Helleiner (1994), and Moses (1994).

16 Generally, tariff levels in these small open economies have always been lower than those in the larger economies. Still, they have varied over time. In the inter-war period, tariffs not only increased, but they were fortified with other constraints in the form of foreign ownership restrictions and domestic cartels.

17 I do not mean to suggest that devaluations are a cost-free economic tool for small economies. Frequent exchange rate adjustments in the same direction can feed speculative ebbs and floods of capital, leading to fiscal instability. Instability and lack of faith in a currency lead to a higher interest rate which discourages domestic investment and growth. In addition, exchange rate changes sometimes affect long-term price developments.

18 This assumes that imports are either luxuries, have domestically produced substitutes and/or they do not play a significant role as inputs in domestically produced goods. To the extent that the Nordic economies are heavily reliant on raw material production and export, and have adequate substitution possibilities, this assumption is largely unproblematic.

REFERENCES

Abrahamson, P. (1971) 'Social class and political change in Western Europe', *Comparative Political Studies* 4: 131–55.

Alvarez, R.M., G. Garrett and P. Lange (1991) 'Government partisanship, labor organization, and macroeconomic performance', *American Political Science Review* 85: 539–56.

Baldwin, P. (1990) *The Politics of Social Solidarity*, Cambridge: Cambridge University Press.

Castles, F. (1978) *The Social Democratic Image of Society*, London: Routledge.

Conybeare, J. (1986) 'Trade Wars: a comparative study of Anglo-Hanse,

Franco-Italian, and Hawly-Smoot conflicts', in K.A. Oye (ed.) *Cooperation under Anarchy*, Princeton: Princeton University Press, 147–72.

Crouch, C. (1985) 'The conditions for trade-union wage restraint', in L.N. Lindberg and C.S. Maier (eds) *The Politics of Inflation and Economic Stagnation*, Washington, DC: Brookings Institution.

Dornbusch, R. and S. Fischer (1994) *Macroeconomics* (6th edn), London: McGraw-Hill.

Esping-Andersen, G. (1985) *Politics against Markets*, Princeton: Princeton University Press.

Frieden, J.A. (1991) 'Invested interests: the politics of national economic policies in a world of global finance', *International Organization* 45: 425–51.

Garrett, G. and P. Lange (1986) 'Economic growth in capitalist democracies, 1974–1982', *World Politics* 38: 517–45.

—— (1989) 'Government partisanship and economic performance: when and how does "who governs" matter?', *Journal of Politics* 51: 676–93.

Gill, S.R. and D. Law (1989) 'Global hegemony and the structural power of capital', *International Studies Quarterly* 33: 475–99.

Goodman, J.B. and L.W. Pauly (1993) 'The obsolescence of capital controls?', *World Politics* 46: 50–82.

Hedström, P. (1986) 'The evolution of the bargaining society: politico-economic dependencies in Sweden', *European Sociological Review* 2: 20–9.

Helleiner, E. (1994) *States and the Reemergence of Global Finance*, Ithaca: Cornell University Press.

Hibbs, D. (1977) 'Political parties and macroeconomic policy', *American Political Science Review* 71: 1467–87.

Høgsnes, G. and T. Hanisch (1988) *Incomes Policy and Union Structure: The Norwegian Experience during the Seventies and Eighties*, Oslo: Institute for Social Research/Department of Sociology, University of Oslo.

Katzenstein, P.J. (1985) *Small States in World Markets*, Ithaca: Cornell University Press.

Kerr, C., J.T. Dunlop, F. Harbison and C.A. Myers (1964) *Industrialism and Industrial Man*, London: Penguin.

Korpi, W. (1983) *The Democratic Class Struggle*, London: Routledge and Kegan Paul.

Korpi, W. and M. Shalev (1980) 'Strikes, power and politics in Western nations, 1900–1976', *Political Power and Social Theory* 1: 301–34.

Kreps, D.M. (1990) *Game Theory and Economic Modelling*, Oxford: Clarendon Press.

Krugman, P.R. and M. Obstfeld (1991) *International Economics*, (2nd edn), New York: HarperCollins.

Lange, P. (1984) 'Unions, workers and wage regulation: the rational bases of consent', in J.H. Goldthorpe (ed.) *Order and Conflict in Contemporary Capitalism*, Oxford: Clarendon Press, 98–123.

Lange, P. and G. Garrett (1985) 'The politics of growth: strategic interaction and economic performance in the advanced industrial democracies, 1974–1980', *Journal of Politics* 47: 792–827.

Lundberg, E. (1968) *Instability and Economic Growth*, New Haven: Yale University Press.

—— (1983) *Ekonomiska kriser förr och nu*, Stockholm: SNS.

—— (1985) 'The rise and fall of the Swedish model', *Journal of Economic Literature* 23: 1–36.

Lybeck, J.A. (1985) *Devalveringar*, Stockholm: Liber.

Maital, S. and Y. Benjamini (1980) 'Inflation as prisoner's dilemma', *Journal of Post Keynesian Economics*, 2: 459–81.

Martin, A. (1994) 'Labour, the Keynesian Welfare State, and the changing international political economy', in R. Stubbs and G. Underhill (eds) *Political Economy and the Changing Global Order*, London: Macmillan, 60–74.

Moene, K.O. and M. Wallerstein (1993) 'Embodied technical progress, wage compression and the centralization of collective bargaining', Unpublished paper, April version.

Moses, J.W. (1994) 'Abdication from national policy autonomy: what's left to leave?' *Politics and Society* 22: 125–48.

—— (1995) 'The fiscal constraints on social democracy', *Nordic Journal of Political Economy* 22: 49–68.

Moses, J.W. and A. Jenssen (1996) 'Nordic accession: an analysis of the EU referendums', in B. Eichengreen and J. Frieden (eds) *The Challenges of European Integration*, University of Michigan Press.

Notermans, T. (1993) 'The abdication from national policy autonomy', *Politics and Society* 21: 133–168.

OECD (1983) *Historical Statistics 1960–1981*, Paris: OECD.

—— (1993) *Historical Statistics 1960–1990*, Paris: OECD.

Offe, C. (1981) 'The attribution of public status to interest groups: observations on the West German case', in S. Berger (ed.) *Organizing Interests in Western Europe*, Cambridge: Cambridge University Press, 123–58.

—— (1984) *Contradictions of the Welfare State*, edited by John Keane, Cambridge, Mass.: MIT Press.

Oye, K. (1986) 'Explaining cooperation under anarchy: hypotheses and strategies', in K.A. Oye (ed.) *Cooperation under Anarchy*, Princeton: Princeton University Press, 1–24.

Panitch, L. (1977) 'The development of corporatism in liberal democracies', *Comparative Political Studies* 10: 61–90.

—— (1980) 'Recent theorizations of corporatism in liberal democracies', *British Journal of Sociology* 31: 159–87.

Parkin, F. (1972) *Class Inequality and Political Order*, New York: Praeger.

Pohjola, M. (1984) 'Union rivalry and economic growth: a differential game approach', *Scandinavian Journal of Economics* 86: 365–70.

Przeworski, A. and M. Wallerstein (1982) 'The structure of class conflict in democratic capitalist societies', *American Political Science Review* 76: 215–38.

Ruggie, J.G. (1982) 'International regimes, transactions, and change: embedded liberalism in the postwar economic order', *International Organization* 36: 379–415.

Scharpf, F.W. (1987) 'A game-theoretical interpretation of inflation and unemployment in Western Europe', *Journal of Public Policy* 7: 227–57.

Stephens, J.D. (1980) *The Transition from Capitalism to Socialism*, Atlantic Highlands, N.J.: Humanities Press.

—— (1994) 'The Scandinavian welfare states: development and crisis', Paper presented at the World Congress of Sociology, Bielefeld, Germany, July 18–23.

Swenson, P. (1989) *Fair Shares: Unions, Pay, and Politics in Sweden and West Germany*, Ithaca: Cornell University Press.

Tranøy, B.S. (1993) 'Styring, selvregulering og selvsosialisering: Staten, bankene og kredittpolitikken 1950–1988', Thesis, Department of Political Science, University of Oslo.

Weintraub, S. (1978) *Capitalism's Inflation and Unemployment Crisis*, Reading, Mass.: Addison-Wesley.

7 Globalization, corporate identity and European Union technology policy[1]

Andrew Wyatt-Walter

INTRODUCTION

The acceleration of EU integration through the European Single Market Programme was in many ways a response to the perceived relative economic decline of Europe in the world economy since the 1970s. Nowhere has European concern been greater than in the area of high technology, where competition from American and Japanese corporations became intense over the past decade. This concern prompted the gradual emergence of a counterpart to the deregulatory strategy of the Single Market Programme, a co-ordinated European high technology policy. Yet the globalization of competition in key high technology sectors has confronted European policy-makers with a dilemma: if the promotion of European high technology sectors is increasingly viewed as a central aspect of Europe's economic policy identity, how should the objects of such policies be defined? Specifically, with the growing physical presence of subsidiaries of US and Japanese firms in the EU and with European firms establishing important operations abroad, what does the promotion of 'European high technology industry' mean?

Such existential concerns have not prevented Europe from mimicking Japanese-style government-sponsored research and development (R&D) industrial consortia over the past decade. At the national level, programmes such as Britain's Alvey programme, France's Programme d'action pour la filière électronique, and Germany's Informationstechnik plan were all aimed at boosting lagging national information technology (IT) champions in the 1980s. By the mid-1980s, there was a growing realization that national strategies alone would be inadequate, leading to the emergence of a European technology programme. The 'Framework Programme' has come to provide an umbrella for the promotion of European high technologies, such as the ESPRIT (information technology), RACE (telecommunications) and BRITE (materials) programmes. At a wider European level, the EUREKA programme has included such important projects as JESSI in semiconductors, and the HDTV project (Okimoto 1989; Fransman 1990; Sharp 1990; Sharp and Pavitt 1993; Mytelka 1991a; OTA 1991; Sandholtz 1991). In recent years, however, the issue of how to treat foreign-owned subsidiaries of American and Japanese high technology firms has arisen, not least because of the realization that they make a major contribution to European output and employment.

This chapter asks why, until now, Europe has tended to allow substantial access for US foreign-owned firms (FoFs) to its technology programmes, but not for Japanese FoFs. This outcome is interesting and requires explanation for the following reasons. First, the Framework Programme, like the Single Market Programme, was designed in large part to promote the competitiveness of European firms *vis-à-vis* both US and Japanese firms. The European industry has been marked by poor profitability, excess capacity and declining world market share. By 1992, European semiconductor producers had only 35 per cent of their indigenous semiconductor market, compared with 85 per cent for Japanese producers and 70 per cent for American producers in their respective home markets. The largest European producers, Siemens, Philips and SGS-Thomson, held a mere 10 per cent of the world market between them in a highly oligopolized industry (*Financial Times*, 17 March 1992: Survey ii, vii).

Pressure from the Roundtable of European Industrialists, a lobby group established in 1983 comprising Europe's largest and most important firms (all of which at the time were firmly in European control),[2] was an important factor in generating support among national governments both for the completion of the single market and the vigorous pursuit of a European technology policy (BRIE 1992: ch. 3). These firms arguably had an interest in restricting the benefits of public R&D funding largely to themselves. Policymakers also felt that European policies ought primarily to benefit European firms. The EU Commissioner for Research, Maria-Filippo Pandolfi, asserted that the aim of the Framework Programme was 'to provide opportunities to European companies in the true sense of the word . . . [and] we would like European companies to remain European'. The Framework Programme has been consistent with a key goal of the Single Market Programme, which has been to enhance 'the ability of firms to become *truly European* at all levels of management, R&D, production, marketing and distribution', so as to enable them to compete at a global level against US and Japanese rivals (Buigues *et al.* 1990: vii; emphasis in the original).

Although at first national responses predominated, there was growing recognition that the promotion of national champions by individual countries in Europe had been a major cause of the competitive failure. The transfer of technology policy in part to the European level, along with the single market, might be said to have represented a shift towards a 'European champion' strategy, or even a 'technological Fortress Europe'. The consensus view in Europe (despite British reservations) was that European industrial policies might succeed where national policies had failed.[3] The apparent success of US and Japanese high technology policies (in the US case, primarily through defence procurement and related research) strengthened support in Europe for a common technology policy to complement the deregulatory impetus of the single market.

Finally, policies in the US and Japan might have been expected to reinforce any tendency towards a technological Fortress Europe. In the late 1980s, both Japan and the US excluded FoFs from their own high technology programmes – the US as a matter of explicit policy.[4] The European rhetoric of the late 1980s also tended to be exclusionary: External Affairs Commissioner Willy de Klerk had argued in a number of speeches in summer 1988 that the benefits of the single market would not automatically be extended to FoFs whose home countries did not provide equivalent access to European firms (Woolcock 1991: 14).

There are a number of reasons, therefore, why substantial participation by FoFs in European R&D projects might not have been expected. We need to explain why participation in European consortia by traditional rivals to indigenous European IT firms like IBM and AT&T, while often controversial, has in fact occurred. In addition, we need to explain why a tendency towards European openness has not been true across the board, particularly with respect to Japanese FoFs.

This chapter is organized as follows. The next section outlines the way in which European policy on the treatment of FoFs in technology programmes has evolved, focusing on some important cases (IBM and ICL-Fujitsu). A subsequent section assesses the reasons for Europe's relative openness to American-owned firms as opposed to Japanese firms. The conclusion considers the implications of this assessment for different theories or perspectives of international political economy (IPE).

The main argument of this chapter is twofold. First, a technological Fortress Europe has not been a real policy option, essentially because neither European champion firms nor national governments have been able to agree on such a policy. The growing difficulty of defining European corporate identity in a context of economic globalization is gradually leading European governments and regional institutions towards a policy based more upon the *location* of economic activity rather than the *ownership* of assets. Second, this has been less true until now for Japanese firms in Europe. The much greater degree of exclusion from European programmes that they have suffered suggests that theories of IPE need to consider more critically the process by which firms achieve insider status within states, in this case in Europe. The cases examined suggest that this is not simply dependent upon the behaviour and activities of individual firms, but also upon broader political, cultural and historical linkages between societies.

THE EVOLUTION OF EUROPEAN POLICY

As already mentioned, the Commission, and in particular the Commissioner for Industry, Etienne Davignon, played an important role in the promotion of EU technology policies in the late 1970s and early 1980s. Davignon and the firms in the European Business Roundtable played a key role in the design and the promotion of ESPRIT and subsequently the RACE programme, lobbying national governments to support them. By the end of the 1980s, these and other programmes were merged into the Framework Programme. The third Framework Programme over 1990–4 was funded at ECU 5.7 billion, and the fourth Programme has recently been extended through 1998. EUREKA, established by nineteen European countries, including the EU Commission, is 90 per cent privately funded, with a budget of ECU 7.4 billion over 1985–90 (OTA 1991: 209). Initially, ESPRIT was restricted to pre-competitive or basic research, but over time has become increasingly oriented towards commercial technologies, as with EUREKA projects (Mytelka 1991b: 187–9).

In practice, EFTA firms have gained good access to the Framework Programme and, along with Turkey, EFTA countries have been members of the EUREKA programme. While this participation was not formalized until recently, with the EU Council of Ministers reserving this for the conclusion of the European Economic Area (EEA) negotiations between the EU and EFTA in 1993, in practice this did not significantly hamper the participation of EFTA firms (*Agence Europe*, 28 November 1990). More controversial has been the issue of US corporate participation. As of 1989, the US firms listed in Table 7.1 had gained access.

As Table 1 shows, large US firms such as IBM, AT&T and Hewlett Packard, as well as many smaller ones, gained access to the first and second Framework Programmes and EUREKA. Not all these firms had European operations as significant as those of IBM or Ford, but nevertheless they were admitted. However, the extent of such participation varies by programme. IBM, for example, was a prime contractor in RACE, but required a major European 'watchdog' partner in ESPRIT. Generally, IBM is allowed to participate in EUREKA projects as the sole computer company (OTA 1991: 222). In JESSI, however, the 1989–96 EUREKA chip project (the basic research element of which is 25 per cent funded through the EU's ESPRIT programme), IBM participation was initially very controversial.[5]

This was complicated by the fact that the US had already launched a comparable collaborative programme with Defence Agency funding, Sematech, which is legally open only to firms which are 'substantially owned by citizens of the United States' and which are 'controlled by citizens of the United States' (Sematech 1988: 2–2.2). Philips, which has US R&D facilities and desired access to Sematech, hoped that IBM participation in JESSI might be made conditional upon reciprocal access for European firms to US programmes. Mark Rochkind, President of Philips Laboratories (US), testified before Congress in November 1989 that 'the denial of participation in JESSI to IBM stems directly from the denial of participation by Philips in the Sematech effort'. Lest he be seen as threatening the US government, he added that 'Philips, in fact, has encouraged JESSI to accept IBM' (Rochkind 1989). Since mid-1989, JESSI and Sematech had been engaged in talks on the

Table 7.1 Participation by European affiliates of US companies in European collaborative R&D programmes, 1984–9

ESPRIT I&II	RACE	BRITE	EUREKA HDTV project
ITT*	ITT*	ITT*	ITT*
IBM	IBM	Donnelly	Captain Video
AT&T	AT&T	Ford	LTV
Digital	Hewlett Packard	Rockwell	Covia
Hewlett Packard	Texas Instruments	Lee Cooper	
Sybase	GTE		
Swift SC	DHL		
Moog Controls	DuPont		
3M	Ford		
DuPont			
Dow Chemical			
Honeywell			
Artificial Intelligence			
Babcock & Wilcox			
Cambridge Consultants			
Intersys Graphic			
Peat Marwick			
McLintock			

Source: Testimony of Bill Bywater, President, International Union of Electronic Workers, to Hearing Before the Subcommittee on Science, Research and Technology and the Subcommittee on International Scientific co-operation of the House Committee on Science, Space and Technology, 101st Congress, 1st session, 1 November 1989, on 'What is a US Company?', exhibit 3.

Note: *ITT companies participating in one or more projects included Bell Telephone, SEL, Face Standard, ITT Europe, ITT Germany and Standard Electrica. controlling interests in many ITT companies were purchased by CGE/Alcatel so these companies' participation as US firms predates such acquisition. An ITT company not controlled by CGE/Alcatel remained active in the EUREKA HDTV project.

possibility of allowing reciprocal access to semiconductor projects (*Financial Times*, 13 June 1989: 2). In June 1989, they set up a joint study group to discuss possible collaboration and in April 1990 announced agreement to work together on two projects. They also agreed to consider the possibility of working on the joint development of semiconductor manufacturing equipment at a later stage. However, little has materialized.

The problem was that Sematech was concerned that it might give more than it would receive. Moreover, even before Sematech had given any concrete indications of allowing European participation, IBM had already been invited by JESSI to submit project proposals. JESSI's president, Raimondo Paletto, claimed in June 1990 that US and Japanese firms which showed 'sufficient commitment to Europe' could participate in JESSI (*Financial Times*, 21 June 1989: 9; 11 April 1990: 14; 7 June 1990: 2). By November 1990, IBM had been admitted to JESSI (though not to its management board). Why did the EU's attempt (led by Philips) to gain reciprocal access to Sematech fail?

There are a number of reasons. First, there was a powerful anti-industrial policy element in the Bush administration which insisted that Defence Department support could be justified only on the basis of narrow security arguments, rather than civilian technology policy arguments. If so, security requirements demanded that participation be restricted to US-owned and controlled firms. This view dovetailed with a more chauvinist but pro-interventionist attitude in Congress that held that the US government had to support its own high technology firms against the interventionist Japanese and Europeans. Sematech was for national security purposes, and foreign participation could not be allowed (de Vos 1989). Europe was not in the position to make a similar argument about JESSI.

Another factor which was important in undermining the initial European pro-reciprocity stance was the lack of corporate consensus. Siemens, which has a DRAM chip technology alliance with IBM, argued for the latter's participation in two JESSI projects on semiconductor manufacturing equipment and lithography. Siemens had deserted intra-European alliances in the past. In 1985, it bought 1-megabit DRAM technology from Toshiba which cut across the objectives of the Dutch–German Megaproject, in which Philips had been a major partner (OTA 1991: 214, n. 93). Siemens did so again in July 1991 when it signed new 16-megabit chip technology development agreements with IBM. Only months before, Philips, SGS-Thomson and Siemens had discussed developing chips jointly, and there had long been rumours of a possible merger of the chip businesses of the big three European producers to create a single, viable European chip producer of world scale (*Financial Times*, 27 April 1991: 2; 5 July 1991: 1). Another problem for JESSI had been the severe financial difficulties of Philips, which led it to withdraw from leadership of a major JESSI SRAM project in 1991. Like the other major European firms, it sought to focus on its strengths through alliances with non-European partners, such as with Sony on interactive compact disk technology and with Motorola on new chip design (*Financial Times*, 5 September 1990: 23; 13 March 1992: 24).

IBM was also steadily conducting its own diplomacy. It said that it supported the European case for participation within Sematech, but that the US government had been opposed.[6] Furthermore, IBM's case for participation was strong: it is Europe's major producer and buyer of chips, has a strong presence in a number of European countries, and conducts 12 per cent of its global research in Europe. It could bring much to the table in terms of technology and R&D capacity, where European firms perceptibly lagged. There were also some in the Commission and elsewhere in Europe, including perhaps Mr Pandolfi, who believed that the IBM–Siemens link could reinforce the European competitive position against the Japanese producers (*Agence Europe*, 4 August 1990). Whether this was true or not was made more unclear in 1992 when IBM, Siemens and Toshiba agreed to develop a next-generation 256-megabit DRAM chip in IBM's American laboratories. Nevertheless, IBM's successful entry into European high technology programmes was indicative of Europe's rejection of the Fortress Europe option, at least *vis-à-vis* American-owned firms.

The different European attitude towards Japanese-owned firms was indicated by the case of ICL, the British computer firm. An original member of the European IT Roundtable and a British national computer champion since the 1960s, ICL was acquired by Fujitsu in 1990.[7] Paletto initially assured the British that ICL could remain within JESSI if Japan could reciprocate in some way over European participation in Japanese projects. Japan was in fact moving towards a policy of unconditional access for FoFs in national technology projects, which MITI dubbed 'technoglobalism'.[8] However, the EU acted in March 1991 to expel ICL from membership of the IT Roundtable and to remove it from three of the five JESSI programmes in which it participated (all in computer-aided design), as well as from JESSI's management committee. JESSI claimed that it acted after consulting other companies involved in projects with ICL whether the latter's continued participation was necessary for the project's success (*Financial Times*, 27 March 1991: 22; 6 September 1990: 7). It appeared as if Europe would act much more decisively to prevent Japanese participation in European technology programmes than it would against US firms, without first exploring the possibilities of reciprocal access for European firms to Japanese programmes. Japanese firms have been conspicuously absent from Framework and EUREKA project teams.

However, total exclusion even in this highly controversial case was not imposed upon ICL. Despite the opposition of Siemens, Olivetti and Bull, ICL was awarded new ESPRIT and JESSI contracts in 1992, which implied a gradual readmittance into the European circle. A number of factors help to explain this. First, Fujitsu's arm's-length treatment of ICL and its promises to float off ICL within five years helped to assuage some European concerns. In early 1992, Fujitsu announced that it was placing some of its US and European operations under the direct control of ICL (*Financial Times*, 21 February 1992: 21). Second, ICL remained one of the few European computer companies with a successful technological track record and was perhaps the only profitable firm in the industry in Europe by 1992. Third, British government support was very important in gaining ICL's readmittance. As in other cases (such as Japanese automobile transplants), Britain was willing to argue strongly within Europe that local commitment was more important than ownership for policy purposes.[9]

Though few of Britain's European partners fully accepted such an argument, a British alliance with less protectionist forces in Europe could generally defeat the more exclusionary-minded Franco-Italian bloc. The French government had requested a Council discussion on the issue of foreign firm participation, which took place on 24 April 1991. Ireland, a host to a number of major US electronics multinational companies (MNCs), was concerned that an exclusionary policy would only concentrate research grants in the large countries, a concern shared by other small countries in Europe.

Germany's position on this matter has been ambiguous, given Siemens's own vacillating position, but its government wished to ensure that Central and East European countries were rapidly admitted to the programmes. Nor did it desire to see Europe turn into a 'research fortress' (*Agence Europe*, 25 April 1991: 8; 29–30 April 1991: 7–8). The Council therefore decided not to adopt general rules for foreign participation in European programmes, but to allow case-by-case assessment. While this considerably strengthened ICL's position, it sent a strong signal to other Japanese-owned firms that they would need to continue to invest heavily in Europe to obtain equal treatment.

ASSESSING EU POLICY

The IBM and ICL cases reveal much about European attitudes to FoF participation in technology programmes. Although European technology policy in the 1980s has in many ways been designed precisely as a means of improving the competitiveness of European high technology companies *vis-à-vis* the likes of IBM and Fujitsu, this did not ultimately prevent their subsidiaries from gaining access to the most sensitive programmes. As suggested earlier, why this occurred requires some explanation, given European policy objectives and the more exclusionary policies of the US and Japan. What also needs explanation is why in general there has been much better access for American-owned than for Japanese-owned firms, which have tended to be largely excluded. The following subsections will examine the preferences and interaction between two of the most important actors in this European policy arena: large firms and national states.[10]

Corporate preferences

As we saw in the second section, different firms in the European industry had divergent preferences regarding the question of FoF participation in European R&D programmes. A number of factors affect corporate preferences in this policy area. First, local firms are likely to look favourably upon the participation of foreign-owned partners which are able to make crucial technological or financial contributions to joint R&D projects, particularly in areas where local firms are weak. Local firms are likely to be less concerned than host states about the actual levels of local content in the operations of FoFs, as long as the transfer of technology and/or finance occurs. The technological strength of firms like IBM and AT&T may be an important factor in their admittance to European projects such as RACE and JESSI. However, this might also be said of many of the large, integrated Japanese electronics firms, which have not so far gained admittance.

A second factor which has pushed against Japanese participation from the European corporate viewpoint has been strategic concerns. As Kenneth Flamm has written:

Because Japanese chip producers were part of larger [computer] systems houses, foreign competitors began to suspect that systems divisions of the same Japanese companies were getting access to leading edge products before their foreign competitors ... Back in the late 1970s, reliance by European systems houses on US semiconductor companies for supplies of advanced chips, though far from welcome, did not pose a strategic problem for European industry. The US merchant chip manufacturers were not, for the most part, vertically integrated into downstream systems.

(Flamm 1990: 247, 262)

Indeed, the success of the Japanese in gaining the leading edge in certain chip technologies in the 1980s was a major factor behind the decision of the major European IT firms to push governments to create the Single Market and a European high technology policy in the 1980s (Sandholtz 1992). The strength of this concern is presumably an important factor behind the reluctance of the major European firms to allow a significant role for the large Japanese electronics firms in European programmes.

A third factor which further complicates corporate preferences on this issue is the growing importance of international strategic R&D alliances between firms in the electronics sector. Firms which acquire such linkages with foreign MNCs may come to prefer greater openness in local technology programmes, at least for their alliance partners.[11] As we have seen, the alliance with Siemens may have been useful for IBM in its quest to gain insider status within European technology programmes. At the same time, however, alliances between European and Japanese firms (e.g. Toshiba–Siemens, Philips–Matsushita, Bull–NEC) have not been sufficient to gain access for the Japanese partner, because there were other factors pushing against Japanese participation, including possible opposition from other major European firms.

A fourth factor behind corporate preferences may be the desire to use access for FoFs to local programmes as a bargaining weapon to gain access to foreign technology programmes. Access to R&D consortia can help FoFs to overcome barriers to market access such as discriminatory government procurement, the difficulty of establishing local supplier networks, and problems relating to different technical standards. It is increasingly important for firms not to be left out of consortia if standards-setting is involved, as shown in the cases of the RACE telecommunications programme in Europe and the various HDTV consortia in Europe, Japan and the US. The desire to make FoF access conditional upon home government reciprocity is likely to be stronger for firms with substantial existing overseas R&D operations (such as North American Philips), rather than for firms (such as Thomson or Bull) with limited foreign R&D activities.

The array of possible motivations behind corporate preferences on the issue of FoF access to European technology programmes suggests that firms are likely to prefer a case-by-case approach to a hard and fast rule. While it is likely that firms would desire access for their strategic partners, it is unlikely that they would desire a general policy of openness which could allow major rivals into consortia.

State preferences

The central question for states is how important ownership is in a sector in which competition is increasingly global. A debate on this question has occurred in recent years between those who generally agree that state intervention in 'strategic' high technology sectors is justified (Reich 1990, 1991; Tyson 1991; Hu 1992). Governments have long sought to ensure that certain industrial activities, which can have a direct impact upon the ability of the state to provide for its defence, are located within state borders. Often, they have gone further to argue that national ownership of the defence–industrial base is important for national control and autonomy. In most contemporary states, foreign ownership in defence-related sectors is restricted, and this is true even for countries such as the US and UK, which have otherwise tended to be highly open to foreign investment. However, there is no necessary reason why state control of particular industries ought to depend upon national ownership (either by the state or by private national investors). In times of war, states can assert control over the operations of FoFs producing within their territory without much difficulty, as did Nazi Germany with GM and Ford subsidiaries during the Second World War (Graham and Krugman 1991: ch. 5).

Complications arise in knowledge-intensive sectors, however, which may make ownership an important consideration. Not only do high technology industries provide a basis for advanced weapons systems and hence national security, but technology externalities or spill-over effects may be important for the competitiveness and long-term growth prospects of other sectors of the economy (BRIE 1992; Sen 1984; OECD 1992; Dosi *et al.* 1990). Many would argue that FoFs are much less likely to undertake substantial knowledge creation outside their home base, so that ownership matters a great deal for the diffusion of technology throughout the local economy (Tyson 1991). At the same time, the perceived growing importance of 'spin-on' from civilian to military technologies provides justification in some quarters for renewed attention to ownership and control issues (BRIE 1992: ch. 1). Although MNCs have recently been internationalizing the geographical spread of their R&D, US MNCs conducted 89 per cent of their total R&D and employed 74 per cent of their total workforce in the US in 1989 (Lowe and Mataloni 1991: 29). The possibility that FoFs may be less likely to utilize locally the technologies developed within a publicly funded programme suggests to some that in practice FoFs should be excluded (Hall 1989; Hecht 1989). However, others argue that there is no reason why FoFs might not locate core R&D activities within host states, particularly if they are encouraged to do so through policies such as local content rules (Reich 1991; Kline 1989a, 1989b).

The academic disagreement over this issue is mirrored in the disagreement among governments in Europe. The French government, for example, has assiduously maintained national ownership and control of firms in high technology sectors and promoted national champions such as Thomson, Bull and Alcatel in the IT sector. The British government, as we have seen, is much more hospitable towards FoFs, and has recently opened its national technology programmes to FoF participation on the condition that the R&D is performed within Britain. Since the UK has received approximately 40 per cent of all Japanese direct investment (and well over half of the R&D laboratories established by Japanese firms) in Europe, one might argue that this policy has become self-reinforcing.[12] Small countries such as Ireland which have been very dependent upon the activities of high technology MNCs have also favoured their admission into European programmes.

Different attitudes across states in Europe created the need for a compromise, since firms were pressing for a clear answer. For the UK, attracting large numbers of Japanese R&D operations, the Japanese were heading in the right direction, something confirmed by Fujitsu's treatment of ICL after 1990. From the French viewpoint, no Japanese firm could be said to have achieved the degree of localization of IBM or some of the other large American MNCs. Even so, requiring substantial local content of FoFs for their admission to European programmes might encourage Japanese firms to do so. Thus, European governments moved towards a case-by-case approach which downplayed the importance of nationality and moved towards a policy based on the contribution of any particular firm to the local economy. Such a policy could safeguard the interests of the major and the smaller European states, despite the disagreement that otherwise prevailed. It also coincided with the overall preferences of the European large corporate sector.

From policy preferences to outcomes

The identification of various factors behind both state and corporate preferences in this area of economic policy is only the first step towards an explanation. To provide a fuller account, it would be necessary to discuss how the preferences of particular states and firms interacted to produce the outcomes outlined in the second section. In the limited space that is available, only the broad lines of such an analysis can be provided.

The argument so far is that the only available compromise for both states and firms in Europe was to adopt a case-by-case approach which allowed these actors some flexibility. However, behind this consensus lurked some major conflicts of interest. In the highly complex political system of the EU or wider Western Europe, power is relatively dispersed between states and firms. Although it might appear that European technology policies have mainly played to the interests of the large European IT firms, it would be wrong to push this argument too far. In fact, despite the visibility of Franco-British conflict over technology policy, the main conflicts have been as follows: first, between mainly small states which are heavily dependent upon FoFs for their presence in high technology and the large states which have attempted to promote their national champions as European champions; second, between states in general, which have increasingly seen local content rules as in their interests, and large firms (including European-owned firms) which naturally prefer to avoid such conditions for access. Neither large states nor large firms have consistently dominated policy outcomes.

The 'small state position', as exemplified by Ireland, which is that ownership should not be important in setting policy, has been relatively successful because Britain and, to a lesser extent, Germany have supported it. In part, this is also due to the norm in the EU that the interests of smaller states should not be overlooked. In a similar vein, initial criticism that the bulk of the funding of the European programmes was going to the major IT firms located in the major states resulted in efforts to divert funding towards smaller firms and states (Mytelka 1991b: 190). As a result, the preferences of the large national champions and their usually supportive governments have not always predominated.

Second, states have at times had an important autonomous impact upon policy outcomes, in part because large firms have not always agreed among themselves. Given the natural suspicion of ICL after the Fujitsu take-over on the part of many other European firms and governments, the willingness of the UK government to argue forcefully that it be allowed to continue as an important participant in European programmes was probably crucial.[13] The ability of European states to insist that FoFs locate sufficient local content (whether in terms of R&D or production or both) in the host economy, something to which local firms may be indifferent or opposed, also suggests that policy is more than a simple mirroring of corporate policy preferences. This may be because high levels of unemployment have become at least as pressing a policy matter for European governments as the fortunes of national champions.

One reason for a weak consensus among large firms on the details of technology policy is that the sensitivity of firms to the sharing of proprietary technology with competitors reduces the scope for common interests. Firms may prefer narrow alliances with trusted partners than participation in national or regional consortia which may have broader objectives (such as local technology diffusion). Shared technological weakness *vis-à-vis* US and Japanese rivals seems to have produced a consensus among European IT firms for moderate trade protection, but there is no similar consensus for wholesale technological protectionism. On the contrary, the very weakness of European IT firms has tended to push them towards technological collaboration with US and Japanese firms.

At the European level, national governments and the Commission may sometimes be more able to resist the demands of national champions than of foreign MNCs. Large, established MNCs such as IBM, Ford and GM, with operations spread much more evenly over Europe than the national champions, can often enjoy more cross-governmental support within European forums. In the words of Hans-Olaf Henkel, CEO of IBM Europe, 'IBM is more German than the Germans, more French than the French, and more British than the British.' The Commission can also play a role in this regard. In recent discussions on information networks in the EU, while the major countries nominated national champions for the preliminary working party (the UK nominated ICL), the Commission nominated IBM.[14] Over time, as Japanese foreign direct investment (FDI) in Europe diversifies towards other European countries, we are likely to see growing acceptance of Japanese firms as insiders on a cross-European basis. It is not clear that the national champions can easily overcome this disadvantage.

FoFs may also engage in the kind of lobbying with single host states that national champions have traditionally excelled in. Over time, rising unemployment and growing state frustration with coddled and uncompetitive national champions have made this easier, with states becoming more willing to compromise on the issue of foreign investment in strategic sectors and technological autonomy. This is even true for France. In early 1992, the French government approved the purchase by IBM of a strategic stake in Bull, the French state-owned computer maker, and technical and marketing agreements between the two firms (the Japanese firm NEC already had a similar arrangement with Bull). This provided the French firm with access to IBM's RISC chip technology, and to IBM's collaborative alliance with Apple and Motorola. Bull has now been slated for privatization, while SGS-Thomson is also collaborating with IBM on chip technology (*Financial Times*, 29 January 1992: 24). The national security state has eroded substantially, although it has not been replaced by a European security identity. This has made it easier for MNCs originating from third countries to become 'policy insiders'.

The result of these factors is an emerging policy consensus in Europe to move away from policies which discriminate based upon ownership towards policies which see location as the primary consideration. This was evident in the late 1980s in the treatment of transplant production by Japanese automobile firms, and it has become evident in the treatment of FoFs in European and even some national technology programmes. In practice, this has meant that local content rules are applied to FoFs only, although in the long run, rules may be applied regardless of whether the firm is foreign or European-owned. Local content rules in technology programmes mean that participating firms should have substantial local R&D facilities which are directly involved in the research programme and which actively foster the diffusion of skills and technology throughout the host economy. Additional requirements may be significant production facilities within the nation or region providing the funding, and the ability to source locally and promote the diffusion of technology in supplier industries. In the latest European Framework Programme, in which Japanese firms will officially be allowed to participate for the first time, FoFs will even be able to participate in some consortia without providing local R&D content, but will be required to do so if they wish to receive European funding.[15]

Until now, however, Japanese firms have been essentially excluded from European programmes, whereas even relatively small US FoFs with a limited local European presence have gained access (Table 7.1). This suggests that factors other than the difference in the degree of globalization/localization of US and Japanese firms have influenced outcomes. In some sense, Europe has tended to treat US firms in general, not just large insiders like IBM and Ford, as part of the relevant policy community, but has not treated Japanese firms similarly. The most likely explanation is Europe's deep political, economic and military relationship with the US, which goes beyond intergovernmental relationships. That is, not only are important countries like Britain, Germany and the Netherlands unlikely to wish to antagonize the US government on this issue, but there appears to be a broader perceived community of interests between European and American societies, including firms. There is no comparable perceived community of interest between Europe and Japan, which helps to explain the greater difficulty its own firms have had in obtaining insider status within Europe.

CONCLUSION

Rather than summarize the foregoing argument, this conclusion will draw out some implications for different theories of IPE. The first is that realist theories, which focus on the security interests of the national state (Waltz 1979), cannot easily account for the way in which corporate and state interests interact to produce a differentiated pattern of outcomes in European technology policy. Greater attention to the impact of transnational corporate alliances and FDI in the policy process is crucial for understanding the way in which policy in Europe has evolved. The role of firms in the policy is evidently crucial for understanding policy developments, even where key 'national security' issues are involved.

Pluralist or society-oriented theories of state policy-making can allow for the impact of sub-state agents upon state policy (Milner 1988; Moravcsik 1993). However, 'corporate diplomacy' of a thoroughgoing kind is rarely allowed for in society-based models of foreign policy-making, which do not usually consider transnational influences on policy. For example, Fujitsu's careful treatment of ICL was an important factor in reducing opposition to ICL's participation in European consortia, and in the British government's ability to defend ICL in European forums. Similarly, IBM's array of alliances with different European IT firms and its strong presence across the various countries provide it with considerable influence in European corporate and government circles, including the Commission. Where powerful actors disagree, apparently weaker actors in technology policy such as small states, the Commission and foreign firms have a greater influence on policy outcomes.

This suggests that the Stopford and Strange model of 'triangular diplomacy', in which firms and states are treated as actors of equal status in a global economy, may be preferable to either the realist or pluralist models of policy-making (Stopford and Strange 1991). The main difference with traditional pluralist models is that here MNCs are seen as influencing the policy process through direct bargaining with host as well as home governments and perhaps with supranational institutions. This model diverges from realist and pluralist models in arguing that these both overplay the role of national actors relative to transnational firms. Yet it has in common with both a focus upon the interplay of interests. There is good reason to think, however, that interest-based models of IPE are not wholly adequate.

First, even if we allow an important role for corporate interests, it is at least as difficult to predict corporate preferences with any accuracy as to predict state preferences in technology policy, given the large number of considerations which go into corporate strategy. This creates a considerable problem for theorists. Second, there appear to be factors at work other than a simple cost–benefit calculation for each possible strategy by individual actors, whether states or firms. Why, for example, should many large Japanese firms with a much greater European presence than some smaller US firms have been excluded, while the latter have been admitted to R&D programmes? This might be because of the length of time during which individual firms have had a local presence in Europe. Yet although it is certainly true for Japanese firms on average, this cannot explain why relatively recent American arrivals have found it easier than their Japanese counterparts to become insiders. European fears about the high degree of vertical integration of Japanese firms, and their close relationship with traditional suppliers, have contributed significantly to their exclusion. Divergent corporate styles and cultures are thus very important. Another factor could be that Japanese firms may not enjoy similar access to established networks of influence of which even newly arrived American firms can take advantage. Finally, the role of cultural factors could be important in providing American firms with an advantage in working through European networks and corporate consortia.

The above considerations raise difficult issues concerning the relationship between the gaining of insider status by individual firms and broader economic and cultural factors, which will require much additional research. It also suggests that globalization is a much more complex phenomenon than 'stateless' firms competing for market share and political influence in various jurisdictions, especially where regional integration arrangements are present. FDI not only reflects changing markets and production structures in certain industries, but it also embodies and is constrained by deeper cultural and historical factors. The relative weakness of European–Japanese societal linkages compared to European–American linkages seems to play an important part in the explanation of Japanese firms' exclusion from European programmes. Approaches which take such factors into account will require development.

A final point is that interest-based models rely upon the ability of the scholar to establish the identities of agents. Yet this is increasingly difficult, at least in Europe, as globalization has made the identification of truly 'European' firms increasingly problematic (Dunning 1993; Humbert 1993; Ostry 1990; Julius 1990). Indeed, there is little agreement as to what a truly European firm would actually look like. Large European firms, like their American and Japanese counterparts, are still predominantly owned and managed by nationals of their home country. However, there are many, particularly those from smaller European countries, whose assets, production, sales and increasingly their R&D lie outside the home base. Even for larger countries like the UK and Germany, the long history of FoF participation in their economies has complicated the issue of European-ness in the context of the deepening of integration in the 1980s. Put differently, the economic and social identity of 'Europe' has always been more diffuse than that of the US, but globalization has made this much more so. While EU firms may have a predominantly national or European base, they are far from disinterested in wider global markets and strategic partnerships. In turn, exclusionary technology policy is difficult to pursue consistently. Critical attention to the manner in which perceived identities evolve over time is important to an understanding of European policy in this and other areas.

NOTES

1 I am grateful to the editors and referees of this volume, and to the participants in the ECPR workshop on 'The Single Market and Global Economic Integration' (Madrid 1994) for helpful comments on an earlier draft of this chapter; they have no responsibility for any remaining errors.
2 These firms were GEC, ICL and Plessey from the UK; Bull, CGE and Thomson from France; AEG, Nixdorf and Siemens from Germany; Olivetti and Stet from Italy; Philips from Holland.
3 The enhanced powers of the Commission to promote competition and to restrict the ability of member-states to provide aid and discriminatory procurement in favour of national champions made a European industrial policy a priority for interventionist countries such as France.
4 Owing to space limitations, this chapter will not discuss US and Japanese policies in any detail.
5 *Agence Europe*, 6 September 1990, p. 7. The objective of JESSI was to produce static and dynamic random access memory chips (SRAMs and DRAMs) and logic chips using 0.3 micron feature sizes by 1995.
6 IBM interview, 28 February 1994.
7 Fujitsu now owns 80 per cent of ICL, though even before this Fujitsu had transferred technology to the British firm on a long-term co-operative basis.
8 *Nature*, 360, 10 December 1992.
9 IBM interview, 28 February 1994.
10 Given space constraints, the role of the Commission will not be examined, but it is fair to say that in such a sensitive area of policy its role has been relatively weak.
11 Analogously, Helen Milner (1988) has demonstrated that rising levels of economic interdependence and international production have led firms to support more open trade policies.

156   *Public policy, globalization and regionalism*

12 Interviews, Tokyo, November–December 1994.
13 A similar argument might be made concerning the UK government's support of Japanese automobile 'transplants' in the EU against French opposition.
14 IBM interview, 28 February 1994.
15 Interviews, Tokyo, November–December 1994.

REFERENCES

BRIE (1992) *The Highest Stakes*, Oxford: Oxford University Press.
Buigues, P., E. Ilzkovitz, and J.-F. Lebrun (1990) 'The impact of the internal market by industrial sector: the challenge for the Member States', *European Economy*, special edition.
de Vos, Ambassador P.J. (1989) Deputy Assistant Secretary for Science and Technology Affairs, Department of State, testimony to House Committee on Science, Space and Technology (1989b).
Dosi, G., K. Pavitt and L. Soete (1990) *The Economics of Technical Change and International Trade*, Brighton: Harvester-Wheatsheaf.
Dunning, J.H. (1993) *The Globalization of Business*, London: Routledge.
Flamm, K. (1990) 'Semiconductors', in G.C. Hufbauer (ed.) *Europe 1992: An American Perspective*, Washington, DC: Brookings Institution.
Fransman, M. (1990) *The Market and Beyond: Cooperation and Competition in Information Technology in the Japanese System*, Cambridge: Cambridge University Press.
Graham, E.M. and P.R. Krugman, (1991) *Foreign Direct Investment in the United States* (2nd edn), Washington, DC: Institute for International Economics.
Hall, R.M. (1989) Testimony to House Committee on Science, Space and Technology (1989a).
Hecht, L. (1989) Testimony to House Committee on Science, Space and Technology (1989a).
House Committee on Science, Space and Technology (1989a) Subcommittee on Science, Research and Technology and the Subcommittee on International Scientific Co-operation, 101st Congress, 1st session, 1 November 1989, hearing on 'What is a US company?'
—— (1989b) Subcommittee on International Scientific Co-operation, 101st Congress, 1st session, 19 July 1989, hearing on 'International technology transfer: who is minding the store?'.
Hu, Yao-Su (1992) 'Global or stateless corporations are national firms with international operations', *California Management Review*, Winter: 107–26.
Humbert, M. (ed.) (1993) *The Impact of Globalization on Europe's Industries*, London: Routledge.
Julius, D. (1990) *Global Companies and Public Policy*, London: Pinter/RIIA.
Kline, J. (1989a) Testimony to House Committee on Science, Space and Technology (1989a).
—— (1989b) 'Trade competitiveness and corporate nationality', *Columbia Journal of World Business*, Fall: 25–32.
Lowe, J.H. and R.J. Mataloni Jr. (1991) 'US direct investment abroad: 1989 benchmark survey results', US Department of Commerce, *Survey of Current Business*, October: 29–55.
Milner, H. (1988) *Resisting Protectionism: Global Industries and the Politics of International Trade*, Princeton: Princeton University Press.
Moravcsik, A. (1993) 'Preferences and power in the European Community: a liberal intergovernmentalist approach', *Journal of Common Market Studies* 31 (4), December: 473–524.

Mytelka, L.K. (ed.) (1991a) *Strategic Partnerships and the World Economy*, London: Pinter.
—— (1991b) 'States, strategic alliances and international oligopolies: the European ESPRIT programme', in L.K. Mytelka (ed.) *Strategic Partnerships and the World Economy*, London: Pinter.
OECD (1992) *Technology and the Economy: The Key Relationships*, Paris: OECD.
Okimoto, D.I. (1989) *Between MITI and the Market: Japanese Industrial Policy for High Technology*, Stanford: Stanford University Press.
Ostry, S. (1990) *Governments and Corporations in a Shrinking World*, New York: Council on Foreign Relations.
OTA (US Congress, Office of Technology Assessment) (1991) *Competing Economies: America, Europe, and the Pacific Rim*, Washington, DC: OTA.
Reich, R. (1990) 'Who is US?', *Harvard Business Review*, January–February: 53–64.
—— (1991) 'Who do we think they are?', *The American Prospect* 4, Winter.
Rochkind, M., President of Philips Laboratories US (1989) Testimony to House Committee on Science, Space and Technology (1989a).
Sandholtz, W. (1991) *High Tech Europe: The Politics of International Cooperation*, Berkeley: University of California Press.
—— (1992) 'ESPRIT and the politics of international collective action', *Journal of Common Market Studies* 30 (1): 1–21.
Sematech (1988) Amended and restated by-laws of Sematech, Inc., a Delaware company.
Sen, G. (1984) *The Military Origins of Industrialization and International Trade Rivalry*, London: Pinter.
Sharp, M. (1990) 'The Single Market and European policies for advanced technologies', *The Political Quarterly*, October.
Sharp, M. and K. Pavitt (1993) 'Technology policy in the 1990s: old trends and new realities', *Journal of Common Market Studies* 31 (2): 129–51.
Stopford, J. and S. Strange (1991) *Rival States, Rival Firms*, Cambridge: Cambridge University Press.
Tyson, L.D. (1991) 'They are not US: why American ownership still matters', *The American Prospect* 4, Winter: 37–48.
Waltz, K.N. (1979) *Theory of International Politics*, New York: Random House.
Woolcock, S. (1991) *Market Access issues in EC–US Relations: Trading Partners or Trading Blows?*, London: RIIA/Pinter.

8 Regional versus global discipline

Export credit insurance in the European Union[1]

Monika Sie Dhian Ho and Klaas Werkhorst

INTRODUCTION

Owing to the importance of exports to the balance of payments and employment in domestic industries, governments have tried to maintain these at a high level by mobilizing large amounts of public funds for export promotion. Export credits are among the more powerful instruments used to support exports.[2] The granting of export credits by exporters, their banks or other financial institutions facilitates trade because foreign buyers are allowed to spread payments over time, instead of paying in cash. Governments support these export credits by subsidizing export credit interest rates (*financing support*) and by providing *export credit insurance*. In the years of rising market interest rates, the costs of interest subsidies escalated and, since the 1982 debt crisis, cumulative deficits on official export credit insurance schemes have mounted up to billions of dollars. As an often decisive, but more and more costly weapon in the competition for export orders, preferential credit and insurance have become a trade issue, discussed at the global and regional levels.

At the global level governments seem to have come to the understanding that some reduction of the level of these subsidies would be beneficial to all exporting countries, providing they can still retain this instrument of national trade policy. With respect to financing support these efforts resulted in the 'Gentlemen's Agreement' of 1976 (later called the Consensus) between all OECD countries except Turkey and Iceland, which is binding for member-states of the EU. In contrast with financing support, which has been one of the main trade issues dealt with by the OECD over the past twenty years (Blair 1993: 7), subsidies in export credit insurance were not brought up in the OECD until the early 1990s.

The public export credit insurance issue has been extensively debated on the regional EU level. In addition to the cost escalation since the debt crisis, factors such as market integration, competition policy and the common commercial policy of the EU have forced policy-makers to examine export credit insurance. Regional efforts to discipline state aids to exports have been slowed, however, by fears of EU member-states that they might disadvantage their exporters *vis-à-vis* non-EU competitors, especially from the US, Japan and the newly industrializing countries. Regional integration, it would appear, can reach limits in the context of global competition. In examining what these limits are, this chapter complements the analysis of securities markets by Coleman and Underhill and of the welfare state by Rhodes and by Moses in this book.

Long the focus of specialists only and the subject of confidential negotiations, the disputes on *financing support* have only recently been described by scholars of international political economy (Moravcsik 1989; Blair 1993). This chapter extends policy studies of export subsidies by examining efforts on the EU and global levels to discipline the other form of support, *export credit insurance* for the account of the government.

The chapter is divided into three sections. The first gives an introduction to the market for export credit insurance; it outlines governments' motives for entering this market and the regulations which already exist at the global level in order to keep this support in check. The second section examines the disciplining initiatives and developments in this issue area within the EU. With state aids increasingly used as a policy instrument to respond to various economic problems, some authors expect that the Commission will have to change its strategy towards *co-ordination* of national instruments of state aid, instead of *prohibition* of the national schemes (Kapteyn and Verloren van Themaat 1987: 323–4). We examine which strategies have been chosen in the case of state aids through credit insurance and which factors have dominated this process. Were they 'supranational' factors like pressure from EU institutions, transnational business interest groups and the European Commission? Or can the process better be explained by 'intergovernmental institutionalism', with interstate bargaining converging towards the lowest common denominator of large state interests and member-states resisting transfer of their future policy autonomy (Moravcsik 1991)? Will an adaptation of the market structure result, with a single European credit insurance facility replacing the national schemes, or will attempts be made to adapt market behaviour and enforce similar credit insurance policies by member-states? In the latter case, is this a real 'common credit insurance policy' or merely transparency and harmonization of techniques with (differing) policy decisions still made at the national level? And if a common policy is to be realized, what will be the financial results – that is, what will be the level of subsidy? The last part of this section describes the interaction between policy-making at the regional and global levels. Unhappy with progress in Europe, the United Kingdom brought the credit insurance issue to the OECD through the British officials within the OECD Secretariat. The third section draws conclusions from the analysis.

PUBLIC INTERVENTION IN EXPORT CREDIT INSURANCE MARKETS

The principal risk in financing exports is that payments for exports will not be received. The cause of such a loss may rest with the buyer (*commercial risks* such as the buyer's insolvency) or with problems in the buyer's country, such as a shortage of foreign exchange, government restrictions on convertibility of currency, war or catastrophes. This risk of losses because of events in the buyer's country, so-called *political risk*, differentiates exports from domestic sales. As the number of buyer countries is relatively limited (as compared with the number of buyers) political risks are characterized by a lack of spread (in contrast with commercial risks). In addition, political risks are interrelated: when a country or region gets into payment trouble, claims will tend to be cumulative and will appear in shocks. Consequently, premiums cannot be calculated statistically in advance to cover the long-term operating costs and losses of an export credit insurance scheme. In addition to political risks, exporters – especially to non-OECD countries – often possess incomplete information on the creditworthiness of foreign importers and countries. Therefore, private insurers normally are willing to cover commercial risks in the OECD area only. For nearly all political risks, commercial risks outside the OECD area or risks with a duration above two years, private parties refuse to provide insurance. Hence the market 'fails'.

Since the 1920s, all industrialized countries' governments have decided to counter this market 'failure' by creating public export credit insurance facilities.[3] Governments usually justify this intervention economically by arguing that market 'failures' make international trade function at a suboptimal level (Baron 1983: 59–85). Intervention may also be driven by the objectives of industrial, employment, strategic trade or even foreign policies. Official support is also justified as necessary if domestic exporters are to be able to compete with government-supported foreign firms. This logic is self-sustaining, of course, as long as there is one government interfering in this market.

Since some governments also provide insurance when the market does not 'fail', the export credit insurance market can be divided into two segments: one where insurance is provided by public insurers only, and the other where both private and public insurers operate. In the first segment, 'non-marketable risks' are insured (mainly for medium-term transactions) by governments, and in the second segment 'marketable risks' (mainly short-term) are covered both by public and private insurers. These forms of government intervention may distort competition in two ways.

First, in the government-only market, competition distortions may appear *between exporters* from different countries, because their respective governments offer different kinds of cover for the same risks. Differences can occur in the quality of cover (covered percentages, covered causes of loss), the price of the cover (premiums) and quantity of cover/underwriting policy ('ceilings' on countries/decisions to withdraw cover for specific countries). Differences in cover and underwriting policy have the highest distorting potential. When troubles in a buying country induce one government insurer to stop cover on that country while another government persists, government-backed firms in the second country can go on exporting, while exporters in the first country have to give up these exports in the light of high risks. Such policy differences may result from different perceptions of risk by governments or from government export credit insurance programmes having different objectives (that is, being more or less dominated by foreign policy, trade policy or domestic employment considerations). These different perceptions or policy objectives may lead to unequal insurance packages for the same transactions for exporters of different member-states. For example, Germany implemented a relatively generous country cover policy on Eastern European countries in order to support the new eastern Bundesländer;[4] similarly, France supports trade with sub-Saharan or Maghreb countries by way of liberal country cover policies.

Second, in the mixed market for short-term credit insurance, distortion arises when governments provide for cover not only when the market fails, but also when risks can be insured by private insurers. If the public insurer can offer more favourable conditions than its private competitor, thanks to its relation with the government (for example, tax exemptions, provision of capital, subsidies or privileged information from the state), a distortion of competition arises *between private and public insurers.*

As early as 1955 the competition distorting potential of government-supported export credit insurance was identified, when the Organization for European Economic Co-operation (OEEC) adopted rules to curb state aids to exports. 'The charging of premiums at rates which are manifestly inadequate to cover the long-term operating costs and losses of the credit insurance institutions' was explicitly prohibited.[5] This rule on credit insurance was transferred to the General Agreement on Tariffs and Trade (GATT), when the OEEC became the OECD. Advising on the implementation of article XVI(4) of the GATT that prohibits subsidies for exports, the GATT working party incorporated the 'no-cost-to-the-government' rules of the OEEC into its 1960 report (Ray 1986: 295–300; Hufbauer and Shelton Erb 1984: 68).[6] In other words, state-related export credit insurance was supposed to function according to the same insurance techniques and self-sustaining principle as a private insurer operating in a private market. This reasoning seems rather paradoxical: private insurers have perceived certain risks to be too uncertain to be profitable, and thus abstain from these markets. States then intervene to provide the coverage refused by the private insurers. Yet, the GATT suggests, this coverage should not end up being a cost to the government.

In practice, the decisions by private insurers to abstain have proved correct: the 1982 debt crisis and more recently the payment difficulties of the Russian Federation have resulted in vast, cumulative claims. In addition, by balancing the break-even principle with motives for intervention, governments are often pulled in the latter direction. Not surprisingly, substantial cumulative deficits on public insurance schemes to an OECD total of 7.1 billion SDR in 1992 have occurred (Kraneveld 1994: 2). As governments are trying to secure later repayment by debtor countries through debt reschedulings, they claim that these cumulative deficits are not inevitably definitive losses. In the latest Paris Club[7] reschedulings, however, considerable debts have been cancelled – not only for the least developed countries, but also for middle income countries like Poland and Egypt. So the GATT's 'no-cost-to-the-government' rule on export credit insurance has obviously not been met (Kraneveld 1994: 4).

EXPORT CREDIT INSURANCE AS A TRADE ISSUE

Although there has not been any effort to enforce the GATT subsidy code in the area of export credit insurance (Abraham *et al.* 1992), there have been several initiatives within Europe to bring the export credit insurance policies of the EU member-states in line with the EEC Treaty articles on state aids (92–94 EEC) and common commercial policy (112–113 EEC). These early efforts have not been very successful, however. Despite the existence of a special Co-ordination Group for Credit Insurance, Guarantees and Financial Credits (CGC), set up by the Council in 1960, and several Commission proposals, concrete results in harmonizing the national schemes and restricting the amount of government support remained quite modest until 1989. Member-states' reluctance could be traced to several factors (Dalvin 1992: 3):

1 the supporting effect of export credit policy on the balances of payment of the member-states;
2 export credit policies' contributions to employment and industrial policy, especially in supporting specific declining industries (for example, shipbuilding) or regions;
3 the relationship between export credit policy and foreign policy of the member-states.

In 1970, after intensive negotiations, the Council adopted two directives on harmonized guarantee conditions. These were never implemented, owing in part to the accession of the United Kingdom (Dalvin 1992). In 1980, the Commission was forced to withdraw similar proposals, aimed at facilitating co-operation between public insurers by harmonizing aspects of the insurance systems. These harmonization efforts dealt with technical aspects of the coverage provided by the member-states, without a clear political direction. The 'real issues' – that is, harmonization of policy aspects linked with national interests, such as premium rates, underwriting decisions, and availability of cover – were not dealt with (Kemp 1989: 58–9). Optimistic plans in the late 1970s for the creation of a European Export-Import Bank were not accepted by the Council. Nor did the member-states give their support to the 1987 proposal of the Commission to create a European Export Credit

Insurance Facility. This European facility would have operated for the accounts of the member-states to support export consortia in which two or more member-states were participating. The only regulations that were decided upon and implemented involved limited co-operation between public insurers in the case of consortium-exports and transparency.[8]

The French initiative: setting the European agenda

Somewhat surprisingly, during its 1989 presidency, France put export credit insurance on the European agenda. Since neither the single market legislation nor the White Paper treated the issue in particular or changed the regulations applicable to official export credit insurance, the EEC Treaty articles had remained applicable. Hence, in 1989, there had been no additional juridical pressure for action. What had changed were a number of factors that affected market conditions. First, whereas increasing cross-border co-operation among EU-exporters had made the need for more flexible export credit arrangements increasingly felt, this trend was not matched by corresponding developments on the supply side. Most insurance schemes remained oriented towards respective national interests. Second, the principle of exclusive coverage for national exporters in member-state policies was bound to be undermined by a growing number of enterprises with affiliates or subsidiaries in other member-states. Finally, the Commission feared that national governments would increasingly rely on various subsidies in response to the fiercer competition that came with a unified market (Abraham 1990: 1).

In addition to these market developments, budgetary pressures as a result of escalating cumulative shortages on the national insurance schemes had helped EU member-states become more willing to deal with the issue. Public export credit agencies are under pressure from ministries of finances and, increasingly, from national legislators to avoid claims (*Financial Times*, 5 May 1994).

France proposed the creation of two expert groups on export credit insurance: one for short-term and the other for medium-term export credit insurance. These were formed by the member-states on 12 July 1989 at a meeting of the Council's CGC. Both expert groups were asked to survey the problems for the twelve existing public export credit insurers that might arise as a consequence of the realization of the internal market and to report their findings to the CGC.

Of particular note here was the emphasis laid on the issue of export credit insurance (by installing two working groups on this issue) and the neglect of the issue of financing supports. Yet these supports had been identified by the Commission as the most important source of export subsidization, 'particularly true for France' (Abraham 1990: 91). Although the level of export financing subsidies may have been restricted by the OECD Consensus agreement, substantial distortions of competition between exporters still existed, because of the lack of harmonization of export financing schemes.

Given the high level of French export financing support, this emphasis on harmonization of credit insurance might be seen as a strategic move.

The first group, chaired by Callut (Belgium), was to concentrate on the mixed market for short-term credit insurance, examining distortions of competition between private and public credit insurers. The second expert group on medium-term export credit insurance (where differences between national insurance schemes influence the competition between exporters), was chaired by Stolzenburg (Germany). An examination of the Stolzenburg group's mandate reveals that member-states preferred to try to diminish possible distortions in competition by targeting market behaviour (national credit insurance policies), while maintaining the existing market structure of twelve different institutions. The Stolzenburg group was asked to conduct a comparative analysis of the existing national schemes and to review the important elements of these public schemes from a competition policy point of view. The group was also asked to examine the existing techniques for co-operation between member-states' export credit insurance agencies and to make proposals for extending them. The mandate did not include inquiries into adaptations of market structure. Member-states agreed that the Stolzenburg group's subject was far more politically sensitive than that of the Callut group because of the importance of national interests (industrial, trade and foreign policy) in medium-term insurance.

Applicability of articles 92–94 EEC on official export credit insurance

In 1989, following the creation of the working groups, Germany and the Netherlands asked the Commission for a statement concerning the EEC regulations applicable to export credit insurance, in order to provide guidance to the technical talks in the two working groups. The Commission responded by arguing that export credit insurance is a violation of the rules on state-aids, *even* if the public insurance facility operated on a break-even basis.

Article 92(1) holds a state aid incompatible with the common market when:

1 an aid is granted by a member-state or through state resources in any form whatsoever;
2 this aid distorts or threatens to distort competition by favouring certain enterprises or the production of certain goods;
3 this aid affects trade between member-states negatively.

In this respect, a distinction has to be made between intra-EU and extra-EU exports. State aid for intra-EU exports would directly affect trade between member-states, while aid for exports to third countries would have an indirect effect, especially when the level of aid was substantial and concentrated in certain industries. This pattern of allocation has characterized both financing support and export credit insurance; both have been found to be directed towards a limited number of industries, such as construction and services, transport equipment, electrical equipment and non-electrical machinery and cars. Abraham also observes that the United Kingdom and France seem to target their export credit subsidies at many of the same industries (Abraham 1990: 92).

Hence, Commission officials had concluded that officially supported export credits and export credit insurance were two of the main forms of export aid. As these forms of state aids were said to affect intra-EU trade, either directly (by supporting exports to other member-states) or indirectly (by supporting exports to third countries), they were seen as contrary to article 92(1). By adding that export credit insurance was considered contrary to article 92(1) even if it did not result in a cost to the government, the Commission had taken an even more strict position than the GATT Subsidy Code.

The proposal for a European reinsurance pool

While the investigations of export credit insurance were proceeding, in November 1990, the Commission (DG I) formulated ideas on the level of market structure in a proposal for a European reinsurance pool, especially for risk on Middle and Eastern European countries.[9] DG I stated that the proposal was based on the principle of subsidiarity: 'the Commission shall offer help or support but [will] not try to replace the national schemes unless it can be proven that for some reason this solution would be much better' (Dalvin 1992: 7). The Commission's objective was to extend the scope of coverage on Middle and Eastern European countries 'to the maximum acceptable from an insurance point of view' and to reduce simultaneously the distortions of competition between exporters of member-states, while limiting changes in market structure to the minimum (Hartog 1991: 15). As a consequence, the proposal was formulated modestly. The member-states' export credit insurance agencies would remain the exporter's 'window' for applications. In the case of exports to one of the six countries with a credit term of more than two years, 60 per cent of the risk would be insured for the account of the member-state and 40 per cent would be insured through the European reinsurance pool. Hence 40 per cent of the risk and 40 per cent of the premium would be redistributed proportionally to the agencies in all member-states.

The pool proposal was embraced by the European Parliament, which added the idea that besides the mechanism of reinsurance, 20 per cent of the risk should be covered through the EU budget. But almost without exception, member-states turned down the pool proposal. They were uncertain about the consequences for national export credit insurance policies and their future policy autonomy. In addition, small member-states feared that costly political motives (aid to Eastern Europe) of some large states would compromise a policy based on sound insurance techniques (Dalvin 1992: 8).

Competition policy or common commercial policy?

By having mandated the two working groups to concentrate on the existing twelve national schemes and by turning down the proposal for the reinsurance pool, member-states had, in fact, excluded measures targeted at market structure. Having thus 'agreed' within the EU that measures should be at the level of national agencies, member-states and the Commission in 1992 entered into new struggles with regard to their respective responsibilities. The disputes were based on the interpretation of articles 92–94 EEC on competition policy and 112–113 EEC on common commercial policy and their respective consequences as a juridical base for measures against distortions of competition.

Because member-states preferred a considerable say in the realization and national implementation of rules for their behaviour in the field of export credit insurance, they preferred article 112 EEC in this respect. This article, which aims for a common policy with regard to trade with third countries, says measures relating to the harmonization of export subsidies must be taken by way of directive, with decision-making by qualified majority. Since this article is within the competence of DG I of the Commission, DG I supported the member-states' preference. As the application of articles 92–94 EEC (on state aids which affect intra-community trade flows) is an exclusive competence of the Commission (DG IV), these provisions were less attractive to member-states.[10]

DG IV, however, had strong arguments for its jurisdictional claim. First, article 112 EEC did not address intra-community trade. Second, DG IV's position was strengthened by two decisions of the European Court: in the case C-63/89 of Cobac against the Council and Commission, articles 92–94 EEC were considered applicable to distortions owing to officially supported export credit insurance.[11] In the case C-142/87 of Belgium against the Commission, the Court widened the scope of articles 92–94 to include extra-EU exports.[12] The Belgian government had supported the exports of tube producer Tubemeuse in a period of European overcapacity in this sector. In its defence, Belgium stated that this support was given to extra-EU exports, and that for state-aid to exports to the former Soviet Union, article 112 EEC was applicable, not articles 92–94 EEC. The Court's judgement, however, supported DG IV, saying that article 112, concerning harmonization of state aid to exports in connection with the common commercial policy, does not exclude the application of articles 92–94 EEC because state aid to extra-EU exports also affects trade flows between member-states.

The first test-case for these matters of competence came following the report of the Callut group on short-term credit insurance, which had finished its work in October 1991. The report demonstrated that member-states' public export credit agencies all received some form of financial support from the government which, in turn, had the potential to distort competition between public and private insurers. Moreover, the report identified those parts of the credit insurance market where these publicly supported credit insurers could be in competition with private market parties: largely all commercial risks for a period of three years or less in the OECD area were considered to be 'marketable risks'.

With the report finished and presented to the Council's CGC, the matter of a policy response arose. Since both DG I (backed by the member-states) and DG IV claimed competence, both made proposals: DG I a concept directive and DG IV a draft communication on short-term credit insurance (based on articles 92–94 EEC). Even though DG IV had a very strong legal position as we have noted, the two directorates remained deadlocked until Commission member Leon Brittan moved from DG IV to DG I. Despite the move, he remained firm in his opposition to state-aids to exports (*Financial Times*, 12 March 1992). It seemed that a compromise had been arrived at between DG IV, DG I and the member-states: the distortions of competition between insurers (Callut dossier) would be handled by DG IV on the basis of articles 92–94 EEC and the (more sensitive from a 'national interest' point of view) follow-up of the reports on competition between exporters (Stolzenburg/later Tuffrau dossier) would be a directive, on the basis of article 112 EEC.

As a consequence, DG IV could prepare a Communication on the application of articles 92–94 EEC on short-term export credit insurance, but it had become clear that member-states would not permit the Commission to dictate their trade policies. DG IV, therefore, chose a cautious approach. It drafted a communication containing a prohibition of state aid to credit insurers which cover 'marketable risks' – that is, risks that can be insured on the private market. The scope of this draft with regard to the definition of which risks are considered 'marketable' was more limited than was identified in the Callut report, clearly in order to avoid disputes on the marketability of the risks concerned. Despite this cautious approach, persistent Anglo-French polemics on the definition of marketable risk have delayed the publication of the communication.[13] Meanwhile, most member-states – except the United Kingdom and Italy – have already adapted their systems, making a distinction between marketable and non-marketable risks and reserving public insurance for the latter category. Consequently, the need for the communication has diminished.

Common credit insurance policy or merely transparency of techniques?

Our analysis of regional EU developments continues with the work of the Tuffrau group an expert group chaired by the French, that had followed up the Stolzenburg group in 1991 and presented its report to the CGC in June 1993. The Tuffrau report focused on medium- and long-term risks; that is, those risks that cannot be insured on the private market. Its mandate called for the development of common principles for conditions of coverage, for premiums, and for country risk assessment.

As most of the so-called 'non-marketable risks' pertain to non-member countries, it is considered that article 112 EEC applies for the formulation of guidelines for policy co-ordination. As mentioned, articles 92–94 EEC could be applicable as well, but DG IV has refrained from exercising its competence, probably because the Commission anticipated that the juridical procedure of articles 92–94 EEC would not be acceptable to member-states owing to trade policy interests.

The Tuffrau report contains proposals for common principles for (1) conditions of coverage, (2) for risk assessment on buyers and buyers' countries and (3) for premium setting. Member-states perceive the principles for risk assessment to be highly political because they intersect directly with aspects of trade and foreign policy. The report ignored politics and covered the subject in a purely technical way. The parameters for country risk assessments were defined and the consequences of the assessments were shown. The report draws no conclusions about the direction of a common coverage policy. The Commission acted as an observer to these discussions, and eventually formulated a draft directive based on EEC 113.

Apart from residual technical questions, there are two main policy issues concerning medium- and long-term credit insurance:

1 Should transparency of techniques and a common methodology lead to a common and binding market behaviour (common credit insurance policy) as well? Given the goal to abandon distortions of competition, the only answer to this question would be yes. If so, which procedures should be followed in this respect?
2 What will or should be the influence of EU guidelines for behaviour on the financial results of governments' credit insurance agencies? Since article 110 EEC advocates a gradual movement towards free world trade, the harmonization of credit policies within the EU should involve a harmonization directed towards a reduction, instead of an increase, in cumulative deficits of the credit insurance schemes.

These two issues were carefully avoided by the Tuffrau group. Possibly, as technical experts, they did not feel competent to make proposals in this respect (although this competence can be deduced from the mandate). It is also conceivable that governments instructed their experts to reduce the discussions on convergence of policy to a discussion on transparency of insurance techniques. In the proposal for a directive that the Commission submitted to the CGC in July 1994, the first of the two questions noted above was dealt with: decisions on common policies should be made by qualified majorities on proposals to be submitted by a working group, chaired by the Commission. The proposals of this working group should be formulated through a procedure in which the Commission has the leading role. Objecting to this procedure, however, member-states have turned down this proposal, which has resulted in a deadlock over the draft directive. The second question above on reducing deficits is dealt with neither in the Tuffrau report, nor in the proposal for a directive.

The British initiative: setting the international agenda

As Coleman and Underhill note in their analysis in this volume (Chapter 11), when deadlock occurs in either the regional or the global sphere, dissatisfied governments can transport the issue to the other sphere. Regional integration and globalization are interdependent processes. Since the issue of reducing deficits was not addressed in the Truffau group, the UK – one of the strongest advocates of the break-even objective – turned from a regional to a more global arena. In his study of trade negotiations in the OECD, Blair asserts that the OECD has proved to be the most

> convenient forum for export credit negotiations, since it included the major extenders of export credits while excluding the major recipients. It was primarily for this reason that the issue was negotiated in the OECD instead of the GATT, where developing countries and centrally-planned economies could have been expected to resist attempts to limit export credit subsidisation.
>
> (Blair 1993: 79)

Thus the UK launched a second offensive within the OECD. Although the European Commission (DG I) represents the EU member-states within the OECD (so the UK is not party directly to the OECD negotiations) British OECD Secretariat officials were able to put the issue prominently on the agenda, expecting to find support from the United States, Canada and Australia. In the Communiqué of the OECD Council Ministerial Meeting of 2–3 June 1993, the ministers called 'for a report at their 1994 meeting on progress in developing guiding principles for setting guarantee premia'. The Secretariat of the OECD added that the starting point for these principles should be the break-even rule of the GATT, although the existing OECD Consensus on financing support is not based on this principle.[14] The OECD Secretariat has recently announced a three-step strategy for the disciplining of export credit insurance (Kraneveld 1994), containing:

1 understanding of the situation (cash flow questionnaires) and the options (analysis of the accountancy and premium-setting process);
2 transparency on the programme level (conversion of the cash flow questionnaires into reporting on financial results) and on the transaction level (notification of long-term transactions insured, comparison of cover policy and premium policy);
3 discipline on covering costs (compliance with the GATT-rule) and on premiums (to eliminate cross-subsidies).

In September 1994 a working group of OECD Consensus members started to investigate various related matters, including country risk classification models, premium benchmarks for different classes of risks, and financial objectives for public export credit insurance systems.

CONCLUSION

This chapter demonstrates the relationship between the processes of regional economic integration and globalization – in this instance of trade relationships. Although on a global level, the violation of the GATT rules on export credit insurance could be ignored, on the regional EU level market integration created pressures to harmonize national credit insurance policies. Since the 1960s, several efforts have been made to discipline export credit insurance within the EU, with all proposals pertaining directly to market structure being turned down by the member-states. Because of the far-reaching consequences for their future policy autonomy, member-states found it unacceptable to create either a European Export-Import Bank, or a European Export Credit Insurance Facility, or a European reinsurance pool for risk on Middle and Eastern Europe. Countries that provide support to exports through export insurance were simply unwilling to give up an important trade policy instrument. In addition, smaller member-states feared the budgetary consequences of a European country cover policy which might be dominated by the interests of the large states.

When assessing the disciplining efforts within the EU, it seems clear that intergovernmental factors have prevailed over supranational/transnational factors (Moravcsik 1991: 19–56). National preferences with regard to harmonizing and disciplining 'official insurance' policy have converged as a consequence of rising cumulative deficits in all member-states and the need to co-ordinate policies to facilitate cross-border co-operation of EU exporters. The resulting negotiation process between member-states has for the most part taken place within the Council's Co-ordination Group for Credit Insurance and two expert groups (which have been created by the CGC, not at the initiative of the Commission). Neither transnational interest groups nor the European Parliament and the Commission have been more than observers in this harmonization process. Transnational interest groups, like the Union of Industrial and Employers' Confederation of Europe (UNICE) found it hard to formulate a common point of view owing to different kinds and levels of support enjoyed in the different member-states.

The Commission did have a strong position though, owing to the judgements of the Court in the Cobac and Tubemeuse case, where articles 92–94 EEC were considered applicable to export credit insurance, even if the support was given to extra-EU exports. The Commission however, has refrained from systematically enforcing articles 92–94 EEC on extra-EU exports for fear of disadvantaging EU exporters against government-backed non-EU competitors. Moreover, the fact that the supported extra-EU exports often are shaped by development assistance and foreign policy objectives could lead to a conflict of objectives with competition policy. When leaving the extra-EU exports to DG I, carrying out harmonization under articles 112–113 EEC (common commercial policy), DG IV clearly hoped that the indirect effects on EU markets of extra-EU export aid would be eliminated, albeit slowly. In return, DG IV could proceed with the communication-procedure for short-term credit insurance, following the conflict on competencies between DG I and DG IV after publication of the Callut report.

This DG IV victory seems rather symbolic, however, since the Callut dossier on competition distortions between insurers is of less concern to the member-states from a trade policy point of view. The Tuffrau dossier on competition distortions between exporters of the various member-states has been dealt with since this time by DG I following a strategy of co-ordination instead of prohibition. Until now, this co-ordination process has taken place within the Tuffrau group on medium-term export credit insurance and has been confined to transparency of insurance techniques.

The regional policy forum has a limited range of activity before issues must be pushed up to a global level. We have shown that the EU forum was more or less appropriate for handling the issue of competition between insurers and for addressing limited co-operation among public insurers in the case of consortium exports. None the less, given the uncertainty about the behaviour of third countries (especially the United States, Japan and the newly industrializing countries), the same forum was not effective for dealing with the trade issue of distortions of competition between exporters. Because changes in the modes and level of insurance support affect the competitiveness of European exporters against government-backed competitors from non-member countries, EU member-states preferred to handle these issues on a global level. Efforts to connect guidelines for market behaviour with the financial objective of having government facilities break even requires global rather than regional agreements.

NOTES

1 The authors would like to thank Bill Coleman, Allan Dalvin, Paul Mudde, Dick Naezer, Éric Philippart, Geoffrey Underhill, Ben de Wilde and Paul Wind for their valuable comments. Klaas Werkhorst's contribution to this chapter reflects his personal views only. Research for this chapter was concluded in August 1996.
2 For related literature see Abraham (1990), Abraham *et al.* (1992), Blair (1993), Fitzgerald and Monson (1989), Kemp (1989), Moravcsik (1989), Ray (1986) and Wallen (1984).
3 National export credit systems have taken on different institutional forms. Support is given by government departments directly (e.g. the Export Credit Guarantee Department in the UK), by public companies (e.g. COFACE in France) and by private companies providing cover for account of the state (Hermes in Germany and NCM in the Netherlands).
4 Hermes, the company which administers the German public export credit insurance scheme, reported a 1993 deficit of DM 5.1bn and a 1994 shortfall of DM 4.3bn. These worst-ever deficits were caused mainly by losses of, respectively, DM 4.5bn and DM 4.2bn on transactions between East German companies and insolvent buyers in the former Soviet Union (*Financial Times*, 26 April 1994 and 13 January 1995).
5 Premium policy is not the only instrument for reaching the break-even objective.

172   *Public policy, globalization and regionalism*

The policy (e.g. terms of re-schedulings) towards debtor countries after claims have been paid to exporters, and especially the policy on the availability of cover and underwriting policy, also influences the financial results of the agency.

6 In the 1979 GATT Subsidies and Countervailing Duties Code (negotiated in the Tokyo Round) this rule has been maintained. In the recent Uruguay Round the word 'manifestly' has been dropped.

7 The Paris Club is an informal group of creditor countries (mainly OECD countries) which meets on an *ad hoc* basis to negotiate with a debtor country to produce a multilateral debt rescheduling.

8 In 1973 (amended in 1976) a Council Directive was adopted, setting procedures for information and consultation to member-states in the case of exports with a credit period of more than five years (73/391/EEC). In 1982 a Council Decision provided for rules for the inclusion of subdeliveries from other member-states in the insurance package that an exporter can get from its government (82/854/EEC). In 1987 additional rules for joint insurance were laid down in a Council Directive (84/568/EEC).

9 *Official Journal of the European Communities*, no. C 302/6–8, 1.12.90.

10 DG IV can draft a communication, which contains the Commission's interpretation of the applicability of articles 92–94 to the field of export credit insurance. Through this communication the Commission informs the member-states of the factors which are considered as trade distorting. Member-states are then asked, in conformity with article 93(1), to adapt their export credit insurance programmes according to the lines of action delineated in the communication. If in the following notification round (after six months) a member-state appears not to have adapted its system, the Commission can take a negative decision. If the member-state does not agree with the Commission's decision, the member-state may appeal to the Court. The member-state may also be summoned to appear before the Court (by the Commission or by another member-state which is involved) if the member-state has not met the negative decision within the time fixed.

11 C-63/89 *Assurance de Crédit and Cobac* v. *Council and Commission* (1991) ECR1–1799, 1848 (&22).

12 Arrêt de la Cour, C-142/87, 21–3–1990, Belgique contre Commission des Communautés européennes, pp. 13–14.

13 The draft communication and most of continental European member-states define marketable risk as short-term commercial risks applying to OECD countries except Mexico, Turkey, the Czech Republic and Hungary. Public export credit insurance agencies, so says the communication, should withdraw from this business. The UK, in contrast, wants to put all short-term export credit insurance (commercial, political, OECD and non-OECD) into the private market – the so-called seamless approach. The UK claims that the European Commission's narrow definition of marketable risk slows down the development of the private sector market, while continental public export credit insurance agencies like the French Coface claim that the UK is trying to develop a market for essentially non-marketable risks (cf. *Financial Times* 31 January 1995, 28 February 1996 and *Project and Trade Finance*, November 1994).

14 The Illustrative List of Export Subsidies attached to the Subsidies Code negotiated in the Tokyo Round prohibits: 'the grant by governments (or special institutions controlled by and/or acting under the authority of governments) of exports credits at rates below those which they actually have to pay for the funds so employed (or would have to pay if they borrowed on international capital markets in order to obtain funds of the same maturity and denominated in the same currency as the export credit), or the payment by them of all or part of the costs incurred by exporters or financial institutions in obtaining credits, insofar as they are used to secure a material advantage in the field of export credit terms'. As

some subsidy of export credit is still allowed by the OECD Consensus (restricted by the minimum interest rates), the OECD Consensus is less strict than the GATT subsidy code. These subsidies are however condoned by the GATT by the following paragraph, implicitly concerning the OECD Consensus: 'Provided, however, that if a signatory is party to an international undertaking on official export credits to which at least 12 signatories to this agreement are parties as of 1 January 1979 (or a successor undertaking which has been adopted by those original signatories), or if in practice a signatory applies the interest rate provisions of the relevant undertaking, an export credit practice which is in conformity with those provisions shall not be considered as an export subsidy prohibited by this agreement'. (Abraham 1990: 15–16).

REFERENCES

Abraham, F. (1990) *The Effects on Intra-Community Competition of Export Subsidies to Third Countries: The Case of Export Credits, Export Insurance and Official Development Assistance*, Brussels and Luxemburg: Office for Official Publications of the European Communities.

Abraham, F., I. Couwenberg, and G. Dewit (1992) 'Towards an EC policy on export financing subsidies: lessons from the 1980s and prospects for future reform', *The World Economy* 15 (3): 389–405.

Baron, D.P. (1983) *The Export-Import Bank; An Economic Analysis*, London and New York: Academic Press.

Blair, D.J. (1993) *Trade Negotiations in the OECD; Structures, Institutions and States*, London and New York: Kegan Paul International.

Dalvin, A.G. (1992) General Directorate for External Relations of the Commission of the European Communities, 'Insuring export credit and political risk' (speech).

Fitzgerald, B. and T. Monson (1989) 'Preferential credit and insurance as means to promote exports', *Research Observer* 4, (1), January: 89–114.

Hartog, E. (1991) General Directorate for External Relations of the Commission of the European Communities, 'The European Single Market and export credit insurance' (speech), Institute of International Finance, London.

Hufbauer, G.C. and J. Shelton Erb (1984) *Subsidies in International Trade*, Institute for International Economics, Washington, DC and Cambridge, Mass.: MIT Press.

Kapteyn, P.J.G., P. VerLoren van Themaat (1987) *Inleiding tot het recht van de Europese Gemeenschappen*, Deventer: Kluwer.

Kemp, R.T. (1989) *Review of Status Options for ECGD*, Export Credit Guarantee Department.

Kraneveld, P, (1994) 'The OECD and export credits; latest developments', London, March (speech).

Moravcsik, A.M. (1989) 'Disciplining trade finance: the OECD export credit arrangement', *International Organization* 43, (1): 173–205.

—— (1991) 'Negotiating the Single European Act; national interests and conventional statecraft in the European Community', *International Organization* 45, (1): 19–56.

Project and Trade Finance (1994) 'Fog in Channel – continent's export', November: 6–8.

Ray, J.E. (1986) 'The OECD "consensus" on export credits', *World Economy*, September: 295–309.

Wallen, A. (1984) 'Export credit subsidization and the consensus arrangement', *Aussenwirtschaft* 39 (III): 261–9.

9 Strapped to the mast

EU central bankers between global financial markets and regional integration

Kenneth Dyson, Kevin Featherstone and
George Michalopoulos

Since the early 1980s, national central banks in Europe have been operating within a dramatically changing environment. First, there has been a process of globalization of financial markets. Financial innovation and liberalization of capital movements, especially under the auspices of the Single European Act, have led to the internationalization of financial markets, thereby altering the systemic relationships that govern monetary policy-making. Foreign exchange market turbulence in the 1980s and early 1990s clearly demonstrates the enhanced power of major financial market actors, illuminates the more powerful constraints on state economic policies and suggests evidence of a crisis of effectiveness of traditional monetary and exchange rate policy instruments. Second, within Europe, the relaunch of Economic and Monetary Union (EMU) in the late 1980s represented a major political challenge to the power of national central banks. It added a second source of uncertainty and potential instability to their operating environment.

In this context of dual assaults from global market contingencies and regional political pressures, central bankers have sought to 'strap themselves to the mast', in the manner of Odysseus, by adhering to a professional ideology of central bank independence. That ideology rested on a professional dedication to the value of price stability, and to the belief that commitment to price stability could only be made credible if central banks were made independent in their use of monetary policy instruments.

This chapter analyses the impact of the European Union (EU) central banking community in the regional process of Economic and Monetary Union negotiations through the signing of the Maastricht Treaty. It highlights the ability of central banks to secure their corporate interests through their participation in the making of EMU. The design of the final stage of EMU was almost exclusively negotiated within the world of central banks. Price stability has become the primary target of EMU, while political and economic independence of the 'new' EU monetary institutions, the European Central Bank (ECB) and the European System of Central Banks (ESCB), has been ensured. We argue that by promoting independence, central bankers were attempting to limit the loss of power they suffered because of globalized financial markets and the regional process of EMU.

Finally, the chapter investigates the factors underlying the renewed power of central bankers. It concludes that traditional theories on central banking behaviour offer little explanation for their ability to determine the content of EMU. A more meaningful explanation has to be sought in a number of structural factors that have been at work, such as the emergence of the Bundesbank as a key actor in the central banking community; the prevalence of a regulatory policy style in the EU; the prevailing unique relationship between central banks and the state; the impact that financial market crises had on the position of central banks in the economy; and the structural change within capitalism related to the increased power of global financial markets and the new credibility that they gave to 'sound money' ideas.

THE ADVANCE OF CENTRAL BANK INDEPENDENCE

Three interconnected changes pushed central bank independence to the centre of the political agenda by the 1990s: the embrace of EMU by the large majority of member-state governments, motivated primarily by considerations of political strategy; structural changes within financial markets and their implications for the effectiveness of traditional monetary policy; and a change in the climate of economic policy ideas. The contradiction between two of these changes (and the new hazards that they engendered) – more exposure to markets and monetary unification in the EU – was more apparent than real. Increased risks of 'destabilization' with more turbulent markets and of political 'irresponsibility' in the rush to EMU were matched by the effort of central banks to police more effectively the interface of policy and markets by institutionalizing the principle of central bank independence at both EU and national levels and by promoting the ideas of fiscal discipline and of structural reforms. The route to EMU and its final design, as sketched in the Treaty on European Union, provides incontrovertible evidence of the renewed ambition of central bankers to control state and EU policies. This ambition stems from corporate interest and represents a fourth factor at work.

The relaunch of EMU and central bank corporate interests

The intensification of regional economic integration through the EMU project was initiated exclusively at the political level (Dyson 1994). Several key factors contributed to the initiation of the process. First, key member-states, notably France and Italy, were increasingly dissatisfied with the asymmetries in monetary policy-making within the European monetary system (EMS). Second, the German political leadership (especially of Foreign Minister Hans-Dietrich Genscher) was receptive to French and Italian proposals for upgrading EU monetary integration. Third, EMU could build on the momentum created by the successful negotiation of the Single European Act, and the evidence of the initial success of the Single Market programme.

Finally, governments had come to accept that freedom of capital movements and stable exchange rates were fundamentally incompatible with independent national monetary policies.

Essentially, the EU central bankers were co-opted into the policy process on EMU. This co-optation came initially in their personal capacity as members of the Delors Committee on Economic and Monetary Union, established at the Hanover summit with the technical task of identifying how EMU could be realized. It continued through the official channels of the Committee of Central Bank Governors (to which the task of drafting the statutes of the ECB and ESCB was entrusted) and of the EU Monetary Committee (whose membership overlapped with the Intergovernmental Conference (IGC) on EMU and where some key decisions on issues related to the transition phase were prepared) (Delors Committee 1989). On issues of political principle, the European Council seized and retained the initiative, forcing the EU central bankers onto the defensive. The central banks' strategy was a combination of damage-limitation to their basic interests on policy, and offensive action on institutional design to secure a cast-iron guarantee of independence for the new ECB and ESCB.

The EU central banks were able to define corporate interests and agreed policy positions on several key issues. First, in the initiation phase, they resisted the EU Commission's early attempt under Delors to promote EMU as a secondary issue attached to the Single Market programme. They supported the notion that the legal framework of Single European Act 'does not suffice for the creation of an economic and monetary union' and that EMU should be based on a Treaty change (Delors Committee 1989: 13).

Second, they secured price stability as the primary objective of the ECB and the ESCB. In fact, the definition of the responsibilities of these institutions in terms of monetary stability is stronger even in comparison to the responsibilities of the Bundesbank as defined in the Bundesbank Act of 1957 (Gros and Thygesen 1992). In order to make the commitment to price stability viable, the ECB and the ESCB were made 'independent of instructions from national governments and Union authorities' (Delors Committee 1989: 22). The power of central bankers in determining the content of EMU is reflected in the fact that most of the recommendations of the Delors report on the third stage of Monetary Union were incorporated into the Treaty.

Finally, central bankers stressed the importance of economic integration and convergence as a prerequisite of EMU and noted the lack of an economic rationale for a timetable of stages for EMU (the Delors Report (1989: 28) concluded that there should be no fixed dates for stages two and three). They strongly supported the need for 'binding rules' for national budgetary policies involving limits on deficits and the abolition of monetary financing of deficits and any privileged access of governments to financial markets. This theme was to be resurrected with the German stability pact proposal of 1995: a tight fiscal ceiling in stage three was to be accompanied by quasi-automatic sanctions. The proposal was strongly backed by the EU central bankers in the European Monetary Institute.

The Treaty on European Union represents, in large part, an EMU for EU central bankers. The central bankers' victory was symbolized by the fact that EMU did not involve the idea of the EU developing an active, co-ordinated fiscal stance. In contrast, the emphasis was on the 'fiscal conditions for a monetary union'; that is, on meeting convergence criteria that were defined in nominal terms and not in real terms of output growth and employment. Measures to promote 'economic and social cohesion' were contained within the Treaty, notably the new Cohesion Fund. They were not, however, added to the convergence criteria, which would have legitimated a more active fiscal role for the EU.

But this evidence of central bankers' strength through cohesion of corporate interests and culture cannot obscure a diversity of motivations in embracing EMU and different conceptions of the kind of EMU that should be sought. In practice, negotiations within the Committee of Central Bank Governors and the EU Monetary Committee proved tough. In the second half of the 1980s, the priority of the Banque de France and the Banca d'Italia was to promote symmetry in the EMS via tightening monetary policy co-operation. The Bundesbank feared that greater symmetry within the EMS would be inflationary. In the subsequent EMU negotiations, the Banque de France and the French government moved out of the 'asymmetry' front to join the 'symmetry' group. The main reason for this ideological shift was that France had gradually moved into the low-inflation club.

More importantly, issues related to the transition stage of EMU, probably because of their political character, bedevilled the negotiations in the Inter-governmental Conference. These issues included: procedures related to the passage to the final stage, like the timetable for stages, and how the decision on the entry to the final stage should be made; the problem of quantification of convergence criteria; and institutional arrangements, especially in relation to the functions of the monetary institution in the second stage and the introduction of central bank independence. On these issues, the final settlement was much the result of intergovernmental negotiations within the Council of Economics and Finance Ministers (ECOFIN), the Monetary Committee and the IGCs. However, the input of central banks in the discussion of issues related to transition, although indirect (that is, through the setting of national positions), was not negligible.

For the French government, central bank independence was the most difficult issue during the IGC. Its opposition to independence reflected mainly the interests of the key bureau in the Finance Ministry, the Trésor, in terms of maintaining control over macroeconomic policy (the Banque de France was not independent during the EMU negotiations).[1] President Mitterrand and his Foreign Minister, Roland Dumas, opposed the Trésor for the sake of diplomatic reality, believing that EMU would only be acceptable to the German government if it came with central bank independence. The German position (largely influenced by the Bundesbank) was that all central banks should become independent at the beginning of stage two, to facilitate convergence in the transition period. This proposal was strongly opposed by the French and UK delegations in the IGCs.

In contrast, France and Italy supported the establishment of the ECB with operational responsibilities in the beginning of the second stage to prepare the co-ordination of monetary policies, a recommendation that was clearly expressed in the Delors report (Smaghi *et al.* forthcoming). The eventual compromise was that 'political' independence of central banks was to be optional in stage two but that their 'economic' independence was to be strengthened by abolishing monetary financing of deficits. Such an outcome was satisfactory to the Bundesbank, whose main concern was that in stage two the principle of indivisible responsibility for the conduct of monetary policy should be retained: hence the nomenclature of a European Monetary Institute (EMI) rather than bank and the lack of operational powers. But the Bundesbank's ability to get its way was enhanced by the unwillingness of key national governments to entertain central bank independence at so early a time. Without central bank independence in stage two, it was easier for the Bundesbank to argue that operational responsibilities could not be given to the EMI. Faced with still-reluctant national politicians, EU central bankers were unable to use the EMU negotiations to promote their corporate interest in a rapid transition to central bank independence.

Outside the realm of central bank independence, there were other issues on which EU central bankers disagreed. On the question of 'economic and social cohesion' the central banks of southern Europe and Ireland took a very different position from the others. Just how tough the convergence criteria should be divided central banks into those (like the Italian) that wanted to avoid precise figures on budget deficits and public debt, and those (like the Dutch and German) that insisted on specific and demanding fiscal conditions.

To summarize, despite disagreements on transitional issues, central banks had strongly promoted their corporate interests with the signing of the Treaty: the priority of the price stability objective was clearly defined; the independence of domestic monetary authorities was to be secured in the end; and fiscal discipline was defined strongly in terms of non-monetization of deficits and the 'no bail-out' clause.

Globalization, innovation and deregulation in financial markets

The defence of the corporate interests of domestic central banks in the context of growing regional integration in the EU was important because they faced additional challenges from deep-seated structural transformations in world financial markets beginning in the 1970s. With globalization, differentiation and the huge increase of scale of financial markets, central banks faced challenges both in regulating banking and financial markets and in operating traditional monetary policy instruments like credit controls.

One aspect was the boom in international lending, represented by the growth of Eurobond issues, international markets in short-term securities or Euro-notes and the increasing importance of cross-border trade in equities (Howell and Cozzini 1991; Porter 1993; O'Brien 1992; BIS 1993a; Underhill 1995). Partly to cover against consequent risk, market operators initiated a process of frenetic product innovation: new financial instruments, like derivatives (swaps, futures and options), expanded rapidly at the expense of spot markets while escaping regulation. The opening of domestic financial markets in combination with these innovations encouraged new entrants into financial markets (particularly from overseas), including insurance companies, mutual investment funds, pension funds and hedge funds. In turn, the important role of these new institutional investors undermined the traditional social and cultural cohesion between central banks and the narrow and exclusive domestic financial communities, a cohesion that had facilitated the operation of monetary policy by central banks, notably the use of moral suasion in a framework of cosy personal relations (Moran 1991). As Coleman and Underhill indicate in this volume (Chapter 11), a further consequence of the rise of transnational corporations was the new dynamics of 'regulatory arbitrage', as such firms sought to migrate to lower-cost regulatory environments. Regulatory arbitrage under the pressure of transnational firms became integral to the dynamics of globalization of financial markets (Stopford and Strange 1991).

This revolution in international financial markets had profound implications for the distribution of political power at the domestic level, opening up new cleavages and remaking political coalitions (Frieden 1991). Overall, it tended to favour the interests of capital over labour, and of owners and managers of financial assets and transnational firms with internationally diversified assets over firms whose assets were tied to specific national markets. In a world of capital mobility, exchange rate politics developed a particular sensitivity as different coalitions emerged over the issues of stability/ flexibility. Export-oriented producers of tradable goods and international traders and investors tend to favour exchange rate stability, in the form of the Exchange Rate Mechanism (ERM); opponents are to be found in producers of non-tradable goods and services and those oriented to domestic markets. As a consequence, the combination of international financial markets with the ERM was exposing EU central bankers to more intense domestic currency politics (Destler and Henning 1989).

Within this process of globalization, perhaps the most fundamental supportive measure of deregulation was the adoption of freedom of movement of capital. Its acceptance by the EU in 1988 as an early part of the completion of the Single Market programme reflected a number of motives. First, there was a growing recognition that financial innovation had rendered capital controls largely ineffective. Second, states with traditionally closed capital markets, like France and Italy, wanted to demonstrate their political will to realize European integration. Third, there was an ideological shift in Europe in favour of deregulation, associated with an efficiency argument: that the allocation of savings and investment in Europe would be more efficient if capital were fully mobile. In these respects, freedom of capital movement was not simply an exogenous shock to which EU states adjusted. It was a rational choice within radically changed structural conditions.

The implications of financial innovation and liberalization for the conduct of monetary policy were apparent: direct credit controls (credit rationing, liquidity constraints, etc.) traditionally employed by many European central banks became ineffective instruments of monetary control. Instead of reducing overall financial expansion, credit controls merely shift activity to markets which are less regulated at home or abroad. Hence, monetary policy in recent years has moved towards the use of indirect policy instruments like open market operations and bank interest rates. Another implication for monetary policy was that the financial revolution has changed the relationship between the intermediate targets indicators (like the M3 so beloved by the Bundesbank) and the final objectives (inflation, nominal income). Thus, the effectiveness of traditional monetary targeting has been called into question, since monetary aggregates are now affected by a wider range of domestic and international factors (BIS 1992, 1993b).

The effectiveness of exchange rate policy was also affected. The increasing power of the financial markets was reflected in the mismatch between the size of central bank foreign exchange reserves and the escalating daily turnover in the foreign exchange markets. According to the International Monetary Fund (1993), the total non-gold reserves of all the industrial countries amounted to $555.6 billion in April 1992, against the background of a daily net turnover of $910 billion in the nine biggest foreign exchange markets in that year. 'Reserve coverage' has fallen sharply for EU countries. Thus, by 1992, a one-day adverse swing in France's current trade payments would absorb almost 6 per cent of its reserves, compared to 3 per cent in 1972. An adverse five-day swing for Belgium would deplete its reserves by one-third.[2] In addition, with the concentration of savings in institutional funds, investment decisions are now in the hands of relatively few professional fund managers. This shift has magnified the sensitivity of exchange rates to changes in market expectations. Hence, foreign exchange market intervention has to be larger than before in order to influence exchange rate movements (BIS 1993b: 145–52).

At the European level, the combination of increasing financial integration and exchange rate fixity resulted in a gradual loss of monetary policy autonomy. Under the arrangements of the European Monetary System (EMS), central banks cannot set domestic monetary targets (interest rates, monetary expansion) independently. Therefore, co-ordination of monetary policies (or a common policy) is necessary to ensure stability in the system. Recognition of this fact led to the 1987 Basle–Nyborg agreements and the EMU initiative. But although EU monetary arrangements imply a reduced power of central bankers in terms of domestic monetary control, they, in fact, provided a powerful check on divergent economic policies. Therefore, central banks were able to advance price and exchange rate stability (that is, their main interests) into primary goals of economic policy.

Market expectations about inflation and exchange rates have become a more potent factor in the mind of the monetary authorities. As a result, credibility and reputation in monetary policy-making have become the indispensable resources of central banks in influencing market expectations. Reputation building is based on a long process of consistent and successful policy-making. In this context, the disincentives to pursue inflationary policies have been increased: market penalties (in the form of increased risk premiums in interest rates) follow from any attempt to depart from a low-inflation policy. Within this framework of quick, sharp market penalties, the capacity of central banks to argue effectively with their governments was significantly enhanced, along with their case for independence.

The dependence of EU governments on their central banks was further increased after the 1992–3 EMS crises: governments rely more on the central banks for the technical expertise in dealing with the 'destabilizing' markets. This reliance leads central banks to argue that the costs of dealing with market pressures could be reduced if the credibility of domestic monetary policies and the reputation of domestic monetary authorities were increased by new measures to establish central bank independence.

Here was an apparent paradox: regionalization advanced the domestic powerbase of central banks. Power appeared to shift to EU states as they took the initiative on EMU, setting new political parameters for EU central bankers. EMU could indeed be presented as a political strategy for recapturing power from the markets by creating a single, much more powerful, world currency. But, as we saw above, it was a strategy whose content was mainly defined by EU central bankers. Meanwhile, as power moved away from states to global financial markets and financial firms, central bankers sought to fill the power vacuum at national and EU levels by reasserting the idea of central bank independence. Independence was the policy project that not only enabled central bankers to negotiate the turbulence created by European monetary unification and by globalized financial markets but also, in the process, promised them increased authority and power at both levels.

The revolution in economic policy ideas

The consolidation of central banks' power was facilitated by a third change, namely the evolution of economic ideas that led into a renewed importance of monetary policy and an emphasis on the goal of price stability. Under orthodox Keynesian thinking, monetary policy was only supportive or subsidiary to fiscal policy in the pursuit of full employment. This attitude was based on the belief that monetary policy had little effect on the economy and it was largely responsible for the inflation of the 1960s.[3] The monetarist challenge established that money does matter for the economy, affecting mainly nominal variables (inflation). Its policy prescription was that central banks should target a constant monetary growth rate to safeguard monetary stability. The central banking profession as a whole was too pragmatic and cautious to embrace monetarism in its purest form. But the monetarist revolution did accord a renewed importance to the policy objectives and instruments of central banks.

The revolution of the new classical economics in the 1970s, under the assumption of the 'rational expectation hypothesis', provided strong support for the neutrality of money: monetary (as well as fiscal) policy does not affect real output and employment but only the rate of inflation; hence, there is no trade off between inflation and unemployment and unemployment remains always at the 'natural level'. This result follows because rational economic agents observe policy changes, evaluate the future impact on the economy and adjust their expectations immediately so that they do not leave room for any changes in real variables (Begg 1982; Sargent and Wallace 1976).

Today, however, the prevailing consensus in the economics profession is that money is neutral only in the long run. In the short run, expectations adjust slowly and thus unexpected inflation (caused for example by an unexpected monetary expansion) could raise output and employment. When the adjustment of expectations is finally complete, real output returns to its natural level and the only permanent effect of monetary policy is on inflation.

These new ideas on the neutrality of money promoted the political idea of making monetary policy 'independent' from the influence of other economic policies, and of focusing exclusively on price stability. The burden of promoting full employment was to be put on supply-side policies, like structural reforms, tax reforms and labour market policies aiming at raising the 'natural level' of output.

Moreover, the new theoretical framework put emphasis on the importance of agents' expectations for the effectiveness of monetary policy. According to this framework, achieving price stability is essentially a problem of credibility and reputation surrounding monetary policy. Lack of credibility means that announced monetary policies fail to restrain inflationary expectations and thus make the disinflation process longer and more difficult. The same line of argument suggests that credibility critically depends on the degree of monetary policy autonomy from political decision-makers.

A central bank which is constitutionally independent from political influence and legally obliged to aim at price stability could enhance credibility of monetary policy for three reasons (Alesina 1988; Swinburne and Gastello-Branco 1991; Pepper 1992). First, it could give a solution to the 'time inconsistency' problem of the optimal policy: policy-makers who have both inflation and employment targets cannot be committed to a lasting anti-inflationary policy because they always have the incentive to exploit the (short-run) trade off between inflation and employment. Thus, they could depart from their publicly announced anti-inflationary policy and create an inflation surprise, in order to achieve short-term output gains. But, by doing so they lose credibility and reputation, making disinflation policies less efficient and more costly in terms of output losses. In contrast, an independent central bank committed to lasting anti-inflationary policy can build up its reputation as a guarantor of price stability.

Second, monetary policies are often manipulated for partisan and/or electoral purposes resulting in sub-optimal fluctuations in money, output and employment (Nordhaus 1975; Alesina 1988). An independent central bank can isolate monetary policy from the impact of the 'political business cycle' or the influence of irresponsible politics.

Finally, central bank independence can enhance the credibility of monetary policy by eliminating government's ability to relax monetary policy and maintain inflation for the purpose of reducing the real value of accumulated debt (Grilli *et al.* 1991). This condition applies particularly to countries where a fragmented political structure (as in Italy for example) has led to an over-accumulation of public debt.

Moreover, exchange rate theory has recently suggested that a central bank could enhance its credibility by adopting an exchange rate rule (like the ERM) which limits its scope for discretionary policy (Giavazzi and Pagano 1988; Barro and Gordon 1983). Actually, the ERM and the EMS have enabled central banks with inflation-prone currencies to borrow credibility from the Bundesbank, the provider of the anchor currency of the system. The increasing degree of exchange rate fixity within the EMS in the 1980s reflects the belief that, on the one hand, there are substantial benefits from sticking to an exchange rate rule, while on the other, devaluations are a costly and ineffective means of macroeconomic adjustment. The rejection of devaluation as a policy variable put pressure on disinflation policies to maintain competitiveness, resulting in a strategy termed as 'competitive disinflation' (Blanchard and Muet 1993). Overall, the EMS has increased the need for a balanced and disciplined monetary policy which aims at lasting low inflation and has thus gradually promoted the divorcing of central bank policy from government influence. Increased domestic power of central banks accompanies rising regional economic integration.

STRAPPED TO THE MAST: THE EXPLANATORY POWER OF TRADITIONAL THEORIES OF CENTRAL BANKING

This analysis leads us to reflect on the extent to which traditional theories of central banking behaviour help us explain this consolidation of the power of central bankers in the process of EMU, particularly their success in establishing the principle of central bank independence in the Treaty on European Union. There are four such theories of central banking: 'public-interest' theories, 'personality' theories, public choice theories and bargaining theories. We show that each has problems for explaining the fate of central banks in the EMU process.

'Public-Interest' Theories

'Public-interest' theories offer an essentially teleological account of central bank behaviour:[4] central banking is an activity shaped by the single-minded dedication of central bankers to the public interest, typically defined as the avoidance of inflation and the stabilization of financial markets (and contrasted with the selfish, short-term behaviour of politicians and market operators). Central bank strategy and tactics are presented as an exercise in applied welfare economics: the task being to maximize the expected value of a constrained social welfare function. The key operative constraint is typically identified as deficient policy intelligence: that central bankers need improved information from economists about the developing state of the economy. Hence economists become central actors within the community of central banking.

The difficulty with this type of explanation is that it fails to consider many factors that affect power over monetary policy. The constraints are more than simply those of deficient economic information. There are problems about matching limited policy tools to complex problems. For instance, central banks will fail to defend exchange rates that no longer reflect economic 'fundamentals'; after financial liberalization in Europe, it is difficult to reconcile an exchange rate regime like the EMS and national monetary policy independence (Padoa-Schioppa 1987). Difficult trade-offs of a politically sensitive nature are required. They enmesh central bankers in complex political bargaining relations and involve the search for politically defensible compromises. To this constraint must be added the problems of co-ordination and control with other actors whose behaviour is significant for monetary policy, notably fiscal authorities and business and labour (in relation to wage bargaining). These constraints undermine the capacity of central bankers to impose unilaterally their idea of the public interest.

The story of the birth of the EMS and of the origins of EMU is of EU central bankers on the defensive, compelled to act reluctantly by politicians; the story of the ERM is of central bankers often forced to act by markets, as in 1987 and 1992–3. In short, the history of the EMS and of EMU – and the victory of the principle of central bank independence – cannot simply be written in terms of the will and capability of central bankers to act on behalf of a general social purpose.

'Personality' theories

Explanations of the influence of the central banking community that focus on the personal qualities and strengths of central bank governors have some attraction (Boyle 1967; Friedman and Schwartz 1963: 411). With reference to the development of EU monetary policy, some central bank governors are more important than others – above all the president of the Bundesbank as the representative of the anchor currency. Following the Hanover summit of 1988 British strategy appears to have relied on the erroneous assumption that the then governor of the Bank of England, Robin Leigh-Pemberton, could block the momentum towards EMU in the Delors Committee (Thatcher 1993: 708). By contrast, Karl-Otto Pöhl, the then president of the Bundesbank, emerged as a much more powerful figure, using the Delors Committee to insert the agenda of the Bundesbank into the EMU negotiations.

The personal beliefs and styles of central bankers are unquestionably important. However, the establishment of the principle of central bank independence at the EU level, and the upgrading of the role of central bankers in EU affairs, did not correlate with the presence of more powerful personalities in EU central banking. Pöhl was a more conciliatory Bundesbank president than his immediate predecessors. It is also worth noting that the tough, abrasive style and independence of Emminger did not stand in the way of the establishment of the EMS in the 1978–79 period, even though Emminger was deeply sceptical.[5] In short, the personalities of EU central bankers offer little insight into the more deep-seated structural sources of change that shape the power of central bankers.

Public choice theories

The third traditional theory of central bank behaviour has its origins in the public choice literature on bureaucracy, with its focus on the micro level of explanation (Downs 1967). According to this theory, the ordering of objectives by central banks, and their choice of monetary instruments and how to use them, is rooted in their private self-interests as agencies in their own prestige and self-preservation rather than in any public interest motivation (Toma and Toma 1986).

In one influential formulation, central bankers are viewed as rational maximizers with their own preference function. Hence they are not neutral, disinterested policy experts. The private interests of central bankers underlie their shared beliefs in widening their discretion over policy. These interests are secured by dampening expectations of their performance by emphasizing the inability of monetary policy to achieve difficult objectives and by inspiring awe or creating confusion amongst potential critics by creating a mythology of monetary technique (Chant and Acheson 1973). The result is that central banks clothe themselves in a 'monetary mystique' to protect themselves from critical public examination; they publish selective information that magnifies their successes and minimizes their failures (Acheson and Chant 1973; Goodfriend 1986).

The theoretical perspective of public choice supports an interpretation of central bank behaviour in the EMS and EMU policy process that emphasizes their 'turf-fighting' to limit the loss of territorial jurisdiction over policy to other EU bodies and maximizes delegation of policy development to themselves. In this respect public choice theories do undoubtedly capture some of the characteristics of central bank behaviour, particularly the element of corporate self-interest behind their shared beliefs. But public choice theories provide little help in identifying why change in the direction of central bank independence took place when it did and how it did. To understand that process we need to focus attention not so much on the self-interests of central banks underpinning their shared belief in independence as on the way in which changes in the macro framework within which they operated favoured the implementation of this policy project.

Bargaining theories and 'scapegoating'

Bargaining theories focus, by contrast, on the essentially political relationships of central banks with external actors, on their political resources in their complex bargaining relations with government ministers and officials, with legislatures, with bankers and financiers, and with economists, and on the incentives from the need to make policy politically defensible for central bankers to play a role as arbiters, balancing opposing points of view behind policies (Woolley 1984; Kane 1980; Canterbery 1967; Goodfriend 1988). This overtly political interpretation draws out the constraints on the capacity of central banks to have an impact on monetary policy.

One variant of bargaining theory – which connects to public choice theory – is the 'scapegoat' thesis to explain central bank independence (Kane 1980). According to this cynical hypothesis, central bank independence serves a political function for government ministers, parties and legislatures in that the blame for policy failures can be shifted to the central bank. Central bank independence involves 'double talk'. Independence serves politicians' interest in having policy scapegoats, and central bankers simply play along for the rewards of longer periods of office and substantial budgetary autonomy.

This approach is helpful in capturing the complex dynamics of tension and change that affect the influence of the central banking community. It shows how central banks are sensitive to external pressures and how the impact of short-term pressures can undermine their capability to formulate, and act effectively on the basis of, their shared beliefs. But the key dimension in the history of EMU was that the political motives and calculations of EU heads of state and government had dominated the agenda-setting phase, not the shared beliefs of central bankers. The perspective of bargaining relations shows how simultaneously the political scope for the impact of EU central bankers was circumscribed (via the European Council's political initiative on EMU) and augmented (by the fresh legitimacy accorded to their shared beliefs by 'sound money' policy ideas). But, useful as the bargaining theory is as a means of analysis of opportunities and constraints on the central banks, it begs as many questions as it answers about the sources of change (which are often structural) and their relative importance.

WHY AN EMU FOR CENTRAL BANKERS?

When it comes to explaining the significant changes in the role of EU central banks in the 1980s and 1990s, the basic problem with each of these theories of central bank behaviour is that they do not take adequately into account the powerful structural forces that have shaped and transformed their position. In particular, they fail to address the impact of the role of the Deutschmark as 'anchor' currency within the ERM in giving structural power to the Bundesbank within European monetary integration and unification. They do not take sufficient account of the peculiar policy style of the EU and of the uniquely intimate relations between central bankers and the state. Nor do they give sufficient emphasis to structural change in the nature and culture of capitalism, and to the impact of economic crises in transforming perceptions of the role and significance of central bankers. Structural change provides a crucial part of the context and terms of interactions within the central banking community.

The Deutschmark and the structural power of the Bundesbank

Since its inception, the ERM's 'anchor' has been provided by the Deutschmark. As the only currency never to be devalued, it had a credibility and reputation in the financial markets unmatched by any other ERM currency. Hence, in order to maintain their parities with the Deutschmark, the domestic monetary policies of other ERM members had to be at least as virtuous as that of Germany. The result was an asymmetry in the functioning of the ERM, with the burdens of adjustment being borne disproportionately by countries other than Germany. In such a context the Bundesbank was able to exert a greater practical power in monetary policy than any other EU central bank. Even more significantly, it emerged as a role model. Consequently, in the process of the debate about the institutional forms of an eventual EMU, the Bundesbank had a moral authority and practical importance denied to any other actor. This factor more than any other helped to ensure that the role model for EMU was central bank independence, Bundesbank-style. The shared beliefs that emerged amongst EU central bankers, and the practical arrangements put in place for EMU, reflected the structural power of the independent Bundesbank and the hegemony of German ideas in the EMS (Dyson 1994).

Moreover, the Bundesbank's systemic position was important in influencing the choice of the approach for the final stage of EMU. Being the issuer of the most stable currency in the system, the Bundesbank was potentially the main loser from any monetary instability resulting from a carelessly designed transition. Thus, because of the Bundesbank's relative weight, the economists' approach prevailed: gradualism, economic convergence and indivisibility of monetary policy became the basic elements of transition (Smaghi *et al.* forthcoming). Similarly, the provisions for fiscal discipline in stage three were pushed powerfully by the Bundesbank in 1995/96.

The regulatory policy style of the EU

In being more closely drawn into the EU environment, both in the operation of the EMS and in the debate about EMU, EU central bankers found themselves in an environment of institutions and rules that was congenial to their influence. The scope and nature of EMU was constrained by one fundamental fact: the EU had very modest resources at its disposal. There is no real opportunity, as for instance in the German and US federal systems, to develop and operate an autonomous EU fiscal policy for the purposes of stabilization and/or redistribution. Given the small size of the EU budget, the only way for the EU to put EMU in place was to focus on the rules-based approach of monetary policy: rules on excessive deficits, 'nominal' convergence and no 'bail outs' for governments, and developing monetary instruments to achieve price stability.

This inbuilt regulatory approach of the EU to policy pervaded the development of EMU in the framework of the EMU negotiations (Dehoussse 1992; Majone 1991; Majone 1993). It threw the burden of work on developing EMU onto the Committee of Central Bank Governors and, from 1994, the EMI. Here, rather than in Delors' office and DG II of the EU Commission, were the resources of technical expertise that were required to develop the EU-level policy instruments for EMU. It also meant that the alternative to an independent ESCB – an EU fiscal authority which in co-ordination with the ECB would decide the appropriate economic policy mix – was not available. In other words, the victory of the central bankers' policy project was mainly due to the absence of a viable alternative power at the EU level. With this victory, the balance of power in the EMS and EMU shifted away from EU governments towards the central banks.

Central bankers and the state

In addition, the victory of EU central bankers in getting an EMU for central bankers reflected the unique relationship that has existed between them and EU states. As we saw earlier, the privileges of central banks were specially granted by states; in turn, governments were dependent on central banks to stabilize financial markets and to finance deficits. Sometimes, as in Germany and Italy, central banks have succeeded in keeping their distance from the state; more normally, as in Britain and France, there have been strikingly close ties in the operation of policy. In the relationship between the very top posts in the Banque de France and the Trésor in the Finance Ministry, these ties have been those of common membership of the Inspectorate General of Finance and were reflected in individual career paths that cross-cut the two institutions.

In Germany and Italy, governments have, for historical reasons, been disposed to defer to their central banks. When the Bundesbank was forced to utter public warnings about the behaviour of the federal government, the government moved promptly to reassure it (as over the establishment of the Franco-German Economic Council in 1987 and the Genscher initiative on EMU in 1988). When the Italian state was faced with an emergency in 1993, it called on the governor of the Bank of Italy to head the government.[6] In France, central bankers have gained an unprecedented access to policy, with the result being an inbuilt voice for central bankers in the EMU negotiations, or a deferential respect for their views. As a result, EU central bankers had a uniquely powerful position within the negotiations leading up to, and consequent on, the Treaty on European Union.[7]

The impact of economic crises: the 'sound money' consensus

To the influence of these powerful institutional factors on central banking's role in European integration must be added the impact of economic crises, notably the ERM crises of 1983, 1987 and 1992–3. These crises represented historical turning points in the development of the ERM. The 1983 crisis of the French franc led to the onset of the *franc stable* policy in the framework of the new, 'hard' ERM and to the policy shift in favour of financial market liberalization. The 1987 crisis precipitated the debate about the need to move from the 'asymmetrical' EMS to EMU. The 1992–3 crises revealed the dependency of EU governments on central bankers in holding together the ERM and making the transition to EMU in the face of market volatility. Their message, at least for those in the ERM, was the need for much closer and more effective monetary policy co-ordination. The central bankers' formula that economic convergence was the precondition for stage three became the conventional wisdom of EU debate.

Exchange rate crises provided central banks with the evidence of the importance of 'sound money' as the primary goal of economic policy. Differences of national success in taking domestic action to curb inflation not only underpinned a distinction between 'hard' and 'soft' currencies but also drew attention to the nature of the domestic conditions that favoured price stability. 'Irresponsible' government use of fiscal policy, particularly reflected in the accumulation of public debt, was increasingly identified as the source of economic problems; the remedies were identified in the realm of monetary policy. The most dramatic change was the new ascendancy of 'sound money' ideas in economic theory, and a revival of interest by economists in the role of central banks in economic policy.

Structural change within capitalism

One long-term structural change within capitalism that has put central banking reform at the centre of the political agenda has been the historical context of contemporary rates of inflation. The inflationary periods of the last thirty years are by no means the historic norm and appear to correlate with the emergence of a world monetary system on a pure fiat standard, a system that emerged gradually after the First World War. This historical acceleration of inflation raised the alternative of either returning to a gold-standard-like system or finding a mechanism for yielding stable prices in the existing framework of a system of 'fiat' money, in which the currency is not backed by some physical commodity. Central bank independence emerged as a lower cost policy reform for this purpose: an independent central bank is capable of restoring rationality in money creation (Bean 1993).

Another structural change within capitalism that has given central bankers an opportunity to present a newly modern image has been the revolution in financial markets. In countries like the US and Britain (and recently France), financial liberalization has led to a remarkable concentration of savings into institutional funds. This development allowed the creation of a stock of privately controlled and highly mobile financial assets (Bishop 1992: 531). In consequence, financial institutions were able to clothe their new market power in the legitimacy of representing the interests of savers in avoiding the ravages of inflation. This development provided central banking, in turn, with a new legitimacy, drawn from a more powerful private-sector constituency of support for its objectives. At the same time, it should be noted that many EU states – and their central banks, like the Bundesbank – remained suspicious of financial market liberalization, for various reasons. In these countries, the legitimacy of the objectives of central banking continued to have a different domestic political base.

To these general underlying changes within capitalism must be added the particular factor of the considerable economic convergence within the EU since the early 1980s: not just in economic ideas but also in economic performance and structure. With respect to inflation and to interest rates, especially long-term rates, the evidence of convergence is impressive. Despite new problems after 1991, performance in convergence of budget deficits and public debt levels has been noteworthy (Barrell 1992). Globalization and deregulation of financial markets have also meant that EU central banks preside over increasingly similar financial structures (Bishop 1992). These structural factors have facilitated a greater professional consensus amongst EU central bankers and the process of defining corporate interests and successfully pursuing them in EU negotiations. As convergence has been towards German-style low inflation, consensus has been based increasingly on the German model.

CENTRAL BANKERS, REGIONAL INTEGRATION AND GLOBAL FINANCIAL MARKETS

The main underlying theme of this analysis is the impact of the EU central banks on the process of negotiating the Treaty on European Union. The principal conclusion is that the central banking community, through its privileged participation in the making of EMU, has managed to secure its corporate interests by promoting the goal of price stability and the independence of the new monetary institutions, namely EMI, ECB and ESCB. It has been emphasized, however, that its impact was absent in the policy initiation phase of EMU. Here the role of political factors was decisive.

In assessing the evolution of the role of central banks, this chapter has identified a connection between globalization of financial markets and the nature of the changes in European integration represented by the commitments to EMU in the Maastricht Treaty. That connection is provided by the policy project of central bank independence. The main arguments are that in promoting this policy project, EU central bankers were responding defensively to their loss of power, first to global financial markets and second in the face of the regional policy initiative on EMU. The basic explanations for the effectiveness of the EU central banking community in pursuing independence are to be found in a conjunction of external political and economic factors rather than simply in the independent actions of central bank professionals or their struggle to amass corporate power.

It should be noted, however, that the impact of central banks in getting their main ideas embodied in the Maastricht Treaty did not necessarily enhance their impact on key aspects of the process of implementing EMU. Central bank independence did not mean that in consequence the EU central banks could readily regain power over exchange rate management from the financial markets. The policy project of independence was attractive mainly because it was perceived as capable of delivering domestic price stability and therefore as an important support of exchange rate stability. But, the short-run behaviour of exchange rates is affected by a set of current and expected future factors. Therefore, independence was regarded as a necessary but not a sufficient condition of market stability.

At first sight, the management of the ERM in the framework of EMU appears to be a testament to the policy impact of the central banks. In the ERM crises of 1992–3, EU finance ministers and central bankers found themselves faced with a strategic choice as they confronted the problems thrown up by the 'inconsistent triangle'. They could strengthen monetary policy integration to avoid conflicting national policies for the sake of exchange rate stability. Alternatively, they could relax the constraint of the 'narrow band' EMS and thus dampen conflicts between external and internal policy objectives. In August 1993, ECOFIN, with the EU central bankers in attendance, opted for the latter choice – that is, widening the ERM's bands. This solution embodied the shared beliefs of EU central bankers who wished to maintain a gradualist approach to EMU, based primarily on economic convergence, and who asserted the indivisibility of monetary policy before stage three. But it is important to remember that the force behind the ascendancy of these beliefs amongst EU central bankers was provided by the structural power of the Bundesbank in the EMU policy process. Perhaps even more significantly, the backing of EU central banks for this solution represented a concession to the power of the financial markets rather than an assertion of their capacity to control them.

The really interesting political question is why central bankers were to prove so influential. The answer is not to be found primarily within central banking itself or even in a failure of political leadership within the EU institutions. It is to be found, in part, in two deeper structural continuities: the regulatory policy style of the EU and the unique relationship between central banks and states. But the crucial factor has been deep-seated structural changes in the nature and structure of capitalism, notably the relationship between EU states and global financial markets and the phenomenon of inflation. The renewed power of central banking reflected underlying structural realities of the international political economy – the nature of the 'anchor' role within the EMS, the emergence of private financial institutions as more powerful economic actors within capitalism and sharing the stability objective of central banks, financial crises and the new prestige of 'sound money' ideas in economic theory. These changes have altered the pattern of incentives and constraints within which EU central bankers operate. They have also bestowed a new legitimacy on central bankers that is likely to have profoundly important practical effects on the process of regional integration in Europe. Such effects are increasingly visible as the central banks' support for strict adherence to Maastricht conditions in the run-up to a single currency proves to be a significant obstacle for those who would prefer a softer approach.

But, in constraining the role of EU governments, both individually and collectively, central bankers may be throwing up wider legitimacy problems as democratic elections lose their relevance as allocators of political values (Underhill 1995). Their dominance of the substantive debate about EMU has not been consistent with a focus on the framework of democratic institutions required to legitimize EMU in the longer term and to enable the political process to restructure the pattern of gainers and losers from EMU.

NOTES

1 For a discussion on the issue of independence of the Banque de France in stage two of EMU see Patat (1992) and Noyer (1992).
2 'Reserve coverage' refers to the ratio between one day's trade payments for an EU country relative to its central bank reserves. See Bishop (1992).
3 For a survey see Chick (1977) and de Grauwe (1992).
4 For examples, see two former presidents of the Bundesbank: Blessing (1966) and Emminger (1986).
5 A personality-focused approach to the Bundesbank is to be found in Marsh (1992). On the role of the Bundesbank in the origins of the EMS, see also Ludlow (1982).
6 For details of the conflicts over the Franco-German Economic Council and over the Genscher initiative see Dyson (1994; ch. 5).
7 For the argument that central bank power and influence stems from their unique proximity and access to state power see Bach (1971).

REFERENCES

Acheson, K. and J. Chant (1973) 'Bureaucratic theory and the choice of central bank goals: the case of the Bank of Canada', *Journal of Money, Credit and Banking* 5: 637–55.

Alesina, A. (1988) 'Macroeconomics and politics', in S. Fischer (ed.) *NBER Macroeconomics Annual* Cambridge Mass.: MIT Press, 17–52.

Bach, G. (1971) *Making Monetary and Fiscal Policy*, Washington, DC: Brookings Institution.

Bank for International Settlements (BIS) (1992) *Annual Report*, Basle: BIS.

—— (1993a) *Central Bank Survey of Foreign Exchange Market Activity in April 1992*, Basle, March.

—— (1993b) *Annual Report*, Basle: BIS.

Barrell, R. (ed.) (1992) *Economic Convergence and Monetary Union in Europe*, London: Sage.

Barro, R. and D. Gordon (1983) 'Rules, discretion and reputation in a model of monetary policy', *Journal of Monetary Economics* 12: 101–22.

Bean, C. (1993) 'The case for an independent Bank of England', *New Economy*, Autumn: 26–31.

Begg, D.K.H. (1982) *The Rational Expectation Revolution in Macroeconomics*, Deddington: Phillip Allan.

Bishop, G. (1992) *Capital Liberalization: The End of the ERM and the Beginning of EMU*, London: Salomon Brothers.

Blanchard, O.J. and P.A. Muet (1993) 'Competitiveness through disinflation: an assessment of the French macroeconomic strategy', *Economic Policy* 16: 11–56.

Blessing, K. (1966) *Im Kampf um Gutes Geld*, Frankfurt: Deutsche Bundesbank.

Boyle, A. (1967) *Montagu Norman: A Biography*, London: Cassell.

Canterbery, E. (1967) 'A new look at federal open market voting', *Western Economic Journal* 5: 25–38

Chant, J. and K. Acheson (1973) 'Mythology and central banking', *Kyklos* 26: 362–79.

Chick, V. (1977) *The Theory of Monetary Policy*, Oxford: Basil Blackwell.

Dehousse, R. (1992) 'Integration v. regulation? On the dynamics of regulation in the European Community', *Journal of Common Market Studies* 4: 383–402.

De Grauwe, P. (1992) *The Economics of Monetary Integration*, Oxford: Oxford University Press.

Delors Committee (1989) *Report on Economic and Monetary Union in the European Community*, Luxemburg: Office for Official Publications of the European Communities.

Destler, I. and Randall Henning, C. (1989) *Dollar Politics: Exchange Rate Policymaking in the United States*, Washington, DC: Institute for International Economics.

Downs, A. (1967) *Inside Bureaucracy*, Boston: Little Brown and Co.

Dyson, K. (1994) *Elusive Union: The Process of Economic and Monetary Union in Europe*, London: Routledge.

Emminger, O. (1986) *Währungspolitik im Wandel der Zeit*, Frankfurt: Deutsche Bundesbank.

Frieden, J. (1991) 'Invested interests: the politics of national economic policies in a world of global finance', *International Organization* 45: 425–51.

Friedman, M. and A. Schwartz (1963) *A Monetary History of the United States, 1867–1960*, Princeton: Princeton University Press.

Giavazzi, F. and M. Pagano (1988) 'The advantage of tying one's hands: EMS discipline and central bank credibility', *European Economic Review* 32: 1055–82.

Goodfriend, M. (1986) 'Monetary mystique: secrecy and central banking', *Journal of Monetary Economics* 17: 63–92.

—— (1988) 'Bureau analysis and central banking', *Journal of Monetary Economics* 22: 517–22.

Grilli, V., D. Masciandaro and G. Tabellini (1991) 'Political and monetary institutions and public financial policies in the industrial countries', *Economic Policy* 13: 342–90.

Gros, D. and W. Thygesen (1992) *European Monetary Integration*, London: Longman.

Howell, M. and A. Cozzini (1991) *Games Without Frontiers: Global Equity Markets in the 1990s*, New York: Salomon Brothers.

International Monetary Fund (1993) *International Capital Markets: Exchange Rate Management and International Capital Flows*, Washington, DC: IMF.

Kane, E. (1980) 'Politics and fed policymaking', *Journal of Monetary Economics* 6: 199–211.

Ludlow, P. (1982) *The Making of the European Monetary System*, London: Butterworths.

Majone, G. (1991) 'Cross-national sources of regulatory policymaking in Europe and the United States', *Journal of Public Policy* 1: 79–106.

—— (1993) 'The European Community between social policy and social regulation', *Journal of Common Market Studies* 2: 153–69.

Marsh, D. (1992) *The Bundesbank: The Bank that Rules Europe*, London: Heinemann.

Moran, M. (1991) *The Politics of the Financial Services Revolution*, London: Macmillan.

Nordhaus, W. (1975) 'The political business cycle', *Review of Economic Studies* 42: 169–90.

Noyer, C. (1992) 'A propos du statut et de l'indépendance des banques centrales', *Revue d'Economie Financière* 22: 13–18.

O'Brien, R. (1992) *Global Financial Integration: The End of Geography*, London: Pinter/Royal Institute of International Affairs.

Padoa-Schioppa, T. (1987) *Efficiency, Stability and Equity: A Strategy for the Evolution of the Economic System of the European Community*, Oxford: Oxford University Press.

Patat, J.P. (1992) 'Quelque remarques sur la question de l'indépendance de la Banque Centrale', *Revue d'Economie Financière*, 22: 5–12.

Pepper, G. (1992) *Restoring Credibility: Monetary Policy Now*, London: Institute of Economic Affairs.

Porter, T. (1993) *States, Markets and Regimes in Global Finance*, New York: St Martin's Press.

Sargent, T.J. and N. Wallace (1976) 'Rational expectations and the theory of economic policy', *Journal of Monetary Economics* 2: 169–84.

Smaghi, L.B., T. Padoa-Schioppa and F. Papadia (forthcoming) 'The transition to EMU in the Maastricht Treaty', *Essays in International Finance*, Princeton University.

Stopford, J. and S. Strange (1991) *Rival States, Rival Firms*, Cambridge: Cambridge University Press.

Swinburne, M. and M. Gastello-Branco (1991) 'Central bank independence: issues and experiences', *IMF Working Paper* No. 58.

Thatcher, M. (1993) *The Downing Street Years*, London: HarperCollins.

Toma, E. and M. Toma (eds) (1986) *Central Bankers, Bureaucratic Incentives and Monetary Policy*, Boston: Kluwer.

Underhill, G.R.D. (1995) 'Keeping governments out of politics: transnational securities markets, regulatory cooperation and political legitimacy', *Review of International Studies* 21: 251–78.

Woolley, J. (1984) *Monetary Politics*, Cambridge: Cambridge University Press.

Part III

Supranational governance and regulation

10 Regionalism, globalization, and 'professional society'

Between state, law, and the market for professional services

Yves Dezalay

Regionalism, globalization, and competition among national models of political economy remain largely misunderstood, and this problem is redoubled when it comes to our understanding of professional services.[1] If globalization has often had the effect of apparent deracination of traditional social groups, this phenomenon can certainly be observed as ongoing in the legal profession. As a result of the opening up of borders, the professional rules, institutions, and more generally the whole framework for economic activity in capitalist countries have become weapons, as well as stakes, in increased international competition. Law and the lawyers are constantly being remade by processes of market competition and global restructuring, even as they remain among the most important participants in these processes.

Yet we can hardly expect this global restructuring to be a homogeneous affair. The national, the regional and the global surely vie with each other. Indeed there is such diversity in the histories of national structures in which the field of professional power is continually being refashioned that such basic notions as the state, professions and the law typically cover quite different realities. In particular, the structures of the law and its place in both the field of the state and that of business are very dissimilar on either side of the Atlantic. Hence, to compare these two models of regulation without taking account of the fact that they do not relate to the same social reality would lead to multiple confusions. One could be forgiven for expecting the predominance of the national and regional, as opposed to the global, in a field as embedded in historical social structures as the legal professions.

Yet the global dimension cannot be ignored since this is precisely what has 'dealt the new hand' in these arenas of professional practices. These 'palace wars' between the elites of different legal traditions are an inseparable part of a geopolitical battle. The exporting of the neo-liberal market economy, as has been said, involves symbolic imperialism. The generalization of the American model of the lawyer as privileged operator of a 'regulatory process' defined in juridical terms is one of the stakes – and one of the supporting elements – in a process of 'globalization' which is also a battle for global domination. In exporting or imposing a mode of economic governance which it can dominate all the better for having been its inventor, the American ruling class is giving itself the means of extending its hegemony over the whole of the planet. After all, it is no accident that the rise of this system of legal production invented on Wall Street, which we have called 'Cravathism', is part of the tidal wave of globalization (Trubek *et al.* 1994). These Wall Street lawyers, or the imitators which they have produced and trained almost everywhere, are the modern mercenaries of this new brand of symbolic imperialism[2] which has been called 'global unilateralism' (Whitman 1984, cited in Strange 1986: 152).

In view of the embeddedness of national legal professions through their rules and institutions (Granovetter 1985), how should we understand this triumph of the global despite extensive, contrasting, and embedded institutions in Europe and the United States, and despite the historical weight of European traditions of the law? This chapter argues that the globalization of the market for legal expertise has decoupled traditional professions from their historical milieux and long-held self-understandings. The opening of borders means a reconversion/restructuring of national legal elites; pecking orders, which were once arranged on a national basis, will be restructured transnationally. The market pressures of professional hierarchy put pressure on older forms of 'collegiality' and introduce a financial rationality born of the global market (Dezalay 1995a: 338). Analysis reveals that this restructuring of professional hierarchies and corresponding discourses takes place across regional variants: the spread of the major (and multinational) US firms leads to the importation of the model of the American Lawyer. Leading global centres (New York, the City of London) push these restructurings into continental Europe and elsewhere. In the domain of international commercial arbitration, this process has even led to forms of 'off-shore justice' quite distinct from state judicial processes (Dezalay and Garth 1995).

This deracination of professional society can be demonstrated by analysing the confrontation of the American and the European models of the legal professions. This comparison allows us to clarify the political and professional stakes involved in this recomposition of national and regional professional arenas, by reminding ourselves of the strategic game in – and by – which they were originally constructed.[3] This is indeed the source of their specificity, but also what gives the competing players their 'competitive advantages' in this 'global market' for legal know-how. We need to reintroduce this political dimension into our understanding of the professional field, especially if we are fully to understand how international negotiations and changes transform professional 'turf battles' into international confrontations. The diversity of national forms of professional power face each other through the opening of borders, leading to a reconversion of national elites into transnational elites. Pecking orders once on a national basis need to be reconstructued transnationally in line with the new pecking order of the market.

Because space is limited, I will content myself with showing how, on either side of the Atlantic, the legal professions originally developed according to two quite different models. In the 'American model', the lawyers play a central part in regulatory processes thanks to the multiplicity of positions they occupy in the fields of the state and politics as well as in business and the academy. By contrast, in the French model it is the '*grands corps*' of the elite groups, with their strong professional bonding based on their selection and training through the *grandes écoles*, which occupy the same positions and visibly play the same role of intermediary between the state and the market. The law in Europe is traditionally marginalized from the field of economic regulation. Yet there is a major and significant difference: the US lawyers claim to represent the Rule of Law, while the French *grands corps* represent State Rule. This difference of terms in fact reflects the contrasting ways in which these national arenas are built and structured, and the different players and rules of the game. It also reveals what is at stake in the game now being played over the law.

The construction of Europe – and more generally the opening of borders – is indeed seen as an excellent opportunity to regain lost ground by a European legal elite which sees itself as having been outranked in the field of power. This demotion is related to its marginalization in the field of governance which has pushed judicial institutions to the sidelines by creating direct links between state agencies and corporate networks (Abel-Smith and Stevens 1967). The new ideologists predict that the law will stage a major come-back as a result of globalization, and that the construction of the European Single Market and the acceleration of the process of economic concentration are reproducing in Europe the socio-political context which on the other side of the Atlantic facilitated the emergence of a legalist model of regulation of economic activity. Judges are the umpires in the 'economic wars' between two modes of production: small business and monopoly capital.

This chapter begins with an analysis of the pressures of globalization on the legal profession, exposing the terrain of the turf battle which has ensued. The second section develops a model of the American legalistic and market-driven legal profession and its relationship to the rise of federal regulatory agencies in the post-war period. The third section focuses on the contrasting European model, using France as a typical example. The final section explains the conversion of the European regulatory arena through the transformation of legal elites into transnational servants of a global market, with the attendant social costs.

'TURF BATTLES' OR 'GANG WARS': TOWARDS A DUAL PROFESSIONAL SOCIETY?

Harold Perkin (1989) has explained the origins of the welfare state as involving the expansion of a professional society which progressively substitutes its scientific rationality (*rationalité savante*) and meritocratic logic for class antagonisms. As the welfare state emerged, an improvement in social protection became the corollary of the advance of productive rationality. Yet he sees this triumph as a Pyrrhic victory, because the professional society is condemned to impotence as a result of internal quarrels. The sectarian jealousies of different groups of experts are exacerbated by a widening gulf between the professionals of the public sector (welfare state) and the professionals of the private sector (market). In this civil war among experts, exacerbated by recession and international competition, each side rediscovers the antagonisms of class struggle which professional society was meant to escape.

Hence Perkin offers a description of what is taking place to a greater or lesser extent in all post-industrial societies, as different models of professional society confront the challenge posed by neo-liberal ideology. The different professional elites attempt to reconvert their position in national structures into a mastery of this nascent transnational market, which demands above all legal–financial expertise, even if this adds to the social cost already posed by unemployment and the exclusion of a growing fraction of the population of Western societies. The split in professional society brought to light by Perkin could be only the muffled echo of a more serious division. Especially in the great metropolitan centres, a dual society emerges where poverty and misery surround the enclaves of power and wealth created by the new generation of professionals (Sassen 1991).

This division between partisans of market freedom and defenders of a 'non-market' public sector, to which Perkin draws attention, hardly matches the homogeneous professional categories we are used to, like law, medicine, or education. His analysis suggests that it is attitudes concerning the market and competition which induce a kind of split in the relative homogeneity of the professional milieu. Whatever the merits of his two categories of partisans,[4] he certainly poses an analogy which we may import for our understanding of the legal profession in global competition. In the legal profession, the split is understandably not produced along the lines of the public/private opposition. Rather, it involves the big firms working for the international market versus small practices, concerned almost exclusively with the everyday problems of individual members of society: property transactions, divorce, traffic accidents. What is taking shape suggests a divergence of interests between national traditions and partisans of entry into the big international market. This emerging political division is just one of the premonitory signs of the recomposition of professional elites. It is a recomposition that has been accelerating since the oil crises of the 1970s where many of the protagonists were recruited from within the legal field of expertise (Dezalay 1993b; Lederman 1992).

Thus it may not be a coincidence that, at the end of the 1980s, an American sociologist produced a book on the 'system of the professions' (Abbott 1988) which also portrayed a profoundly fragmented and divided professional society in Britain. This sociologist takes as his inspiration the quasi-permanent skirmishes engaged in by urban gangs in order to redefine their respective territories. The confrontation is less fratricidal than interprofessional; rather than being self-destructive, on the contrary it is fundamental to a self-regulation of this 'eco-system of the professions'. The victorious professional 'species' in this Darwinist struggle for survival is the one best adapted, or most adaptable, to transformations in the environment.

The law once purported to incarnate the ideal of a policed universe wherein the cult of knowledge, competence, and conviviality combined harmoniously with the vocation of public service. The ultimate of the gentlemen professionals, lawyers kept the material and the vulgar at arm's length. In contrast, Abbott advances a schema in which the competitive laws of the jungle rule more than the laws of honour. The organizing principle becomes not *noblesse oblige* but the survival of the fittest. The model is inspired overtly by the observation of street gangs which established the reputation of the Chicago school of sociology.

The apparent incongruity of this transposition of conceptual categories developed to account for another social milieu gives the analysis its heuristic force. It surprises and shocks because it reverses all the conventions of common sense which tend to present the professional universe as a triumph of rationality and civility. Since these legal experts produce rationality and civility there is a tendency to see them – and for them to present themselves – as if they were the most exemplary manifestation of these qualities. Thus law firms were once able to boast of being 'the most perfect example as well as the final refuge of Athenian democracy'. It is no longer possible to sustain this myth.

Yet the new global market and its exacerbation of international and intraprofessional competition have led this milieu to promote an image of the expert who does not hesitate to display 'creative imagination' in order to defend his clients' interests aggressively (Eisler 1991). The market big bang has transformed them into conglomerates of professional mercenaries in the service of big financial interests. The smug pictures of the activities of modern yuppies of law and finance offered to us by the practitioners themselves (Lewis 1989; Lederman 1992) contrast sharply with the journalistic investigations devoted to unravelling the structures of junk bond markets (Stewart 1991) or the mechanisms for laundering dirty money (Ring and Frantz 1992; Truell and Gurwin 1992). These probes give an image of professional practices closer to gang warfare than to the practices of the medieval clerks in monastic cloisters, an image to which the legal profession long aspired in the UK and Europe.

The relations which this professional 'system' maintains with other neighbouring social fields, such as the state or politics or the production of knowledge, are nowhere presented in a systematic way. There certainly exists, however, an implicit hierarchy which takes account of the positions of the various professions in the field of power and knowledge and their accumulated social and scientific capital. The most 'noble' professions attract the best endowed 'heirs' as well as the most brilliant – or most ambitious – *'arrivistes'*. They know that by aspiring to a prestigious professional title they will benefit automatically from the collective capital of renown that it represents. According to the logic of the corps, individual success is conditioned by the group's renown, and vice versa. However, this system of hierarchical positions and the struggle for prestige is certainly far from being inviolable, it runs its course parallel to the territorial struggles for the occupation of new markets.

The law has done well in these battles for turf and prestige, and the profession is at the centre of the process of reproduction and transformation of elites in the emerging global market. The internationalization of the legal field and, particularly, business law, has helped redefine a whole series of pecking orders which were once established, and more or less stabilized, on a strictly national basis. Thus it is not only the small minority of applicants for admission to this transnational elite who feel concerned in the stakes, but also all of their colleagues whose symbolic capital risks finding itself brutally devalued, or revalued, on the new transnational market of professional competition. The restructuring of the legal professional landscape in the 1980s was not only quantitative, but qualitative. The opening of borders speeds up the transition of the profession from gentlemenly partnerships to enterprises. Due to this process of economic concentration, the whole division of labour and the internal hierarchy of competencies are affected, as are the positions lawyers occupy in the field of power. At the same time, the importance of the capitals raised by these multinationals of expertise – as well as the importance of the profits they are likely to generate – introduces financial rationality into professional milieux which previously prided themselves on keeping their distance from the logic of the market. The pressure of the bottom line does not sit well with the ideal of collegiality and public service.

This restructuring is all the more brutal as it takes place from the inside of the profession, as of necessity national fields for the production of legal expertise become competitive in international competition. In short, the entire mode of production and legitimation of professional know-how finds itself implicated in this game of international competition (Dezalay and Trubek 1993). In fact, the different kinds of expertise in the complex game are tightly interwoven around multiple legal and regulatory devices. These resemble those which claim to guarantee free competition by forbidding dumping or monopoly practices, or more generally all those which work towards enframing an activity of production or exchange. The export or import of a specific model of expertise is indissociable from the import or export of the hierarchy of know-how linked to the wider market for production and exchange. Thus to import the model of the American lawyer is to adopt a social set up which enables this professional category to lay claim to the role of orchestra conductor in multidisciplinary teams of experts advising business, as if this leadership was due by right and not the result of politics. In this race for power, the victors are those who succeed in building up their capital of transnational renown by taking a leadership position in highly visible international business. From then on, the concentration of resources becomes a decisive factor.

But by moving from the status of *primus inter pares* to that of enterprise boss, these 'learned clerks' are obliged to adopt an economic rationality in terms of profit that is far removed from the ideal of gentlemen's professions. In this palace revolution, the modernist fraction of the legal elite sacrifices on the altar of the professional market a great deal of the tradition and 'habitus' (Bourdieu 1967: 175; Bourdieu and Wacquant 1992: 120) constitutive of the homogeneity and identity of national or regional professional fields. Clearly it comes up against the protests of the 'guardians of the temple' who are all the more vehement as the possibility of their personal reconversion and profit are limited. But the position of reformists in the national field is strong. Rightly or wrongly, in an international confrontation amongst tribes of legal experts given free rein by the relative absence of the nation-state in the global market, ironically they appear as 'champions of national know-how' to their peers. The 'institutional schizophrenia' of lawyers (Gordon 1984) makes them the perfect 'guardians of collective hypocrisy'. This chapter now turns to the confrontation of the European and the American models of the legal profession, demonstrating how the deracinated merchants of law have forged a new transnational professional elite in tandem with the new market realities of the global era.

THE 'AMERICAN MODEL': LEGALISM AND MOBILITY

To describe the American model of regulation as a legalist one may today seem either obvious or banal. Yet this legalization of economic relations is diametrically opposed to the 'non-contractual relations' revealed by Macaulay's classic study (1963). Could this legalism be a recent phenomenon? Could legal regulation be limited strictly to the domain of intervention by federal agencies? A proper reply to these questions – especially the last one – requires a historical approach. It does indeed seem to be the case that the role of law in these arrangements has greatly increased, especially in the past two or three decades. This is as much due to the intervention of federal agencies as to the specific dynamic of the legal field. My central hypothesis is precisely that these two types of phenomena are closely interrelated. The emergence, the rise, and more generally the impact of the federal agencies can only be understood if one takes into account the positions and strategies of their protagonists within the legal field. Conversely, it was by the deployment of the authority and state-derived legitimacy of the regulatory institutions that the business-law practitioners were able gradually to come to dominate the field of business as professionals in the formalization of economic relations. Relational capitalism as described by Macaulay still exists, but the management of these relations has been professionalized and they are increasingly cast in legal forms.

In the earlier model of regulation, judicial intervention in the regulation of economic activity was fairly rare. Daily business matters – meaning those which did not involve major political stakes – were regulated 'in the shadow of the law'. It was only relatively late that this pattern began to be upset, and for various related reasons. Political crises or technological innovations help to make and unmake social networks. Thus, at the end of the last century, it was the relentless acceleration of the process of capitalist concentration and restructuring which allowed the anti-trust judge to impose himself as the umpire between two worlds which were ignorant of and hated each other almost to the verge of a civil war. The oil crisis and monetary upheavals of the 1970s, and the intensification of international competition, set off a profound and lasting restructuring of the business field that upset the stable alliances and networks which supported informal regulation. At the same time, the mushrooming of law schools and the rise of a market for regulation facilitated the entry of a meritocracy into the market for business law, which was especially enthusiastic to use the courts tactically in economics. Those essentially were its special skills, as it did not have the wordly wisdom or the social capital of its elders. This meritocracy used the federal regulatory bodies for its apprenticeship both in the courts and in the business world. The emergence of a regulatory field therefore played a key role in the juridification of the field of business and the rise of the legal profession. Conversely, it is because the law and lawyers were for a long period at the centre of the political game that these new state regulatory devices were cast in a legal mould.

Judges very soon found themselves in the position of umpires between the different social groups fighting each other in the state arena. As Sklar (1988) has shown, the anti-trust laws made the judge the arbiter of a political equilibrium between the appetites of the big Wall Street financiers, who wanted to profit from carrying through the necessary rationalization of the apparatus of production, and the fears of a middle class of small entrepreneurs whose populist ideology expressed their desperation to fight off the threats to social structures and their mode of production.

Paradoxically, in putting themselves forward as strict defenders of the traditional conception of a competitive market in the face of a federal authority which was more responsive to new arguments in terms of macroeconomic equilibrium and efficiency, the Supreme Court judges were acting in conformity with a professional ideology and with social origins which predisposed them to be defenders of the 'little' against the 'big'. They were also contributing to the institutionalization of the power of the big Wall Street lawyers as necessary and legitimate intermediaries in the market for corporate restructuring. The complexity and seriousness of the legal and juridical provisions made the lawyers indispensable to the financiers who employed them. They also allowed them to demonstrate a certain autonomy in relation to those over-powerful clients who were always tempted to reduce them to the status of 'hired guns' (Gordon 1984).

This example already contains all the essential ingredients which characterize the American model and have ensured, if not its success, at least the prosperity and the social attainments of those who were both its inventors and its operators. What is striking is the complementarity of roles between those who appear as the guardians of the general interest and those who defend private interests. Indeed this structural complementarity is so strong that both these roles can be carried out by the same person – whether successively or even simultaneously. Gordon (1984) gives a perfect description of this 'institutional schizophrenia' of the elite of the New York Bar. Its members attempted to preserve the ideals and the 'civic virtues' of the gentleman lawyer, while showing no embarrassment or scruples in their mercenary activities in the service of the 'robber barons'. In contributing to the development of an ideal of the law, the members of this professional elite developed rules to which they subjected themselves (and above all perhaps their collaborators and competitors who were even less scrupulous, being more careerist). These rules were just so many fire-breaks to shelter them from the demands of clients who could have created dangers for their ultimate credibility and legitimacy by making them appear too openly as simple instruments in the service of capital. Their position condemned them to be 'double agents', now public servants, now mercenaries, fashioning with one hand the rules which they were striving to evade with the other. The more they undermined the image of the law by appearing as 'hired guns' in the service of the highest bidder, the more they had to augment in parallel the authority of the law which is the basis of their social power. Although very profitable, such a double game is also a very delicate one to play. So it is confined to a small elite, skilled at accumulating positions and titles. This fact also explains the large contribution which these great business lawyers made to the growth of the great law schools. By subcontracting this double role of learned authority and moral conscience to a special category of professional, a solution was found to that dilemma. An 'institutional schizophrenia' was transformed into a rational division of symbolical labour.

The law schools, therefore, came to play a central role in the emergence of these arrangements of legal regulation. The great professors such as Pound or Frankfurter wanted to be reformers and 'social engineers' and tried to inculcate this public service mission in their best pupils. Obviously, the moralism of this education was not enough to make the majority of these graduates turn aside from the career mapped out for them in the big Wall Street firms. At least it maintained the schizophrenic predispositions of these white Anglo-Saxon Protestant gentleman lawyers who saw themselves as an enlightened elite. None the less, this appeal to build an 'alternative' elite ready to devote itself to the service of institutions embodying the general interest[5] was bound to strike a very strong chord among the minority fraction of the young graduates for whom, because of their social origins, the royal road to a legal career was closed. This was even more so in the periods of crisis when the Wall Street elite could give their prejudices free rein, due to the slowdown in the business law market.

During the New Deal period, all these conditions came together: 'It [public service] attracted young, upwardly mobile, minority-group lawyers whose professional advancement within traditional channels was thwarted by the Depression and frustrated by the social structure of the bar' (Auerbach

1976: 173). Roosevelt could fish in this breeding-ground of brilliant social outsiders to recruit lawyers whose competence matched their predisposition to dress his reformist programme in legal clothes, the better to defend it from the attacks of the legal establishment. Contrary to what happened in Europe, if the crisis of 1929 did not result in the United States in the disqualification of legal forms as a means of governing the market, the credit goes to this alternative elite. While opposing the political views of the legal notables, they shared their devotion to the law. They were all the more legalist since they had to make up for the weakness of their social capital by an additional investment in legal techniques and belief in the virtues of the law.

This shared belief greatly facilitated the ultimate reconciliation of these opponents and the integration of this meritocracy of combative outsiders into the dominant institutions of the business law world. It is true that these 'prodigal sons' did not return empty handed. They were bearers of this entire new market of economic regulation, the intricacies of which they knew better than anyone since they had helped fashion them. By welcoming them as partners, the big law firms were at the same stroke acquiring a slice of expert capital and of contacts which ensured their mastery of this new and rapidly growing market, for the benefit of their big business clientele.

So we come to the usual account in which these state agencies are used as a sort of 'passing lane' for those professionals who enter the market for regulation by the 'side-door'. Taking the detour through these institutions whose esteem is as low as their pay-rates provides a second chance for those young people who – for educational or social reasons – could not get access to the big firms where the most high-flying and prestigious careers are made. This apprenticeship allows them to acquire practical knowledge and contacts, which the more ambitious – or lucky – ones will be able to cash in by rejoining the private sector after some years of 'purgatory' in the service of the state (Spangler 1986).

The path taken by the leading lights of the law in the field of regulation was quite different from that of this hard-working meritocracy who only gained entry by the 'side door'. The royal road which allows you to play the role of 'power broker' in the regulatory field is that of lobbying in the wings – or sometimes also on the main stage – of the big federal institutions. What counts in this power strategy is the amassing of positions, relationships, and titles which allows these persons always to be in the right place, while wielding the social resources and symbolic skills necessary to insert themselves everywhere as indispensable mediators. Due to the extraordinary mobility and multi-positioning of the Washingtonian elites, the lines of force between the public and private poles are extremely variable.

These two career paths for regulatory agents – by the side door or the main entrance – are therefore central to the American regulatory system. It explains both the strengths and weaknesses of the system, as well as its dynamics. Nevertheless, the domination of this field of practices by the spokespersons for private interests (or those who aspire to this role) should not be seen as simply the 'capture' of the regulatory agencies. If there is a capture, it has a double meaning. The mobility of the agents also entails a degree of dissemination of a public order logic – one which takes account of the major elements of social equilibrium – even into big business. In this scenario, the professionals play the main role of courtier, but also that of 'double agent', between the state and the market. The intersection of these two worlds of public and private can be seen either as a delegation of public authority and responsibilities to the entrepreneurs, or as the introduction of competition and of merchants into the world of the state and the constitution of a market in public order – indeed a market in expertise and state legitimacy (Dezalay 1993a).

To summarize, the central place of law and lawyers in regulatory processes is in no way natural or immutable. It is continually reconstructed by a professional elite, which is both exclusive as well as relatively open to entry by the more successful of a meritocracy of social outsiders. In terms of imagery, it could be said that it is an order of legal knights which has managed to take advantage of crises periodically to re-gild its coat of arms at the cost of accepting some alliances with those more lowly newcomers who had accumulated some valuable social capital by opening up new markets and new spaces of influence for the law. This strategy of forming lowly alliances has allowed it to keep its positions in the fields of state and economic power. The two are inseparable. It is vital, for a professional group which lays claim to the role of mediator, to keep a balance between these two poles of power, since they are mutually complementary. Law's authority – and hence the value of lawyers – in the field of business is based on the mastery of the spaces and the instruments where the regulation of economic activity takes place.

THE 'FRENCH MODEL': THE MARGINALIZATION OF LEGAL PROFESSIONALS

In contrast to this American schema of a field of regulation which expands until it merges with that of the practitioners of business law, the history of Europe[6] provides a sort of counter-example where regulatory processes develop at the margins of the law and largely avoid judicial institutions. On the American side, the circulation of members of the elite between its various fractions helps to ensure the relative homogeneity of a regulatory process which is both at the heart of the field of business law and closely involved with that of economic power. On the European side, the distance between the state, the judicial institutions and the business world is so great that it is quite difficult to speak of a single field.

These multiple processes of 'corporate governance' in Europe are defined and constructed by their opposition to each other. When they nationalize large firms, or intervene more or less directly in their management through the terms of credit, industrial policies, or 'indicative' planning, the supporters of the welfare state claim to correct or prevent market disequilibrium. They denounce the economic inefficiency and social injustice of a juridico-economic order which follows a strictly commercial and contractual logic. Indeed, often they do not stop at suspending or modifying the freedom of contractual relations, they also ensure that judicial institutions are kept in the background (Abel-Smith and Stevens 1967). According to the well-known formula, 'state rule replaces the rule of law'.

Conversely, 're-legalization' is directly tied to the success of neo-liberal policies in dismantling a state machinery which was denounced as costly, clumsy, and inefficient. The great majority of legal practitioners openly rejoice in this 'restoration' of the rule of law, which they expect will bring an end to a long period of political marginalization and social decline. At the same time, they have embarked on the 'reconquest' – or more accurately the conquest – of the position which they consider they deserve in the management of business. Depending on the positions they occupy, the learned European lawyers contribute in various ways, direct or indirect, to this strategy of challenging, or even denouncing, 'relational capitalism'. The new generation of business lawyers, trained in the American style, is trying to profit from the process of restructuring of the field of economic power, accelerated by the crisis and internationalization, to promote a legalized, American-style managerial system. At the same time, the eminent lawyers are trying to extend the economic powers of state bodies by using the creation of the European Single Market and the establishment of a 'level playing-field' to press for powers of judicial review over the corporatist-style self-regulatory bodies (Bancaud and Boigeol 1995). Finally, even the learned lawyers who are apparently the furthest removed from the business world make their own contribution, although a more indirect one, to this attempt to juridify economic relations. They use the court bench to denounce as corruption the more or less hidden financial arrangements linking the political class with the world of business (*mani pulite* in Italy: Nelken 1996).

The articulation between all these arrangements for governing the economy, therefore, was not based on any rational division of regulatory tasks, but rather on a competitive drive between agents who were more likely to denigrate each other than to co-operate. The major characteristic of this European market in legal competence was – and remains – its closed nature. Legal practitioners and juridical institutions play only a small role, although for the past few years, due to the development of European integration and more generally of internationalization, they have been busy building up their positions.

To understand this phenomenon of exclusion and of marginalization, it is necessary to go back into the history of the legal field – all the more so since the same conflicts and accusations can be seen in the past (Charle 1992). Throughout the Third Republic, the elite of the well-heeled and well-educated Parisian bourgeoisie gradually distanced itself from the main institutions of the legal field, which were increasingly identified with a static or even conservative image. Subjected to political power and recruited essentially from among provincial notables, the judiciary became a bastion of moral order. Even at the heart of the Bar, not without its Republican political activists, the legal world sheltered mainly amateurish and conservative notables, usually from the provinces. *Rentiers* or careerists of modest origins, what these fractions had in common was the distance that separated them from the world of business. This is what explains the ideology of 'disinterestedness' which predominates in the Bar (Karpik 1995): whatever their other differences as regards class and divergences of opinion, the *avocats*-political activists and the *rentier*-notables of the Bar were agreed on the denunciation of any involvement in the business world as meddling with 'trade'. Even if it was for very different reasons, neither group was keen to strike out into a world which was very unfamiliar to them. Moreover, the emergence of a market in business law would have endangered – even more than today – the image of unity which the Bar carefully cultivates because it allows it to defend its collective prerogatives.

This denunciation of the practitioners of business law did not prevent them from prospering, but their success occurred at the margins of the legal professional world in the strict sense of the term.[7] Rejected by their peers, the lawyers who became interested in the business world had no option but to join it officially by themselves becoming 'men of affairs'. This change of designation somewhat modified their role: they acted as intermediaries in commercial transactions which they helped to 'put into legal form' and in which they sometimes intervened for their own account. Elsewhere, they could be called upon as mediators of conflicts, often informally but sometimes in the commercial courts. In short, it was doubtless these rejects from the world of 'noble' legal practices who were largely responsible for the rise of the processes of self-regulation and of private justice 'in the shadow of the law'.

If the denunciation of involvement in 'trade' by the Bar shows the widening gulf between the 'active' and the *rentier* fractions of the bourgeoisie, the creation of the Ecole Libre des Sciences Politiques (1872) demonstrates that the most intellectual and dynamic layers of the ruling class also remained remote from a world of law that they left to the provincial notables and the tribune-*avocats*. This Ecole's project was openly elitist: its aims were to train statesmen, or more precisely to select and educate the scions of the ruling classes and turn them into 'government professionals' (Damamme 1987). But this project, the promoters of which were themselves situated at the intersection of the economic, intellectual and political fields, was aimed at the most intellectual or innovative fractions of the *haute bourgeoisie*. Convinced that 'it was the University of Berlin that won the battle of Sadowa' (Damamme 1987: 33), these reformers were immersed in positivism and scientism, and intended to construct a modern bureaucracy whose dowry included the double legitimacy of birth and knowledge.

This School identified itself with the political sciences also because it was designed as a weapon to wage war on the law faculties which are so 'rooted in their doctrinal traditionalism and their corporatism' that they refused to open themselves up to new fields of knowledge and new practices establishing themselves around the sciences of the state and the economy (Le Van Lemesle 1983). This was precisely the gap which this School – sponsored by innovative scholars, top civil servants, and the leading entrepreneurs in business or banking of the period – was to fill.

The educational project and the political ambitions of these reformers conformed to their social positions: they were thus the very opposite of what the law faculties represented. The latter at that time were notorious for the weakness of their teaching and the absenteeism of their students.[8] The latter, it is true, had little reason to be motivated by their studies, since they mostly came from not very intellectual backgrounds. They knew instinctively that their careers would be determined much more by the patronage that they could obtain than by the technical skills that they might acquire.[9]

By recruiting its students preferably from the most open and intellectual fraction of the Parisian bourgeoisie and by paying much more attention to their educational environment, the Ecole Libre quickly and easily came to dominate the market for training the new state elites. Ever since then, the fame of the '*sciences po*' went along with that of the '*grands corps*' which in many ways constituted the new learned nobility. More exactly, they are its heirs to the extent that they have facilitated the conversion of the old learned bourgeoisie into a 'state bourgeoisie' (Bourdieu 1989). Indeed, not satisfied with co-opting the most brilliant heirs of this fine old urbane and intellectual bourgeoisie which traditionally supplied the elite of the legal field, these '*grands corps*' also borrowed the juridical model on which the learned lawyers had built their legitimacy. The Conseil d'Etat and the Cour des Comptes are organized along the lines of tribunals, and the Inspection des Finances prosecutes its investigations on the lines of an adversarial hearing.[10] That is not all. Charle (1992: 197, 228) shows that the analogy goes much further. Just as the learned nobility of the *ancien régime* claimed to 'constitute an autonomous social force in relation to its progenitor the king', this new state aristocracy allows itself to judge and censure the state. Today, as yesterday, their *esprit de corps* allows a small, privileged and high-born elite to pool their social and intellectual capital for a better defence of their positions in the field of power.

Just as in the past the landed wealth of the judiciary allowed it to maintain its independence, today the top civil servants and politicians carefully nurture their network of links and influence in the business world to ensure their access to lucrative livings which are also positions of power.[11] Thanks to their opportunities and strategies, they can be simultaneously inside and outside the state. In this dual role, they can ensure that the state's influence extends into the field of business much further than the already large area of it occupied by public enterprises.[12] Thus, they occupy this 'pivotal position between administration and politics, law and administration, or more generally between the state and civil society' which allows them to 'intercede in the complex game of interacting powers'.

French-style planning perfectly illustrates this close interaction between the state and the economy where the legitimacy of the state nobility depends on its ability to handle the technological advances which underpin social progress. 'The plan itself became the high priest of high technology' (Hall 1986: 179). During the 'thirty-year boom', the supremacy of this interventionist state model was hardly challenged, except at the political and populist level. This state of affairs remained at least until the oil shocks and the crisis of the Fordist model challenged the legitimacy of this 'developmental state' and forced this state nobility to restructure itself around new power bases . . . and perhaps to borrow, for this purpose, the clothes of the law, or more exactly of the American lawyer.

FROM STATE TECHNOCRATS TO INTERNATIONAL EXPERTS

Having sketched out the very contrasting examples of the construction of national legal professions and corresponding regulatory arenas in the US and France, the logical next step would be to show how they are recomposing with the help of the increased pace and especially the institutionalization of globalization. And since the two models represent virtually the two extremities of the gamut of arrangements for governing the economy, one legal and the other bureaucratic, one managed by legal entrepreneurs, the other centralized or co-ordinated by the state, one is tempted to ask whether globalization implies the creation of competition between these two technologies of power. In short, is the conflict between the market economy and the welfare state best summed up as a competition between lawyers and technocrats? Unfortunately it is not quite so simple.

To understand how and why 'regulatory regimes' of apparently quite different inspiration come into being, they must be approached as constructions – continually being reconstructed – in a professional field which has its internal differences and struggles as its principle of transformation. These 'regulatory regimes' do not have an objective existence in themselves. They can only be understood and analysed in relation to the 'palace wars' which retranscribe into symbolic language the confrontational games of the field of economic power.

This distinction is even more indispensable if the focus of interest is on the international competition played out, in part, on the terrain of global or regional institutions and techniques of government. In contrast to the widespread rhetoric of 'globalization', it is helpful to describe the emergence of an international field of expertise by analysing first what is nourishing it, and second how it is simultaneously transforming the various national fields from which it is constituting itself (Dezalay 1993b, 1993c). Far from sparing the necessity of an analysis of national specificities, on the contrary this object of research requires a deepening of the structural history of the national fields in which these internationalization strategies are inscribed. Hence, there is no split or contradiction in the ways in which the 'global' and the 'local' should be approached, nor any fundamental difference between these levels of analysis.

By definition, the legal field of economic regulation is a site of confrontation between different groups or categories of producers, each continually attempting to redefine the rules of the game, or to modify the conditions of their application, in their own interests. Far from being homogeneous and rational, regulatory space is characterized by the co-existence of highly typified systems, each bearing the marks of the social context and the political compromises by – and for – which it was devised. It is particularly hard for producers to circulate since this space is partitioned up between institutions and rationalities, each jealously defending a particular territory. Furthermore, many of these producers are far from interchangeable, since they are 'marked' by their social origin and/or their career trajectory. If ideological affinities or disciplinary and institutional affiliations are largely the result of the positional system in the field of expertise, they also tend to introduce into it divisions which can turn out to be particularly rigid when they are combined with an *esprit de corps*. Indeed, their influence will be all the stronger since such affiliations often do no more than reinforce choices and orientations which owe much to '*habitus*' and to social trajectories.

The field of expertise offers a wide spectrum of situations among which entrants are distributed more or less according to their ambitions and to the type of capital they command. Despite everything, whatever room for manoeuvre there may be (and in any case it is relative) there is a far from exact correspondence between social position and institutional function. This relative lack of correspondence is perhaps indeed one of the keys of the transformation of the machinery for governing the economy. As we have seen above in relation to the New Deal lawyers, this type of shift can stimulate new entrants into the market for expertise to invest their capital of specialist competence into new institutions more appropriate to their convictions or their ambitions.

This same logic can also be found in the process of construction of an international market for expertise in matters of law and regulation. The increase in trade – symbolic as well as economic – provides opportunities for a greater number of producers of expertise to try to export their techniques to new territories. 'Globalization' offers an excuse or a banner for strategies of symbolic imperialism which are supported by many learned or institutional networks. Very often, beyond the politico-academic objectives which they proclaim, these 'epistemic communities' are aiming above all to create an international market for techniques, in which national producers can exchange 'localized' social capital for a cosmopolitan competence. In the absence of a world state, the latter is guaranteed collectively by this small elite of traders in 'universal' expertise which substitutes its pseudo-learned authority for political legitimacy (Dezalay 1993a). As a corollary, the spread of these 'borderless' jurisdictions tends to downgrade purely national techniques as second-class competencies. This phenomenon is particularly characteristic of dominated countries which thus find themselves 'provincial-ized' by the new symbolic imperialisms. Hence, international competition in the market for regulation, both by its causes and its effects, refers back into the positional systems which are constituted around nation-states.

In sum, to understand how – and by whom – the continual recomposition of the mosaic of legal and regulatory mechanisms is carried out, it is impossible to avoid analysing, at least in schematic terms, the main characteristics around which this social space comes to be organized. In particular, we must assess the terms of trade between the different forms of capital – economic, academic, or cultural – which circulate there and which determine the hierarchy of techniques in the field of the state. For it is these objective positions which, in the last analysis, determine professional strategies, and hence the institutions or the forms of representation which circulate in the field of power.

'Palace wars' and globalization

Clearly, these 'palace wars' both nourish and feed off the political battles provoked by a process of globalization which upsets the revenue redistribution processes established by the welfare state to guarantee social peace. Thus, international competition provides a convenient excuse to justify the elimination of a wide range of regulations or of bureaucratic interventions, which the adherents of free trade denounce as fetters on the spirit of free enterprise, or handicaps in relation to heightened international competition. In this emerging market order a new kind of law is born in Europe, and the effects of these neo-liberal policies are very soon felt. Since the early 1980s, with the rise in real interest rates, the gulf has again widened between the small minority which has benefited handsomely from the extraordinary revival of the international capital market and the mass of wage-earners (or of unemployed) who have lost the protections or advantages which they previously enjoyed.

International economic restructuring not only challenges the system of social pacification built around the welfare state, it also weakens the positions of the inheritors of the Ecole Libre, those who embodied and managed that search for social consensus. It introduces a new power relationship into the field of the state, as well as that of professional knowledge. The globalization of economies thus helps to accelerate a process of recomposition of ruling elites, especially those linked to the state apparatus. Centralism and state planning had been efficient enough to organize the economic take-off of the economies of the third world or European post-war reconstruction. Once these objectives had been achieved, however, these state or party technocracies found it much more difficult to manage complex economies, especially those which are closely tied into international exchange. Their foreign business partners – who are also rivals – are quick to complain about dumping, as soon as public subsidies become too large or too visible. Further, the instruments of planning or incentives lose their efficacy because the economic actors can easily find alternative solutions by using external markets to find capital, clients or suppliers. Finally, as Hall (1986) emphasizes, this state technocracy loses much of its political legitimacy once the rise of unemployment reveals its powerlessness to resolve an economic and social crisis which has been continually worsening. Hence it is not only a regulatory model which is in crisis, it is also the credibility of those who embody it.

In such a position of weakness, these holders of state power increasingly sense the pressures from the new cosmopolitan technocracy of economists, lawyers, and consultants that has grown up with the expansion of the multinational firms and the penetration of a financial capitalism with global ambitions. Almost unanimously, this new group fights for the flexibility of work, against wage 'rigidities', for a reduction of social protection and of the tax burden, and more generally in favour of privatization and of a weakening of the role of the state.[13] To accompany the integration of their country into the world economy, while themselves joining the nascent international elite, 'converted' national economic managers have strong incentives to distance themselves from the interventionist bureaucracies which are losing momentum and to build the legal mechanisms of the global market.

The clothing of the lawyer is perfectly suited for the new role being adopted by these state technocrats or party cadres. It is well adapted to the deployment of skills of a generalist sort where personal relations have a predominant role. Above all, as we have seen in relation to the United States, this ambiguous position, poised between the public and the private, permits the mobilization of state or political resources, while claiming complete independence from the state. In the traditional European model of legal practice, however, this double game is harder to play. The gap which has been created between the social state and legal institutions has made it more difficult to lead this double career of legal practitioner and statesman simultaneously. In recent years, in contrast, it is precisely these two types of skills and experience which are essential for an international competition played out on the borders of law and the state, because this competition requires the construction of quasi-state arrangements to ensure the regulation of a market economy encircling the planet.

The opposition between the market and the state is not, actually, as clear – or as schematic – as some militant (or scientistic) discourses would have us believe. As Hall emphasizes, 'Markets are themselves institutions ... depend[ing] on an ancillary network of social institutions, often generated and sustained by state action' (1986: 282). The conversion of the defenders of the state and the public sector into dealers in regulatory expertise thus cannot be reduced to the sacrifice of the general interest in favour of private profits. The credibility of these experts rests not only on their skills but also on their claims to incarnate universal values. These credibility claims are especially true for lawyers. As we have seen, these dealers in law are in a certain manner condemned to be 'dealers in virtue'. To sell legal services, they are indeed forced to invest in the legitimacy of the law. Rivalry in the market for regulation and economic management therefore also produces law, and even forms of state.

Competing for 'universals'

The management of economic disputes through international commercial arbitration can serve as an example in which the same public–private dialectic is to be found: the privatization of the state engenders a market for the universal (which means, in this case, a market for justice; Dezalay and Garth 1996a). And this international competition produces the state (in this case, the embryo of a transnational law and jurisdiction). Certainly, for this specific example as well as more generally, it is far too early to forecast the final outcome of this process of restructuring of state processes. One must settle for an analysis of the internal struggles which delineate the first main outlines of this field of international juridical practices and the apparent dominance of American legal forms in this transnational domain.

During the 1980s, there was a successive series of reforms of the laws of arbitration in many countries. These reforms all had the same objective: to try to attract a larger portion of the market in international arbitration by reducing as much as possible the constraints involved in state governance over this private justice. And the various promoters of these reforms vaunted the special facilities offered by their own country in the creation of a sort of 'legal free-port'. Here, the parties would be perfectly free to administer their litigation in their own way, choosing their judges and their law, without any interference by the state's courts.

The competition between the great arbitration centres acts as a justification for strategies of bidding up deregulation and bringing down the prerogatives of national courts. Indeed, the latter are all the more reluctant to abandon a long tradition of mistrust of this private justice, often considered to be an 'inferior justice', since the right of oversight is also the best protection of the monopoly of national practitioners of law over the market for managing disputes. Strong arguments are therefore needed to persuade them to give it up, and by the same action to open the door to foreign competitors.[14] These arguments emphasize a state of rivalry that is above all at the level of rhetoric.

In fact, contrary to the media image of these arbitration centres engaged in a no-holds-barred struggle for this rapidly growing market, this field of practices can be compared to a club of insiders where personal ambitions must give way to a collective logic. Indeed, all the members of this community are perfectly conscious that the credibility of this private justice is too new, and too fragile, to tolerate strategies of marketing which might be too daring or aggressive. In any case, the rate of growth of this market is probably far from being as miraculous as it is made out to be.

Furthermore, in this small world where personal relations are very close, there is extensive interpenetration between the networks which cluster around the different arbitration centres or institutions. To gain credibility, each of these centres subtly gilds its list of arbitrators by including representatives of other arbitration circles. This relative openness to 'outsiders' is the price to be paid to justify the pretensions to universality, which is often no more than an international marketing drive launched by a few local practitioners. At the level of the management of arbitral cases, it translates into a complex system, albeit one which is also closely codified and monitored, of favours and counter-favours, which ensures more effectively than any rules of procedure the smooth functioning of this extra-normal justice.

In short, this field of practices is quite the opposite of the image of an open and very competitive market which is implied by the rhetoric of global competition. On the contrary, it resembles a closed market where the producers are closely hemmed in, as much by their mentors as by their peers. Personal relations at the heart of networks operating on the basis of complicity and reciprocity reinforce the stability of this market. Since, above all, access is still very tightly controlled by the small core of founding fathers who select the aspirants according to the deference that they show to the values of arbitration, this private justice for traders is therefore, in many ways, further removed from the market – and perhaps better protected from its temptations – than is state justice. It is true that the importance of the financial or political stakes in this type of international dispute requires a certain vigilance, especially taking into account the fragility of this institution which does not have the benefit of a guarantee from the state.

But the national legal authorities in fact do not give up their statutory prerogatives without a quid pro quo. Often, in order to facilitate this mutual recognition, one or other of the members of a local legal elite is co-opted and enthroned in this closed circle of arbitrators which is one of the keys for access to an international legal field which is being constructed. In return, these new recruits act as intermediaries between these two worlds which until now were alien to each other. In one, they put forward the specific merits of their national legal culture; in the other they act as guarantors for the legitimacy of this international private justice.

Since it lies at the intersection of the European and American legal cultures, this field of practices creates a breach in the national legal monopolies based largely on their mutual ignorance. Narrow though it may be, this footbridge creates the possibility of a confrontation. The result may be, if not the creation of effective competition, at least a sort of mutual evaluation. The different local elites learn to take the measure of each other: the UK barrister compares himself to the continental professor or to the senior partner of a large American law firm.

Whereas these comparisons were formerly mere academic exercises, global competition now substitutes a real and substantial test: the effectiveness of each when confronted with a specific problem, or when they compete in an actual case. This evaluation is based on a system of trading between the different fields of practices. It allows a small group of eminent figures in national law to convert into cosmopolitan fame the authority which they possess within the local courts. It also facilitates many other trading transactions: academic lawyers can use it to acquire familiarity with and contacts in the business world; conversely, the business lawyers can use it to acquire the legitimacy and patina of learning.

In short, the market for arbitration operates like a trading floor where the transactions concern the different forms of legal authority and legitimacy. In this way it helps to establish their relative values, and to continually readjust them. From this perspective, there really is a process of competition between national legal systems. It represents the opportunity to redefine the rules of the game – and the resources which the players can mobilize. This new deal has facilitated the relative autonomy of arbitration which has become a sort of 'off-shore justice' which is both decentralized and delocalized. More importantly for this chapter, this outcome was the result of an encounter between a small coterie of learned European lawyers and some multinational law firms of American origin. The 'transnational' was constructed from a competition among national legal practices, whether the concern was the protection of the environment, human rights and constitutionalism, securities regulation, or international commercial arbitration. International commercial arbitration itself is therefore an amalgam of national approaches in which the US approach to litigation has recently gained the upper hand. Although the process is far from uni-directional, this work of social construction can be described as a rationalization in the Weberian sense and also as an 'Americanization' that has permitted US litigators to shape the rules to favour their adversarial skills and approaches (Dezalay and Garth 1995).

This does not mean that international commercial arbitration is necessarily destined to remain like US litigation. Competition is an ongoing process, especially in the shadow of the emerging EU single market and its associated legal practices. None the less, to the extent that US-style litigation has gained in importance, it opens the door to further US influence in the field of business law as the Wall Street firms and practices take hold. The ongoing competition among national approaches to the law and to the governance of business conflict has been determinant in the simultaneous reconstituion of the national and constitution of the transnational.

CONCLUSION

The true nature of the market revolution in the global economy cannot be understood from the simplistic standpoint of emphasizing one or the other of either external constraints on national systems of governance or internal dynamics of change. This revolution must be understood simultaneously from both inside and outside national structures and elites. The professional field of the law provides a focus for developing this important argument concerning the social construction of globalization. Global and regional pressures are mainly effective through their reinterpretation in the context of local struggles and individual or collective strategies at the local and national level. What counts is the relative value of international social capital in local battles. The social cost for the economically weak is rising.

This chapter is largely the story of the penetration of the US legal model into the regional and national legal and regulatory processes which have accompanied economic globalization. The venerable legal fields of the UK, France, and the rest of Europe have given way, at least partially, to the practices of the Wall Street multinational business lawyers. Those national professional elites who have embodied this trend have seen rapid growth in their capital in the market for prestige and material gain. The construction of Europe may offer new opportunities for a reconversion of this emerging transnational legal field, recentring European law towards an enhanced regional model of the legal profession, no doubt with implications for the Wall Street lawyers as well. The European single market brings the European legal elite into a regional game of transnational business law, but their contact with the global and, hence, the American, will not disappear in their transatlantic world.

Furthermore, similar processes are under way elsewhere in the global economy. The advent of the North American Free Trade Agreement presaged a reconversion of economic and legal elites in Mexico through the same inside–outside dynamics (Dezalay and Garth 1996b). In this case, legal and economic elites in Mexico are leading a challenge to the patrimonial state dominated by the traditional PRI (Institutional Revolutionary Party) at the same time as they remain embedded in the state and its social constructs. Mexico's economic powers are increasingly served by legal intermediaries who can go between business and the state. All the while they are building on their social capital and their 'made in USA' legal expertise (Dezalay and Garth 1996b: 78). Globalization is revealed as a series of simultaneous local and transnational battles, where regions and the national remain embedded in the global.

NOTES

1 This chapter draws on a number of earlier works, presenting a broad series of arguments concerning the globalization of markets and the legal profession, in particular Dezalay 1995a; Dezalay 1996; Dezalay and Garth 1995, 1996b.

2 Just as, in another age, the European legislators (at the side of the missionaries and teachers) took up the baton from the colonial armies to reinforce the subjugation of those populations by imposing on them a Western legal system presented as universal and liberating.

3 This historical approach is complementary to the work I have published elsewhere on the current confrontation between the 'American model' and the 'European model': in particular, on the management of the market for corporate control (Dezalay 1992, 1995b) and the constitution of a field of international arbitration (Dezalay and Garth 1996a).

4 Perkin himself has great difficulty making clear the line of demarcation between these two groups whose antagonism does not, as he sometimes implies, reduce to

an antagonism between the public and the private. In fact, this hypothesis of a division of the 'professional Society' between public and private sectors scarcely makes sense in countries like France where professional elites circulate cheerfully from one to the other (Marceau 1989), or to the United States where, according to Gordon (1984), they 'suffer' a kind of 'institutional schizophrenia' (cf. Auerbach 1976).

5 Frankfurter's ambition was to set up in the United States an elite civil service on the British model (McCraw 1984). Thus he became a 'job-broker', directing his pupils towards those New Deal agencies which for this meritocracy represented a 'unique opportunity for upward professional and social mobility'.

6 Given the length of this chapter, and to be able to go beyond generalities, it has seemed better to focus on the 'French model' since it is in sharp contrast to the 'American model'. However, it would be wrong to see this as exceptional in European terms. The enclosure of the regulatory arena, the marginalization of the legal professions in the business field and the dominant role of state-based processes are present to various extents in most European countries, even if the routes towards them have been very different (cf. Abel-Smith and Stevens 1967; Hall 1986).

7 Particularly by taking the part of banker or intermediary, or one related to less 'noble' professional groups such as accountants (Sugarman 1993).

8 This description was still applied, according to Dahrendorf (1969), to the German law faculties in the 1960s.

9 This generalization – which applies to France, as well as Germany (cf. Dahrendorf 1969), and to Latin America (Perdomo 1981, 1988; Falcao 1979, 1988) leads to a reconsideration of the idea that the professors played a dominant role in these systems based on codified law, often described following Max Weber as the '*professorenrecht*'. At the same time, the low-level educational recruitment characteristic of these institutions explains their increasing marginalization in the field of reproduction of elites, especially after the arrival of new institutions and the growth of competition creates a surplus of educational qualifications (Bourdieu 1987). The French situation is thus not as exceptional as might be thought. It only anticipates a more general development.

10 This formalism is mostly a façade. The interventions are essentially negotiated on the basis of the relations of power and networks of influence represented by former colleagues who have moved into cushy jobs at the head of the big public enterprises or firms controlled by the state and the *grands corps* (Mamou 1987: 77, 280; Bourdieu and de Saint Martin 1976). As Hall (1986: 153) points out, adapting a remark by Tocqueville, the government only passes strict and general laws to make it easier later to negotiate case-by-case exceptions which allow it to exercise its discretionary power. Naturally, these arrangements exclude any public debate and differing opinions.

11 This phenomenon, which is referred to as '*pantouflage*', has grown over time. In 1973, 43 per cent of directors of the 100 biggest firms were former top civil servants (Birnbaum 1977: 141; also Bauer and Bertin Mourot 1994).

12 As is remarked by all observers (Birnbaum 1978: 85; Grémion 1974: 173), these top civil servants see no contradiction between these two roles. On the contrary, this symbiosis between state and business leaders is considered as a trump card contributing to the success of industrial policies favouring growth and technological progress.

13 Thus, in its June 1996 report on employment the OECD's experts wrote that 'it is necessary to rethink the whole range of economic and social policies to facilitate the adaptation to the emerging modes of production and exchange'.

14 In Great Britain, the advocates of a reform of arbitration had thus estimated at several hundred million pounds the lost potential gains to the British balance of payments – and to the London practitioners – resulting from proposed legislation

which was perceived by their foreign colleagues as too restrictive and too expensive. These same people today admit quite freely that these figures, which were widely quoted in the press, were pure whimsy. This does not stop them from again brandishing these alarmist threats when the House of Lords is about to give its decision on the question of its right to adjudicate on 'security for costs' in an arbitration (D. Egan 'Splendid Isolation', *Legal Business*, May 1994).

REFERENCES

Abbot, A. (1988) *The System of the Professions: An Essay on the Division of Expert Labour*, Chicago: University of Chicago Press.

Abel-Smith, B. and R. Stevens (1967) *Lawyers and the Courts: A Sociological Study of the English Legal System, 1750–1965*, London: Heinemann.

Auerbach, J. (1976) *Unequal Justice: Lawyers and Social Change in Modern America*, Oxford: Oxford University Press.

Bancaud, A. and A. Boigeol (1995) 'A new judge for a new system of economic justice', in Y. Dezalay and D. Sugarman (eds) *Professional Competition and Professional Power*, London: Routledge.

Bauer, M. and B. Bertin Mourot (1994) *Les Enarques en entreprise: 30 ans de pantouflage*, Paris: CNRS-Boyden.

Birnbaum, P. (1977) *Les Sommets de l'Etat*, Paris: Seuil.

—— (1978) *La classe dirigeante française*, Paris: PUF.

Bourdieu, P. (1967) *Esquisse d'une théorie de la pratique*, Geneva: Droz.

—— (1987) 'The force of law: towards a sociology of the juridical field', *Hastings Journal of Law*, no. 38.

—— (1989) *La noblesse d'état*, Paris: Editions de Minuit.

Bourdieu, P. and M. de St Martin (1976) 'Le patronat', *Actes de la Recherche en Sciences Sociales*, nos. 20–1.

Bourdieu, P. and L. Wacquant (1992) *An Invitation to Reflexive Sociology*, Chicago: University of Chicago Press.

Charle, C. (1992) 'Les grands corps', in P. Nora (ed.) *Les lieux de mémoire, III, Les France*, Tome 2, Paris: NRF.

Dahrendorf, R. (1969) 'Law faculties and the German upper class', in W. Aubert (ed.) *Sociology of Law*, London: Penguin.

Damamme, D. (1987) 'Genèse sociale d'une institution scolaire: l'Ecole Libre des Sciences Politiques', *Actes de la Recherche en Sciences Sociales*, no. 70.

Dezalay, Y. (1992) *Marchands de droit: L'expansion du 'modèle américain' et la construction d'un ordre juridique transnational*, Paris: Fayard.

—— (1993a) 'Professional competition and the social construction of transnational regulatory expertise', in J. McCahery, S. Picciotto and C. Scott (eds) *Corporate Control and Accountability*, Oxford: Oxford University Press.

—— (1993b) 'Des notables aux conglomérats d'expertise: Esquisse d'une sociologie du 'big bang' juridico-financier', *Revue d'Economie Financière*, no. 25.

—— (1993c) 'Multinationales de l'expertise et "dépérissement de l'Etat" ', *Actes de la Recherche en Sciences Sociales*, nos. 96–7.

—— (1995a) ' "Turf battles" or "class struggles": the internationalisation of the market for expertise in the "professional society" ' *Accounting, Organizations and Society*, 20 (5): 331–44.

—— (1995b) 'Technological warfare: the battle to control the mergers and acquisitions market in Europe', in Y. Dezalay and D. Sugarman (eds) *Professional Competition and Professional Power*, London: Routledge.

—— (1996), 'Between the state, law and the market: the social and professional stakes and definition of a regulatory arena', in W. Bratton, J. McCahery, S. Picciotto and

C. Scott, *International Regulatory Competition and Coordination: Perspectives on Economic Regulation in Europe and the United States*, Oxford: Oxford University Press.

Dezalay, Y. and B. Garth (1995) 'Merchants of law as moral entrepreneurs: constructing international justice out of the competition for transnational business disputes', *Law & Society Review*, 29 (1).

—— (1996a) *Dealing in Virtue: International Commercial Arbitration and the Emergence of a New International Legal Order*, Chicago: University of Chicago Press.

—— (1996b), 'Building the law and putting the state into play: international strategies among Mexico's divided elite', *American Bar Foundation Working Paper no. 9509*, Chicago: American Bar Foundation.

Dezalay, Y. and D. Trubek (1993) 'Global restructuring and the law: the internationalisation of legal fields and the creation of transnational arenas', Paper presented to the National Assembly on the Future of the Legal Profession, Case Western Law School, June 1993.

Eisler, K. (1991) *Shark Tank*, New York: Penguin.

Falcao J. (1979) 'Lawyers in Brazil: ideals and praxis', *International Journal of the Sociology of Law* 7: 355–75.

—— (1988) 'Lawyers in Brazil', in R. Abel and P. Lewis (eds) *Lawyers in Society*, Vol. 2: *The Civil World*, Berkeley: University of California Press.

Gordon, R. (1984) 'The ideal and the actual in the law: fantasies and practices of New York City lawyers, 1870–1910', in G. Gawalt (ed.) *The New High Priests: Lawyers in Post-Civil War America*, Westport: Greenwood Press.

Grémion, P. (1974) 'La concertation', in M. Crozier (ed.) *Où va l'administration française?*, Paris: SEDEIS.

Granovetter, M. (1985) 'Economic action and social structure: the problem of embededdness', *American Journal of Sociology* 91: 481–510.

Hall, P. (1986) *Governing the Economy: The Politics of State Intervention in Britain and France*, Oxford: Oxford University Press.

Karpik, L. (1995) *Les avocats*, Paris: Gallimard.

Lederman, L. (1992) *Tombstones: A Lawyer's Tales from the Takeover Decade*, New York: Farrar, Strauss and Giroux.

Le Van Lemesle, L. (1983) 'L'économie politique à la conquête d'une légitimité (1896/1937)', *Actes de la Recherche en Sciences Sociales*, nos. 47–8.

Lewis, M. (1989) *Liar's Poker: Two Cities, True Greed*, London: Hodder and Stoughton.

Macaulay, S. (1963) 'Non-contractual relations in business', *American Sociological Review* 28 (1).

McCraw, T. (1984) *Prophets of Regulation*, Cambridge, Mass.: Harvard University Press.

Mamou, Y. (1987) *Une machine de pouvoir: La Direction du Trésor*, Paris: La Découverte.

Marceau, J. (1989) 'France', in T. Bottomore and R. Brym (eds) *The Capitalist Class: An International Study*, New York: New York University Press.

Nelken, D. (1996) 'The judges and political corruption in Italy', *Journal of Law and Society* 23 (1); 95–113.

Perdomo, R. (1981) 'Jurists in Venezuelan history', in C.J. Dias *et al.* (eds) *Lawyers in the Third World: A Comparative and Developmental Perspective*, New York: International Centre for Law in Development.

—— (1988) 'The Venezuelan legal profession: lawyers in an inegalitarian society', in R. Abel and P. Lewis (eds) *Lawyers in Society*, Vol. 2: *The Civil World*, Berkeley: University of California Press.

Perkin, H. (1989) *The Rise of Professional Society: England since 1880*, London: Routledge.

Ring, J. and D. Frantz (1992) *A Full Service Bank*, New York: Simon and Shuster.
Sassen, S. (1991) *The Global City*, Princeton, N.J.: Princeton University Press.
Sklar, M.J. (1988) *The Corporate Reconstruction of American Capitalism, 1890–1916: The Market, the Law and Politics*, Cambridge: Cambridge University Press.
Spangler, E. (1986) *Lawyers for Hire*, New Haven: Yale University Press.
Stewart, J. (1991) *Den of Thieves*, New York: Simon and Shuster.
Strange, S. (1986) *Casino Capitalism*, Oxford: Blackwell.
Sugarman, D. (1993) 'Qui colonise l'autre? Réflexions historiques sur les rapports entre le droit, les juristes et les comptables en Grande Bretagne', in Y. Dezalay (ed.) *Batailles territoriales et querelles de cousinage: Juristes et Comptables européens sur le marché du droit des affaires*, Paris: LGDJ.
Trubek, D.M., Y. Dezalay, R. Buchanan and J.R. Davis (1994), 'Global restructuring and the law: studies of the internationalisation of legal fields and the creation of transnational arenas', *Case Western Law Review* 44 (2), Winter: 407–98.
Truell, P. and L. Gurwin (1992) *False Profits: The Inside Story of BCCI*, Boston: Houghton Mifflin.
Whitman, M. von N. (1984) 'Persistent unemployment: economic policy perspectives in US and Europe', in A. Pierre, *Unemployment and Growth in the Western Economies*, New York: Council on Foreign Relations.

11 Globalization, regionalism and the regulation of securities markets[1]

William D. Coleman and Geoffrey R. D. Underhill

INTRODUCTION

The complexities of the relationship between the growing number of regional economic agreements and associations, including European integration, and the process of global economic integration are not yet well understood in international political economy. Global markets, regional integration patterns and individual states are bound up in an intricate web of interrelationships which require painstaking analysis to unravel. As the EU is largely driven by political will, and is the most institutionalized and advanced among regional integration processes in the global economy, so it is in relation to Europe that this puzzle presents itself most persistently. 'Can regional patterns of market integration be looked at as a step down the road toward the increasing globalization of the international political economy, or is a world of closed economic blocs emerging?' (Stubbs and Underhill 1994: 331).

Differing conceptions of European integration, from 'Fortress Europe' to a liberal market model fully integrated with the global economy, would appear to provide distinct answers to this question. The fortress model is often coupled with ideas of resurgent economic nationalism in an era characterized by declining American willingness and capacity to underpin a liberal international economic order (Gilpin 1987). The 'Triad' economies of Europe, Japan and the US are conceived as being involved in increasingly 'head-to-head' economic competition (Thurow 1993). Other literature (Busch and Milner 1994; Milner 1988) argues that the rise of economic nationalism, whether through regional organizations or traditional nation-states, is an unlikely outcome. In examining the policy options of states and the preferences of economic actors and their representative associations, these authors postulate that regional economic associations or integration processes such as the EU, North American Free Trade Agreement (NAFTA), or Asia-Pacific Economic Co-operation forum (APEC) are compatible with globalization (Busch and Milner 1994). Indeed, they cannot be well understand without considering globalizing factors. Through FDI and other financial flows, trade, and the production strategies of firms, there are important and developing *inter*-regional linkages among the major regional integration processes.

Of course, there are also more developed patterns which are *intra*-regional. Although these integration processes at national, regional, and global levels are ongoing, simultaneous and compatible over time, they still face obstacles internally and pose contradictions from time to time across levels.

The dichotomy between 'fortress' and 'globalization' is therefore an inappropriate oversimplification. That there should be conflict as these parallel regional and global processes take place is not surprising. That this conflict should express itself through the political institutions of states and the EU is even less surprising. Both globalization and regional integration entail an intensification of competition and force on citizens, firms and states a process of economic adjustment in which winners and losers are starkly defined. Changes in economic structure are accompanied by various forms of legal and regulatory change; change that will make winners of some and losers of others. Accordingly, political resources are spent attempting to affect the outcomes of these changes. But even this political game is a complex one. Many of the most powerful economic agents are simultaneously active at domestic, regional and global levels, particularly in the domain of financial markets. A battle lost in one domain might be recouped in another. If the various markets these firms are involved in are difficult to separate, these firms might also work towards regulatory change that will bring elements of convergence across markets. Such change is also bound to create considerable tension across national, regional, and global space as the question arises: who will converge on whom?

This chapter examines political conflict arising from the interaction of domestic, regional and global levels of governance in the process of regulatory adaptation in securities markets. The chapter suggests that a limited process of international regulatory convergence has been taking place, with the key evidence coming from the agreements reached within the EU and from the results of 'global' international co-operative processes taking place under the auspices of the International Organization of Securities Commissions (IOSCO) and the Basle Committee on Banking Supervision (Basle Committee). We demonstrate that this process of convergence necessarily involves elements of regulatory competition between states and regions, occasioning some open political conflict (McCahery *et al.*, 1996). State regulatory agencies and their traditional market constituencies face difficult choices in bargaining on these issues. Tension has been particularly high between the EU and the US, as the dynamics of the emerging European Single Financial Area have allowed the Europeans to flex new-found political muscle.

THE ARGUMENT

Beginning in the mid-1980s, a previously insignificant body, IOSCO, became increasingly the vehicle for promoting international agreement on a more harmonized set of rules at the domestic level. The IOSCO discussions were joined by a parallel process centred on the Basle Committee on Banking Supervision which had begun to look at the question of banks' risks from their rising levels of securities business. The resulting regime has come to supplant more and more the existing private or self-regulatory arrangements and to favour the harmonization of domestic state regulation (Porter 1993).

Coincident with the emergence of a nascent interstate regime on a global level, the European Union began its single market initiative. In the area of financial services, it was postulated that this initiative would require new directives in banking and in investment services. A second banking co-ordination directive and accompanying directives on own funds and solvency were agreed to in 1989. These agreements gave additional impetus to the idea of an investment services directive that would provide non-bank securities firms with the same European passport that would be available to banks (Underhill 1997a). The Investment Services Directive (ISD, European Communities 1993b) and its associated Capital Adequacy Directive (CAD, European Communities 1993a) were a long time coming, with final agreement not accomplished until early 1993 (Brown 1997).

The EU process should, however, be distinguished from the globalization process. The EU's programme was a deliberate exercise of political will to carry the financial integration of domestic markets to more radical lengths than parallel global integration processes which occurred initially through the attempts of firms to avoid national regulatory jurisdictions. In fact, the EU programme of market integration has often been explained as an attempt to take better advantage of global transformations, and to promote an efficient process of capital formation and a competitive European financial services sector well adapted to the exigencies of global competition.[2]

The coincidence of these two financial integration processes raises a number of important issues. First, what is the relationship between the first steps towards a global interstate regime for regulating securities and the definition of a regional European regime for securities markets? Are the two processes compatible? Or will the development of a single European financial market slow down developments towards a global order? Second, how have key European states dealt simultaneously with EU and global attempts at regulatory co-operation? Have their policy strategies assumed compatibility or conflict between the two instances of regulatory co-operation? Third, what constraints has the global process of regulatory and supervisory co-operation placed on the drafting of EU directives? In turn, what effects has the EU legislation had on global patterns of co-operation? In short, drawing on a case study of governance of securities markets, this chapter examines linkages between national, regional and global policy-making.

In his study of securities regulation in Britain, Japan and the US, Michael Moran (1991) notes that policy had traditionally followed a private, self-regulatory, corporatist path. With the onset of internationalization and the accompanying opening up of domestic securities markets, this self-regulation came under sustained pressure. Self-regulatory regimes often masked cartel arrangements among a set of domestic firms. Complex systems of interest intermediation underpinned these contrasting domestic regulatory arrangements (Coleman 1996). They also functioned on the basis of informal understandings and mutual trust that were difficult to sustain once foreign firms crashed the party. Policy-makers had to take a more direct interest in supervisory and regulatory policy. Policy systems in the Anglo-American democracies and Japan were shifted from pure, private self-regulation to a more strongly state-supervised self-regulation (Moran 1991; Coleman 1994). Moran describes these changes as a 'revolution in regulation' involving the reconstruction of corporatist self-regulation along similar lines in different economies. Common to all countries was a codification of rules governing the markets, an increased penetration of law into the regulatory system, and a more prominent role for formally constituted organizations, both public and private (Moran 1991: 13).

Moran adds that understanding this convergence requires a close look at the role of the US. US institutions, particularly the Securities and Exchanges Commission (SEC), have been the main agents diffusing an approach to regulation that emphasizes codified rule-making, statutory development and strong state oversight. The US regulatory culture supports a more intensive oversight of markets by the judiciary and by the national legislature (the Congress). It also favours a formal approach to rule-making, enforcement and discipline, often relying on legal prosecutions to accomplish its ends. In the US view, markets should be transparent, trading should be concentrated on markets that provide investors with the maximum of information, and dealing on the basis of 'insider' information is anathema (McCahery 1997).

We argue that the processes of globalization of financial markets and the erection of a single market in securities for European financial services firms have brought some convergence on the US style of securities regulation. This finding supports Moran's own analysis of domestic changes in the US, the UK and Japan. In this sense, regional and global trends complement rather than contradict one another. This finding is not surprising given that the major firms in US, Japanese and EU markets are largely the same transnational entities seeking to facilitate cross-border and cross-exchange dealing by reducing regulatory costs.

This 'convergence hypothesis', however, must be qualified in a number of respects. Although the regional process of regulatory change in Europe has followed, in part, the international lead developed at Basle, the EU's position on investment services has pre-empted a component of the IOSCO negotiations. This outcome has jeopardized co-operation between IOSCO, the Basle Committee and particularly the US. Because it has gone beyond the harmonization achieved to date internationally, the EU has solved some problems that had been intractable at the broader interstate level, particularly in IOSCO. In taking the lead, the EU has thrown down the gauntlet to the wider international community on defining the policy instrument of capital adequacy for securities market risk in particular. The EU definition poses a challenge for the American Securities and Exchange Commission's long-standing approach to safety and soundness in the markets. To complicate matters, the Basle Committee at the global level has since moved the supervision of bank securities business in the direction of the EU's standards. The US banking supervisor, the Federal Reserve Board, has accepted this and is therefore at odds with the US securities regulator, the SEC.

One cannot therefore think of 'convergence' as a one-way adjustment of EU and other national regulatory systems towards the US position. Convergence, as the analysis of capital adequacy harmonization illustrates below, is at least a two-way street with increasingly complex patterns of traffic flows. Despite the convergence which has undoubtedly taken place towards a more US-style juridified and institutionalized regulatory system, other factors come into play which mean that the global, regional, and domestic levels often present disjointed regulatory standards in what are undoubtedly markets undergoing a rapid process of integration.

First, the desegmentation of traditional barriers between the banking and securities sectors on a global basis, combined with the breakdown of barriers between national financial markets, have led to a more market-oriented order with greater emphasis on competition among the formerly discrete sectors of activity. This 're-regulation' (Cerny 1993: 51–2) to ensure adequate supervision and fair terms of competition in itself contributes to an 'attenuation of institutional differences' (Bliman *et al.* 1993: 185) among financial systems and their regulatory organs. US and other authorities alike find themselves constrained by this dynamic, resulting in a degree of pulling and tugging among national regulatory systems and standards.

Second, there was an independent intra-EU dynamic at work which was just as important as pressures for convergence towards the US. EU members, of course, had to co-operate to achieve common prudential and regulatory standards, but EU financial policy communities were none the less competing among themselves for European (and global) market share: the European exchanges sought 'primarily to retain trading in their own domestic securities' and also 'to attract listings of non-domestic stocks, and most of all US and Japanese equities . . . [so as] to be a vital part of an effective concentration of financial services in its own capital' (Knight *et al.* 1993: 166–7). Internal EU bargaining, therefore, did not always take place with reference to the US position.

This means that, third, the temptations of global 'regulatory arbitrage' also come into play. Firms seek to migrate to jurisdictions where regulatory and prudential standards, while not necessarily lax, do not impose undue costs on securities operations, which are notorious for their narrow margins. The EU (and especially London as the major marketplace) showed some willingness to play this game by implementing less costly capital standards, thereby halting convergence towards US policy on capital adequacy somewhat.

Finally, domestic-level traditions and processes, as they bear upon policy goals, content and instruments, do not dissolve as a result of either globalization or European financial integration. Despite the political dynamic wherein firms and their associations will put pressure on regulators to move in the desired direction, state regulatory agencies do not always respond and will seek to defend their own regulatory turf, even if this puts them at odds with 'global' regulatory trends. This has been the case for the US SEC, which to start with is accountable to the American Congress. The SEC has furthermore regarded its market as retaining a significant role for the small private investor[3] and thus places a high priority on investor protection (as opposed to competitiveness issues) with regard to capital adequacy (GAO 1992: 44–51). Even though the SEC's counterpart in terms of banking supervision, the Federal Reserve Board, has joined the global trend, the SEC still resists acceptance of common standards in IOSCO. In the light of such distinctive concerns, conflict will be inherent as financial interdependence drives regulatory authorities to increased levels of co-operation.

In sum, Moran is correct when it comes to convergence of policy style: more codified, institutionalized and juridified forms of regulation and prudential supervision of the sort applied by the US since the Depression. But when it comes to the adoption of internationally accepted minimum standards, the outcome is far from obvious. The American SEC has sought to gain broad acceptance of its methods and standards, with greater success on some issues than on others. On the question of capital adequacy, the US now faces the prospect of being forced to converge to the EU-Basle standards on market risk for securities dealers and bank securities trading-book activities (Underhill 1997b).

This argument is developed in the following steps. The next part of the chapter examines the process of 'globalization' with respect to the securities industry. The fourth section traces the development of the EU's investment services directive (ISD) and capital adequacy directives (CAD). The complex and overlapping tugs of war involving universal banking traditions versus investment banking traditions, on the one hand, and 'Club Med' or Roman Law countries versus the self-regulatory 'Old Boys' Club', on the other, will be illustrated. We show that these directives move Europe closer to the US regulatory model (particularly on issues regarding market transparency and fraud), occasioning in the process significant domestic changes in member countries. The fifth section then examines the developments taking place at IOSCO and their relationship to EU developments, which includes co-operation between the Basle Committee and IOSCO negotiators. In this case co-operation has been more difficult. The position adopted by the EU on capital adequacy has proved anathema to the SEC. Agreement on global capital adequacy standards has subsequently been impossible for IOSCO, but the Basle Committee has now accepted the controversial EU position. If there is to be further convergence, it will involve the US moving towards the EU position, not the other way around.

GLOBALIZATION AND SECURITIES MARKETS

The globalization of securities markets and corresponding regulatory trends are complex processes and hence require preliminary explanation. This complexity derives first of all from the remarkable range of securities markets to be found. They include markets for the creation of new debt or equity securities, an activity often termed primary market operations or investment banking. Debt securities may be short term, ranging from a few days to a year, and these are sold on money markets. Longer-term securities such as bonds are sold on capital markets. In addition, securities which have already been issued are purchased and resold on secondary markets, with firms acting as principals (taking positions in the name of the securities firms) or as market makers (standing ready to quote prices for purchases and sales of a given security – OECD 1987: 8). Still another activity involves the organizing and managing of groups of individual securities that are offered to the public and traded as single investment shares. These instruments take various forms and include mutual funds, unit trusts or investment trusts. They may include money market securities, capital market securities or equities.

Over the past two decades, new types of securities have also appeared on primary, secondary and collective investment markets. The more globalized financial system that emerged with the abandonment of the Bretton Woods System significantly increased the volatility in foreign exchange markets, in interest rates, and in equity and commodity prices. In response to this volatility, financial services firms developed derivatives, 'financial instruments that derive their value from that of an underlying asset or index' (Steinherr 1994: 14). These new instruments – futures, forward contracts, options, swaps – have commodified the risk of price changes in foreign currencies, interest rates, equities and commodities. Derivatives permit investors to change the risk characteristics of securities, allowing them to pursue the most advantageous investment or borrowing opportunities. As a recent IMF study notes, 'the new instruments and techniques permit the separation and unbundling of risk, the pricing of its separate components (credit risk, liquidity risk, market risk), and the redistribution of risk to those best able to manage it' (IMF 1994: 1).

Given, then, this range of securities instruments and how they are marketed, globalization of securities refers to a series of related changes to these market structures. First, international markets in securities have grown up alongside traditional domestic markets. There has been a spectacular growth in foreign exchange transactions in all major financial centres with the collapse of the fixed exchange rate monetary system. During the 1970s and 1980s, 'Eurobonds' (bonds issued in a currency other than the domestic currency of the borrower, usually in several foreign centres) became major competitors to domestic and conventional foreign bonds in many financial centres. In 1991, Eurobonds or 'global bonds' accounted for 5 per cent of all international bonds. By 1995, this figure had more than doubled to 11.1 per

cent (OECD 1996: 68). The same period saw the development of international markets in short-term securities or 'Euro-notes'. 'Cross-border'
trades in equities (a firm's stocks are purchased on the firm's local stock
exchange by foreigners) have grown importantly over the past two decades. In
1990, 11.8 per cent of all equity trading was in cross-border equities (Howell
and Cozzini 1991: 25). In addition, 'cross-exchange' trading occurs (a firm's
stocks are purchased on foreign exchanges) in many locations, with the most
important being SEAQ International in London. Cross-exchange trading has
grown by a factor of eight since 1986. When cross-exchange trading is combined with cross-border equity markets, we find that they account for 17.7 per
cent of all trading in 1990 (Howell and Cozzini 1991: 24–5). Growth has
continued in the 1990s. In 1991, international equities were valued at 23.4
billion dollars; five years later the figure had risen to 41 billion dollars
(OECD 1996: 74). Finally, growth in derivatives has been spectacular, with
the notional value quintupling from an already high $7,198 billion in 1989 to
$17,463 billion in 1992 (GAO 1994: 35).

Second, spurred in part by the growth of such international markets and in
part by the availability of suitable information technology, domestic money
and capital markets have become much more closely integrated with each
other. Crises in one domestic market now have much more immediate effects
in other markets. The combination of these first two changes – the emergence
of new international markets and the growing interdependence of domestic
markets – has produced a third change that is a dimension of globalization.
National policy-makers have acted to 'deregulate' domestic securities markets, breaking up long-standing domestic oligopolies, and admitting foreign
firms to compete on national treatment terms, and 'desegmenting' financial
services firms or sectors once clearly divided between banking and securities
activities.

Each aspect of 'globalization' (see below) has increased competition,
raised the degree of risk faced by financial services firms, and added a measure of instability to securities markets. Not surprisingly, this process of internationalization has brought important changes to the way in which securities
are regulated at both the national and international levels. As Porter (1993:
ch. 4) has hypothesized, an increasing level of atomistic competition in both
domestic and international markets has favoured the development and
strengthening of an interstate regime for regulating securities. This interstate
regime necessarily overlaps with regulatory change in the EU single market
for financial services and the domestic financial reform efforts of individual
states. The remainder of the chapter analyses this set of interrelationships.

THE SINGLE MARKET AND INVESTMENT SERVICES

The Second Credit Co-ordinating Directive adopted in 1989 marked a victory
for the universal bank concept.[4] The Directive provided a list of the activities
in which credit institutions might engage and which would be recognized as

legitimate by all Community members. These activities included, among others, participation in the issuing of securities, in portfolio management and investment advisory services, and in the safekeeping of securities. Admittedly, these activities do not cover all investment services, but they do embrace what is normally understood to be the core of the securities business. Accordingly, it was clear that when the Single Market provisions took full effect, banks would receive a passport to engage in key investment services throughout the Community.

From the perspective of non-bank investment firms, the Second Credit Directive heightened the need to agree on another directive that would provide them with their own European passport. Otherwise, they would be in a weakened competitive position *vis-à-vis* universal banks. The push for a European passport for investment firms, however, quickly raised several fundamental issues that also stood in the way of harmonizing securities regulation in the global context: different regulatory cultures between investment firms and universal banks, the relative transparency of markets including the place of regulated versus over-the-counter (OTC) markets, and the respective roles of state and self-regulatory bodies. The European discussions thus provided a second forum for issues that had arisen in the global context. In the end, by resolving some of these issues, the European solutions have had a decided impact on global developments.

Investment firms versus universal banks

Non-bank investment firms and banks have traditionally operated in two, quite distinct regulatory worlds. We can begin to understand these differences by examining the basic concept of capital adequacy. Capital adequacy refers to a test performed by a regulator to determine whether the financial resources available to a firm are at least equal to a calculated total. This total takes into account the risks to which the business is exposed at any given time. For banks, this determination has come to be based on a weighted evaluation of risks associated with different types of assets (mortgage loans, a claim on a government, corporate loans and so on), referred to as 'credit risk' (Porter 1993: 64–5). An international agreement in 1988 thus established a target standard ratio of capital to these risk-based assets. Behind this calculation was the central concern to provide safeguards for depositors' funds, a relatively liquid liability, and systemic stability for the emerging transnational banking system.

Capital adequacy for an investment firm takes different risk factors into account. The most important of these is 'market' or 'position' risk, i.e. risks associated with a firm's position in the market: changes in market prices may produce losses when firms come to sell securities they have been holding. There are two forms of market risk: 'specific risk' related to price levels of a specific security, and 'general' market risk related to the risk of an overall fall in the market. Other forms of risk include: settlement risk, counterparty risk, interest rate risk and exchange rate risk. Capital adequacy must take rather detailed account of the kinds of securities held and the particular set of risks associated with each. In addition, investor protection has come to extend well beyond capital adequacy to include issues such as market transparency, business conduct (fraud) rules on insider trading, marketing and advertising controls, the segregation of client money and investments from those of the firm, and investor compensation schemes.

Regulators for universal banks had not developed systems that took detailed account of securities risks. From the point of view of investment firms, if banks could continue to be regulated in their traditional way, the 'playing field' would not be level. The problem was becoming more acute as the 'securitization' of bank activities meant they were increasingly devoting their energies to securities markets. Banks would be able to operate under the apparently 'looser' regime of the Second Credit Directive (*Financial Regulation Report* (*FRR*), February 1990). In contrast, universal banking countries like Germany strongly resisted the idea that their banks' securities activities should be governed by the ISD and the CAD. German banking leaders viewed this proposal as a direct attack on the universal bank structure in favour of specialized and autonomous securities subsidiaries such as those in Britain (Arnold 1989: 14). They preferred that the banking policy be extended to investment firms, an idea the latter resisted fearing higher overall capital levels and therefore higher transaction costs in a low-margin business.

The resolution of this dispute took over two years, with the eventual accord bringing the universal bank countries closer to the Anglo-American approach to regulation, wherein banks and securities houses are regulated on a separate basis. The CAD defines the concept of a 'trading book' which includes holdings in transferable securities, units in collective investment schemes, derivative products such as financial futures and options, and exposures due to securities lending, fees and commissions related to most securities transactions (*FRR*, July 1992: 2–4). Not only investment firms, but also banks whose securities business thus defined accounts for more than 5 per cent of their business, would be required to maintain a trading book. A capital adequacy test based on traditional securities definitions of risks would then be applied to the trading books of banks and securities firms alike. Accompanying this approach to capital adequacy were other well-established procedures for investment firms that would now also be applied to banks' trading book activities: administrative and accounting procedures, rules for the segregation of client funds from those of the firm, and various business conduct rules relating to market transparency.[5] Convergence towards the US position on these latter issues (such as insider trading) was less controversial and parallel discussions had been under way in IOSCO for some time.[6]

Universal banks did not lose all the battles. First, in the final agreement on levels of capital required, the amounts were definitely higher than British firms were accustomed to. Hence, many investment firms would have to add core capital whereas banks generally have sufficient resources already. Second, the directive used the 'building block' approach to position risk proposed by the Germans, rather than a 'comprehensive' approach favoured by the US, the UK and Japan (*FRR*, November 1991: 9). This put the entire EU at variance with American practice, which eventually became significant for debate within IOSCO. Third, they sought and gained (eventual) access to securities exchanges previously closed to them. Finally, the ISD extends certain procedures common to banking regulation to securities firms, including the requirement that firms monitor and report large exposures to single clients, and supervision on a consolidated basis.

Regulated and transparent markets: Club Med versus the Old Boys' Club

In the autumn of 1990, France put forward a proposal, since named 'the concentration principle' that became a major sticking point in the ISD negotiations. The principle stated that member-states may require transactions relating to investment services to be carried out on a 'regulated market'. A 'regulated market' was a market in any of the instruments covered by the ISD (securities, money market instruments, financial futures, options, interest rate and exchange rate swaps, units of a collective investment fund) (European Communities 1993b). As such, the market is constituted and recognized by a member-state, functions regularly, has provisions governing the operation of the market, access and trading, and complies with ISD requirements on record-keeping, transparency and reporting (*FRR*, April 1991: 2). All the EU's main stock exchanges and financial derivatives exchanges would satisfy the requirement.

Member-states could invoke the principle if the investor were established in that member-state, if the investment firm carried out the transaction through an establishment in that member-state or on a cross-border basis, and if the trade was related to an instrument traded on a regulated market in the member-state. In addition, if a state were to invoke the principle, it had to permit the investor the right to authorize an investment firm to trade instruments off-exchange and the member-state could not prevent an investor from obtaining an investment service from a firm situated outside that state.

Cutting through these technicalities, the effect of the application of the principle would be to restrict significantly the amount of securities trading that could take place 'off-exchange' or 'over the counter'. Germany and Britain had the most to lose from adoption of the principle because significant proportions of securities dealing in both countries have taken place outside the established stock exchanges. Based on early versions of the principle as developed by France, it was also possible that the highly successful London screen-based system, SEAQ International, would not qualify as a regulated market.

France, with strong support from Italy, Spain, Belgium, Portugal and Greece (quickly branded 'Club Med' in Brussels), offered three reasons in support of its positions. First, the principle would reinforce the transparency and security of transactions; securities markets work best when they are highly liquid.[7] Second, the principle increases the capability of markets to offer sound investor protection. Finally, France argued that the principle would provide key support to two other securities directives already approved – one on insider trading and the other on take-overs.

Behind these reasons, one finds a deep-seated concern about the future of domestic financial markets in the Club Med states. They had already witnessed the migration of significant amounts of securities business to London, with its less regulated, off-exchange markets like SEAQ International. They feared that without some intervention their own markets might dry up in favour of London.

Britain, Germany, the Netherlands and Ireland mounted a stout attack on the concentration principle. This 'Old Boys' Club' argued that off-exchange dealing promoted competition between exchange products and those sold over the counter. It enabled deals to be tailor-made to investors, and it constituted a kind of research and development laboratory for new products. These countries added that professional investors tended to make most use of off-exchange markets and they were less in need of investor protection measures. They concluded by noting that if the Community restricted off-exchange trading, given existing technology, it would simply move to another site and all of Europe would be a loser (*FRR*, April 1991: 3).

Complementing the concentration principle, France also called on all regulated markets to provide a minimum level of price transparency. Investors had to have a clear picture of market prices so that they could assess the prices at which they were trading. Again this proposal constituted a frontal attack on British securities markets. On UK domestic equity markets, prices of large trades are published only ninety minutes after they have taken place so that market makers have time to reduce their exposure. On SEAQ International, trade details are not published at all: 'the large investors who use this professional marketplace prefer it that way, the London Stock Exchange says' (*FRR*, June 1991: 12).

The Club Med countries achieved a significant victory when a final version of the ISD was approved. The concentration principle, as articulated by the French in the autumn of 1990, appeared virtually unchanged in article 14. The only concession to the Old Boys' Club appeared in the opt-out clause where it said that member-states authorizing an investor to opt out had to take into account 'investors' differing needs for protection and in particular the ability of professional and institutional investors to act in their own best interests'. The article added that authorization must be given under conditions that 'do not jeopardize the prompt execution of investors' orders' (European Communities 1993b).

Article 21 also contained a significant commitment to market transparency by providing for regular publication of prices in all regulated markets. Investors will be able to know high and low prices, and aggregate volumes and prices of trades. These are to be reported at the start of trading and on a rolling basis throughout the course of the day. Similar provisions were to apply to 'quote driven' or 'order driven' markets – that is, to off-exchange markets such as those in the UK. One significant concession to the British was for the possible reduction in these requirements in circumstances where the relevant trade is exceptionally large in the context of the particular stock as traded on the market in question. Despite this concession, it was evident that regulated, transparent markets would be the instrument of choice when the ISD came into effect in 1996.

Placed in the broader international context, these policies on regulated markets and price transparency move European securities policy closer to the US approach. The French position illustrates how internal EU dynamics were important, and probably derived some benefit by being closer to the US position in a long-standing US–UK debate over the role of the state and the importance of market regulation in securities. Price transparency and careful regulation of markets have been long-standing pillars of US securities policy. None the less, it remains difficult to assess the impact of these measures in the longer run. By early 1996 only three EU countries had actually managed to implement the directive, and important barriers to market integration remained (*FRR*, January/February 1996: 17–18). A number of EU countries were undoubtedly uncomfortable with the free-wheeling model of market globalization represented by the UK position, and some have even argued that the concentration and transparency clauses in the ISD are likely to be employed as effective instruments of protectionism (*FRR*, March 1996: 2–4).

An enhanced role for the state

When the ISD and the CAD are placed in the context of other securities initiatives of the Community over the past fifteen years, the implications for the role of the state become clear. Together, these initiatives have pushed member-states to reconsider and to reorganize how they regulate securities. For a country like Germany, where domestic reform had been slow in coming (Moran 1992), the organizational changes required were sufficiently wide-ranging that it insisted on an implementation date of 1996 for the ISD and the CAD rather than 1993, and others had similar sorts of temporary deroga-tions. For most of the continental European countries, the CAD brought a completely new approach to measuring capital adequacy and to assessing risk. This approach will require investment firms and banks to differentiate among different types of market risk and to report to supervisory bodies on capital holdings matched to these risks. The ISD adds several reporting requirements related to price transparency, rules of conduct, prudential rules, consolidated operations and large exposures. These directives join the Insider Trading Directive that had already forced some reconsideration of domestic regulatory policy in many member countries. Finally, 1990 marked the com-ing into effect of three directives that sought to establish an EU-wide information policy on securities by co-ordinating a number of rules relating specifically to securities that have been admitted to official stock exchange listing or where admission is being requested.[8]

All these EU policies have pushed member-states towards a more statutory and codified system of securities regulation, as Moran anticipated in his study. The state, rather than private self-regulatory bodies, is called upon to play the lead role. Article 22 of the ISD defines 'authorities' as 'either public authorities, bodies recognized by national law or bodies recognized by public authorities expressly empowered for that purpose by national law'. We illustrate this point briefly by looking at two member-states – France and Germany.

In France, legislative and regulatory changes moved the country much closer to the US model and set the stage for its championing of the concentration principle and increased market transparency. The changes began with stock exchange reform that abolished the monopoly held by recognized brokers or *agents de change* and changed their status to private commercial companies or stock exchange firms (*sociétés de bourse*). As commercial companies, the new stock exchange firms were able to open their ownership to other financial services firms. By the end of 1990, close to 80 per cent of the firms were owned by banks with insurance companies taking over some others. Very few independent companies remained.[9]

The Stock Exchange Reform Act of 1988 also changed the approach to regulation and supervision from the *tutelle juridique* of the Trésor, to the state-supervised self-regulatory approach found in the Anglo-American countries. A new body, the Stock Exchange Council (Conseil des Bourses de Valeurs), composed primarily of stock exchange firms plus a representative of the Trésor, was given the tasks of setting up the general rules for the functioning of the market, of accepting securities for the market, of licensing stock exchange firms, and of disciplining firms and their employees (Jurgensen and Lebègue 1988: 150). A second body, the Stock Exchanges Corporation (Société des Bourses Françaises), owned by stock exchange firms, received responsibilities for implementing the regulations and for managing the market.

Finally, the authorities renewed the structure of the Stock Exchange Commission (Commission des Opérations de Bourse), pushing it somewhat in the direction of the SEC model. First, the Commission was granted a measure of independence not common in the French government;[10] the National Assembly even removed from its board the government commissioner who represented the finance ministry. The president was guaranteed a single six-year term.[11] Second, the Commission was granted some rule-making powers, while having its disciplining functions reinforced.

Reforms in Germany came several years later and were triggered largely by the emerging EU policies. The first important reform was the founding in 1989 of the German futures and options exchange, DTB. As Moran (1992: 147) notes, by German standards, the exchange was an extraordinary innovation. Not only was it fully computerized, but also it broke with the principle of regional stock exchanges and operated country-wide. The centralization process continued with the founding of a national securities data centre and the merger of the local clearing systems into the Deutscher Kassenverein.

With a prospective agreement on the ISD and the CAD looming and the Insider Trading Directive already in place, the German federal government pushed the reform process further with the publication of the finance minister's policy paper, *Konzept Finanzplatz Deutschland* in January 1992. This paper set out a clear strategy of action for the building of an internationally competitive financial centre in Frankfurt. The paper was followed by the privatization of the Frankfurt exchange and its re-emergence as a national stock exchange, the Deutsche Börse AG, jointly owned by the banks, the regional stock exchanges and the stock exchange brokers.

The minister's paper also noted the inadequacy of current regulatory arrangements (italics in original text).

A mere legal supervision of stock exchanges, as now performed at the regional level, is no longer satisfactory. There must be market supervision, as in most leading international financial centres ... Supervision must therefore include a number of regulations taken from outside the strict limits of the stock exchange, such as the EC guidelines on matters of insider trading and publicity. The question of whether and with which content the EC Investment Services Directive is adopted will be decisive for the area of supervising authorities' competence.[12]

Translation of the paper into policy came through a second *Finanzförderungsgesetz* which was discussed and debated in 1993.

Perhaps the most important proposal in the law was for the establishment of a central, federal securities supervisory agency, the Bundesaufsichtsamt für das Wertpapierhandel. The new agency receives responsibility for supervising insider trading, monitoring publicity of information on transactions of significant shareholders of listed firms, defining and monitoring rules of conduct, and collaborating in the international sphere with other national agencies (Gammerdinger 1993; Lütz 1996). The same legislation extends the legal and market supervisory responsibilities of the *Länder* and links these with the new federal agency. Finally, the legislation directs the stock exchanges to become more professional self-regulatory bodies. They are required to set up an autonomous division to oversee trading and business settlement and to take on professional management staff (Gammerdinger 1993).

In short, even in a system where universal banking had treated securities as an integral concept of banking and where banks dominated securities exchanges, the international model based on the US approach could not be resisted. By 1996, Germany had a more codified, institutionalized and juridified system of securities regulation. The state will be playing a stronger oversight role at both the federal and *Land* levels (Coleman 1996; Lütz 1996). And

Germany has its own SEC-like agency to deal with harmonization issues on the EU and international levels.

INTERNATIONAL REGULATORY CO-OPERATION: IOSCO, BASLE AND US–EU TENSIONS

Co-operation among national securities regulators is a relatively recent phenomenon. Historically, securities markets have been either local or national in scope with little in the way of transnational activity. The securitization of banking activities and the emergence of cross-border and cross-exchange dealing changed this pattern substantially. It gradually became clear that no one national regulator could cope with the demands of prudential supervision in the rapidly growing transnational markets. Pressure from the industry and others mounted to deal with the new regulatory issues. IOSCO was founded in 1984 and by 1986 had been pushed to resolve international regulatory problems (Guy 1992: 291).

IOSCO's members are the official national securities regulators responsible for their respective markets. As a club of regulators, it considers itself a non-governmental international organization;[13] membership at the end of 1992 was 102 (IOSCO 1992a) including 'associate' and 'affiliate' members. Associate membership caters to countries with more than one securities regulator, as in federal jurisdictions, but each country is only allowed one vote. Affiliate members are self-regulatory agencies or trade associations with self-regulatory responsibilities. They do not vote but their involvement is considered crucial to the success of the organization.

The key aspect of IOSCO's structure for our purposes is its committee organization. The membership is split into the Development Committee (members representing countries with so-called 'emerging markets', including those in the former East Bloc) and the Technical Committee on International Transactions, which consists only of members from 'the most developed markets' (Guy 1992: 293). The Technical Committee is the most important body in the organization when it comes to international regulatory and supervisory co-operation.

The organization seeks to obtain co-operation among members in promoting and establishing regulatory standards in order to facilitate international securities transactions, including mutual assistance, surveillance, and enforcement of standards so as to ensure the integrity of the markets. The overall aim is to provide 'the benefits derived at the domestic level' on a global scale (IOSCO 1991). The organization's main objective has been the removal of regulatory and other barriers to the enforcement of standards, which necessarily involves a degree of harmonization across regulatory boundaries. To these ends, the Technical Committee established four working groups. Each addresses an issue of importance to the objectives of the organization, with particular emphasis on examining 'impediments to international transactions and [proposing] ways of eliminating these impediments' (Guy

1992: 294). The working groups were: (1) Multinational Disclosure and Accounting Standards; (2) Regulation of Secondary Markets; (3) Regulation of Market Intermediaries; (4) Enforcement and the Exchange of Information; a fifth working party on Investment Management was established later (IOSCO 1992a: 8, 18).[14] In addition, the organization has worked on facilitating international equity offers through the harmonization of information requirements and prospectuses.

Working Parties 1 and 4 have proved relatively uncontroversial, but such cannot be said about the other two. For our purposes, the Working Party on Market Intermediaries is the most crucial. The supervision of financial conglomerates has received considerable attention and there has been a large measure of agreement since the London annual conference of 1992 (IOSCO 1992b). This consensus matches the efforts of the Basle supervisors in the banking sector. More contentious, however, has been the definition of capital adequacy for firms operating across jurisdictional boundaries. Behind the mild rhetoric of the 1992 Annual Report lies a severe blockage between the US Securities and Exchange Commission and the EU. The global convergence pressures have come face to face with regional interests.

The important players in this drama are the SEC, the EU (under pressure from France and the UK) and the Basle Committee banking supervisors, with Japan making important contributions periodically. Underlying the situation were different regional market structures. The London market is a wholesale market; most of the operators are subsidiaries or branches and they have a sound and more tightly regulated parent in the background. In a wholesale market large institutions with sound market and risk information place orders with broker-dealers and have little need of protection. The regulator therefore worries more about systemic failure brought about by the collapse of a major player. In contrast, the US market is a market with a substantial presence of small investors, and so customer protection is a primary objective.[15]

What is surprising is that convergence on the issue of capital adequacy initially looked fairly straightforward. There was (and still is) broad agreement that an internationally acceptable minimum standard for capital adequacy for securities traders, including the risks associated with banks' securities activities, is desirable. Success would mean a comprehensive international agreement among the major banking and securities supervisors and regulators to underpin the activities of the emerging financial conglomerates. The problem was that different regulators had different systems of measuring capital, and different interpretations as to what was 'sound' in a volatile and innovative market environment. It is useful to discuss these differences briefly even though some aspects of the discussion were covered in the second section of the chapter. What follows covers only the issue of market or 'position risk' – the risks associated with a firm's position in the market – but the reader should bear in mind that other risks are included in capital adequacy requirements such as settlement risk, counterparty risk, interest rate risk, size of firm, subordinated debt, and so on.

In particular, reflecting a conservative stance perhaps related to the broader retail base of US markets, the SEC insisted on measurement of capital on a 'gross' basis; firms operating in US markets are not allowed to 'net' their long and short (buy/sell) positions. When this principle is operationalized, a firm must hold a minimum of 15 per cent of its market position as capital to offset risk (GAO 1992: 28, 34). Furthermore, the US measures capital reserves based on the 'comprehensive' approach. Capital must cover a combination of specific risk (risk of a fall in the price of a specific security) and general market risk (risk of a general fall in the market). The comprehensive approach stipulates so-called capital 'haircuts' which pare required levels of provision down to a minimum acceptable component of the total risk to which a firm is exposed as a result of its market position at any one time (in the US case, a haircut of 15 per cent). Total risk is essentially the net worth of the firm's market position.

Contrast this approach to the 'building block approach' which we saw was proposed originally by Germany in the EU negotiations. Germany's market was similar in one respect to London's; it was predominantly a wholesale market. In addition it was dominated by large, well-capitalized, banks. It was much less concerned with investor protection for small consumers than the US. This approach allows different levels of provision for specific as opposed to general risk, and the components are then added together. This approach also permits netting with respect to general risk, wherein evenly matched long and short (buy/sell) positions can be balanced against each other to obtain a more 'realistic' assessment of the risks involved. There is, therefore, a percentage provision required for gross market positions in an equity, and a separate percentage required for net provisions, and again the two can be combined. In concrete terms, a regulator might require 8 per cent capital on gross positions to cover specific risk, and 15 per cent on netted positions to cover general risk.

Ironically, in view of later developments, the Technical Committee of IOSCO came to an agreement in principle on capital adequacy levels in January 1992. This agreement was for minimum acceptable international standards; authorities with more rigorous standards (i.e. the SEC) were under no obligation to lower their guard. The aim was to prevent the dynamics of regulatory arbitrage from getting out of hand and pushing standards below levels acceptable to the major regulatory agencies. The agreement settled on the building block approach then under discussion as the basis of parallel EU negotiations. The interim IOSCO agreement was a '4 + 8' accord: a minimum of 4 per cent provision would be required against a firm's gross position in an equity to cover specific risk, and a minimum of 8 per cent of the net position as provision against general market risk, and there was support for this accord in the Basle Committee. It appeared that securities and banking supervisors were on the brink of a historic global agreement.

The joker in the pack proved to be the EU negotiations on the CAD. For some time the draft CAD had been a 4 + 8 agreement as well. Under the British presidency of the Council, however, an additional provision had been put up for discussion: the French and British had proposed (echoed by a British proposal in IOSCO) that under certain circumstances a '2 + 8' provision could apply. A firm with a highly diversified and liquid portfolio could reduce the 4 per cent provision on gross positions for general risk to 2 per cent (*FRR*, November 1992: 8–9). This provision would apply only to certain sophisticated market players (more common in London than elsewhere) with the capacity to net their long and short positions perfectly (a 'hedging strategy' based on a complex computer-generated 'portfolio model' of risk) across the diversified portfolio (*International Securities Regulation Report (ISRR)* 5 (23), 03/11/92). The approach is in line with current 'portfolio theories' of securities regulation.[16]

This clause in the CAD, which was eventually agreed, proved anathema to the SEC, which was already uneasy about the whole idea of the more liberal building block approach – the US authority is not in favour of netting.[17] In response to the EU directive and a parallel UK proposal in IOSCO, the then Chairman of the SEC (Richard Breeden) dashed hopes of an IOSCO–Basle accord at the October 1992 annual conference of IOSCO by withdrawing SEC agreement on even the 4 + 8 proposal. It appeared to matter little that the CAD would include a provision for amendment in the light of an eventual global accord.

'So why, the Europeans ask, did [Breeden] sign up to the earlier agreement?' (*Economist*, 31 October 1992). The answer is far from clear. Certainly the US authority has always been under the scrutiny of Congress, and the 1987 market crash had focused attention on the issue of safety and soundness. Breeden claimed to have done calculations which demonstrated that EU firms would have been insolvent in the crash under the 2 + 8 provision (a point refuted by the Europeans), and he went on to argue that adoption of the formula would only encourage firms to restructure their portfolios so as to reduce capital provisions. If portfolios are perfectly matched (or 'netted'), the 8 per cent net requirement is effectively void, leaving only 2 per cent against the gross position (*FRR*, November 1992: 9).

Consequently, the IOSCO proposal did not succeed because the US, supported by Japan and Canada, preferred the comprehensive approach to capital standards. In fact, with 75 per cent of equity trading between Japan and the US alone (*ISRR*, 5 (23), 03/11/92: 9), this might have appeared a hegemonic position. The Basle Committee on Banking Supervision, however, remained committed to the interim IOSCO deal and accepted the EU's approach with respect to capital standards for bank securities trading activities. When Basle proposals on market risk for bank securities activities were released for consultation with the industry on 30 April 1993, they broadly shadowed the CAD, but minus the 2 + 8 clause. They also contained an explicit commitment to pursue further discussions with a view to convergence with the CAD so as to avoid undue competitive inequalities between banks and investment dealers. By the time of the Basle Committee's revision of the proposals (and following intense industry criticism of the earlier draft), they contained an explicit commitment to the use of bank's internal portfolio models, unacceptable to IOSCO. This development constituted 'a sea-change in the philosophy of regulation, as supervisors distance themselves from the day-to-day measurement of risk, and emphasise instead the setting of risk parameters and the validation of management's own internal risk controls' (*FRR*, April 1995: 2).

In the light of the Basle–EU position, which looks like an emerging global minimum standard, the SEC appears seriously out of step. Convergence towards the US model has proved a non-starter on capital adequacy. Several reasons might account for this surprising development.

First, domestic constraints on the US authority have played their part, but these are not sufficient in themselves to explain the abandonment of the 4 + 8 deal. Second, the intra-EU dynamic meant that the pivotal position of the London markets, in combination with France and Germany's big banks, held sway. In this regard we need to look more broadly to the crucial effects of capital adequacy standards on the transaction costs of firms. Although high standards offer competitive advantages to large multinational firms over their less capitalized competitors (large firms can meet the standards more easily), complex hedging techniques offer even more substantial cost advantages to the big players. Small firms simply cannot meet the conditions of the 2 + 8 provision and cannot afford the 'rocket scientists' required to run the mathematically complex portfolio models. From here the dynamic of regulatory arbitrage takes over: the London markets have always prospered on the basis of the UK's ability to provide a more market-oriented and self-regulatory environment to multinational firms. Once London won the debate in the EU it was unlikely that the Union would give up the ghost in the face of US pressure. The competitive advantage of the London regulatory approach may yet take its toll on the US share of international dealing.[18]

Third, much of the innovation in 'over-the-counter' (i.e. off-exchange) derivatives and new financial instruments in the US takes place within unregulated affiliates of broker dealers who have not been subject to SEC capital standards. These instruments would normally attract high capital charges owing to their high risk nature. In contrast, the UK (and Japanese) authorities insist on regulating these operations (GAO 1992: 28–9). This escape option of US firms is not therefore available in London and the EU. The EU can little afford to regulate these activities and restrict hedging activities. Derivative products are all about hedging against risk.

The pressure on the SEC to change its approach may yet prove overwhelming. In this eventuality, convergence will indeed take place, even on capital standards, but towards the EU's approach and not the US model. In the meantime, the SEC draws attention to 'the market for safety, soundness and integrity'.[19] The agency believes that firms will seek to operate in the US market with its high standards over the long run, despite the pressures on firms to reduce costs. Officials point out that large firms have seldom even come close to the 15 per cent minimum US standards in active trading. Only a large and well-capitalized firm can play a serious game, and tend to have excess capital in the hundreds of percentage points. If such is the case, one might add, what is the worry about the 4 + 8 proposal? As is perhaps usual, political disputes may depend on how big firms vote with their feet in this high stakes game of regulatory arbitrage.

A growing complication for the SEC comes from the Basle Committee's recently released final draft of the market risk amendments to the original Capital Adequacy accord of 1988 (*FRR*, January/February 1996: 7–10). This governs the securities operations of G10 banks in international markets and is, as was proposed in earlier drafts in 1993 and 1995, a decisive move towards the EU position. Crucially for the SEC, internal portfolio models for risk management are accepted in the rules, but the new standards also pose problems for the EU, which must now amend its CAD after all the wrangling to get agreement in the first place (*FRR*, May 1996: 18).[20] The new Basle standards are tougher than the EU agreement in significant ways, and in particular do not include the 2 per cent provision for diversified portfolios; the accord is an 8 + 8 standard with a 4 per cent exception for diversified portfolios. IOSCO has still been unable to agree to internal risk management models because of continuing US recalcitrance, but slowly the principal securities regulators and their banking counterparts appear to be struggling towards a commonly accepted global standard.

CONCLUSION

Policy convergence has its (at least temporary) limits, even in this globalizing era. There has been considerable progress on harmonizing regulations with respect to insider dealing and 'transparency' issues. These policies were not in question once domestic reform programmes began to respond to the emergence of a more market-oriented transnational financial system. The breakdown of traditional barriers to competition among sectors of the financial services industry and rapid product innovation required re-regulation to ensure enhanced transparency and a guarantee of fair competition. These changes represented a clear movement towards a US-style of regulation and prudential supervision. Even Germany, with its tradition of universal banking and its reliance on the market-stabilizing effects of securities trading within bank structures using inside information, accepted the principle that insider trading constitutes fraud in its 1992 domestic reform programme, *Finanzplatz Deutschland*. IOSCO discussions on this issue progressed well, especially as regards the sharing of information among regulatory authorities.[21]

The IOSCO negotiations, however, are blocked on the issue of capital adequacy. There is an emerging EU–Basle standard which challenges the US approach to capital adequacy. The dynamics of regulatory arbitrage appear to have ensured that the EU, under pressure from the UK and the London markets, prefers the building block approach. Furthermore, the portfolio approach (risk management models) to capital standards is in place, despite the EU imperative to raise its numerical standard to 4 per cent. The major firms in London, the largest of which are often American and Japanese, have clearly argued their case successfully and the EU is bidding to increase its share of the global securities business.

How should one understand this apparent incompatibility of EU and US rules? Is EU financial integration thus rendered incompatible with the broader process of globalization? Have the limits of convergence been reached? We argue not. In fact, regulatory arbitrage under the pressure of the multinational firms and other forms of conflict among political jurisdictions must be understood as integral to the dynamics of globalization and convergence across national, regional, and global levels. A complex pattern of co-operation and conflict can be expected to emerge in the process of transnationalization and liberalization of financial markets. States, in this case including the EU, have powerful incentives for co-operation to ensure the safety and soundness of the financial system. This pressure is particularly intense in the face of market desegmentation, which implies increased inter-linkages among banking and securities firms and the emergence of financial conglomerates. These developments have increased the risk of a systemic failure being generated in the securities sector and spilling over into the banking system.

In the final analysis, regulatory policy is part of the ongoing distributional conflict inherent in economic restructuring and integration processes, and political jurisdictions remain in competition with each other in the international system. This competition enables private (particularly large transnational) firms to place pressure on regulatory authorities to bring standards down, to decrease costs and to facilitate further globalization. In the longer run, the US may in fact be forced down the road of convergence to EU standards. A report of the US General Accounting Office (1992: 51) to Congress has admitted as much, arguing that the US may have to alter the balance between investor protection and competitive considerations in its administration of prudential standards.

Thus the transformation of market structures plays itself out across institutional levels in the global political economy. The emergence of the EU single financial market, with its significant harmonization of member-state regulations, is the most radical development in this regard. Similar co-operation among NAFTA members may be expected to intensify as the agreement works itself into the fabric of domestic policies. It is none the less highly unlikely that distinct regional patterns will remain highly incompatible with the globalization process. After all, it is the same large firms which dominate each of the major markets and which are capable of articulating their policy preferences in several regulatory iurisdictions at once. Blockage of the IOSCO process may therefore be seen as part and parcel of the way in which the regional EU integration process is in fact compatible with global trends. It is natural for increased global financial interdependence to occur in this heterodox fashion. Given a choice, the 'constellations of private interests' joined in alliances with constellations of regulatory agencies (Moran 1991: 130) prefer lower costs: the dynamics of regulatory arbitrage are intrinsic to the international political economy of liberalization. Left out of this calculus, unfortunately, is the broader public interest in a stable financial environment, and the importance of this stability to economic development in democratically organized societies (Underhill 1995).

NOTES

1 Funding for this research was generously provided by the Social Sciences and Humanities Research Council of Canada, Research Grants 410–88–0629 and 410–91–0974, and by the Economic and Social Research Council of the United Kingdom's Global Economic Institutions Programme, Grant L120251029.
2 This point has been made often by EU officials and commentators alike; see, for example, Giovannini and Mayer (1991: 1–2) and Geoffrey Fitchew (Director-General DG XV; Financial Institutions and Company Law, Commission of the European Communities), Paper presented to the Centre for European Government Studies, University of Edinburgh, 15 January 1988.
3 Confidential interviews, Washington, DC, September 1992.
4 Admittedly, the concept of a universal bank is slippery. The German banking historian and analyst, Oswald Hahn (1992: 925–6), has noted that no country in practice has a fully universal banking system. For our purposes, we will use the term to refer to banks that engage in the full line of deposit-taking and credit business plus primary and secondary dealing and trading in securities.
5 On transparency, see European Communities (1993b), especially pp. 30, 36–7.
6 IOSCO members have signed numerous bilateral 'Memoranda of Understanding' (MOUs) with respect to information sharing to protect against securities fraud. See IOSCO, *Annual Report*, various years, and copies of the MOUs in the public domain. However, McCahery (1997) argues that despite apparently similar legislation in the EU and the US, considerable differences in the implementation of regulations means that there is some way to go before convergence is in fact achieved, if ever.
7 Interview, Commission Bancaire official, 28 January 1991.
8 A directive agreed to in 1979 co-ordinated conditions for admission of securities to official listings of stock exchanges. A second directive adopted in 1980 and amended in 1987 co-ordinated requirements for the drawing up, scrutiny and administration of the listing particulars for admission and provided for full mutual recognition of these particulars. A third directive sets out the information that must be published on a regular basis by companies whose shares have been admitted to an official listing.
9 Confidential interview, Association française des sociétés de bourse, 25 October 1990.
10 In discussing the changes to the Commission, Raymond Benoît (1989) notes that it now has a relatively original status 'dans le paysage administratif français, d'autorité administrative indépendante'.
11 The other dimensions of the Commission's independence are outlined in Benoît (1989) and in Bézard (1989).

12 Theo Waigel, Minister of Finance, *Konzept Finanzplatz Deutschland*, translated by *FRR*, February 1992: 6.
13 Interview with Paul Guy, IOSCO Secretary-General, Montreal, Canada, 10 December 1991.
14 There has in fact been some ongoing rationalization and changes among working parties since they were set up in 1989–90.
15 Interview sources, Washington, September 1992. The concern with investor protection is corroborated by the GAO report (1992: 51–2). However, it is not clear that the small investor is as important to the US markets as claimed; major investors often deal off-exchange, sidestepping regulations (interview sources, GAO 1992: 28–9), but investor protection is certainly a major concern of the Congress.
16 See paper by Elroy Dimson and Paul Marsh (1994) 'The debate on international capital requirements: evidence on equity positions risk for UK securities firms', City Research Project, London Business School. Dimson and Marsh argue that the SEC approach to capital adequacy is inefficient and outmoded, and that the portfolio approach is superior.
17 GAO (1992) and confidential interviews, Washington, September 1992.
18 The GAO (1992: 44–52) has explicitly discussed this scenario in its report: 'The firms we talked to . . . pointed out that some foreign standards – particularly those in the United Kingdom – recognise a wider variety of hedging strategies than the US standards *and might encourage US firms to move their hedging activities overseas*' (emphasis added).
19 Confidential interviews, Washington, DC, September 1992.
20 The CAD always anticipated this possibility, and the original directive contained a clause committing the EU to harmonization with eventual international standards.
21 Interview with Paul Guy, Secretary-General of IOSCO, Montreal, Canada, 10 December 1991.

REFERENCES

Arnold, W. (1989) 'Trennbank- oder Universalbanksystem: Wohin führt die EG-Bankrechtharmonisierung', *Börsen-Zeitung*, 30 September: 14.
Benoît, R. (1989) 'La Commission des Opérations de Bourse après la réforme d'aôut 1989', *Regards sur l'actualité* no. 155: 23–9.
Bézard, P. (1989) 'Le nouveau visage de la Commission des Opérations de Bourse', *Revue internationale du droit comparé* 4: 929–57.
Bliman, M., C. Bruno and J. Le Cacheux (1993) 'L'espace bancaire et financier européen', *Observations et Diagnostics Economiques: revue de l'OFCE* no. 43, January.
Brown, P. (1997) 'The politics of the EU Single Market for investment services: negotiating the investment services and captial adequacy directives', in G.R.D. Underhill (ed.) *The New World Order in International Finance*, London: Macmillan, 124–43.
Busch, M.L. and H.V. Milner (1994) 'The future of the international trading system: international firms, regionalism, and domestic politics', in R. Stubbs and G.R.D. Underhill (eds) *Political Economy and the Changing Global Order*, London: Macmillan, 259–76.
Cerny, P.G. (1993) 'The deregulation and re-regulation of financial markets in a more open world', in P.G. Cerny (ed.) *Finance and World Politics: Markets, Regimes, and States in the Post-Hegemonic Era*, Aldershot: Edward Elgar, 51–85.
Coleman, W.D. (1994) 'Keeping the shotgun behind the door: governing the securities industry in Canada, the United Kingdom, and the United States', in J. Rogers

Hollingsworth, W. Streeck and P. Schmitter (eds) *Governing Capitalist Economies: Performance and Control of Economic Sectors*, New York: Oxford University Press, 244–69.

—— (1996) *Financial Services, Globalization, and Domestic Policy Change: A Comparison of North America and the European Union*, London: Macmillan.

The Economist (1992), 'Capital spat', 31 October.

European Communities (1993a) 'Council Directive 93/6/EEC of 15 March 1993 on the capital adequacy of investments firms and credit institutions', *Official Journal of the European Communities* (legislation), no. L141, vol. 36, 11 June (CAD).

—— (1993b) 'Council Directive 93/22/EC of 10 May 1993 on investment services in the securities field', *Official Journal of the European Communities* (legislation), no. L141/26, vol. 36, 11 June (ISD).

Financial Regulation Report (FRR) (1990) 'Severe differences of opinion on the Capital Adequacy Directive', February.

—— (1991) 'ISD – the concentration principle – the impasse remains', April: 2–4.

—— (1991) 'Investment Services Directive in trouble', June: 12–13.

—— (1991) 'Developments on the Capital Adequacy Directive', November: 9.

—— (1992) 'Capital Adequacy Directive agreed', July: 2–4.

—— 'Continuing debate on capital standards for securities business', November: 7–10.

Gammerdinger, D. (1993) 'Zur Entwicklung der Wertpapier- und Börsen-aufsicht in Deutschland', *Zeitschrift für das gesamte Kreditwesen* 46, November: 976–9.

General Accounting Office (GAO), United States (1992) *Securities Markets: Challenges to Harmonizing International Capital Standards Remain*, Washington, DC: GAO (March).

—— (1994) *Financial Derivatives: Actions Needed to Protect the Financial System*, Washington, DC: GAO (May).

Gilpin, R. (1987) *The Political Economy of International Relations*, Princeton, N.J.: Princeton University Press.

Giovannini, A. and C. Mayer (1991) 'Introduction', in A. Giovannini and C. Mayer (eds) *European Financial Integration*, Cambridge: Cambridge University Press for the Centre for Economic Policy Research, 1–8.

Guy, P. (Secretary-General of IOSCO) (1992) 'Regulatory harmonization to achieve effective international competition', in F.R. Edwards and H.T. Patrick (eds) *Regulating International Financial Markets: Issues and Policies*, Dordrecht: Kluwer Academic.

Hahn, O. (1992) 'Universal- und Trennbanksystem: Unklarheiten', *Zeitschrift für das gesamte Kreditwesen* 45: 925–6.

Howell, M. and A. Cozzini (1991) *Games Without Frontiers: Global Equity Markets in the 1990s*, New York: Salomon Brothers.

International Monetary Fund (IMF) (1994) 'Banks and derivative markets: a challenge for financial policy', *IMF Survey*, 21 February.

International Organization of Securities Commissions (IOSCO) (1991) *By-Laws of the International Organization of Securities Commissions*, Washington, DC, September.

—— (1992a) Annual Report, Montreal: IOSCO.

—— (1992b) *Principles for the Supervision of Financial Conglomerates*, Montreal: IOSCO.

International Securities Regulation Report (1992) Vol. 5, no. 23, 3 November.

Jurgensen, P. and D. Lebègue (1988) *Le Trésor et la politique financière*, Paris: Montechristien.

Knight, J., S. Mazey and J. Richardson (1993) 'Groups and the process of European integration: the work of the federation of stock exchanges in the European Community', in S. Mazey and J. Richardson (eds) *Lobbying in the European Community*, Oxford: Oxford University Press, 162–76.

Lütz, S. (1996). 'The revival of the nation-state? Stock exchange regulation in an era of internationalized financial markets', *MPIFG Discussion Paper 96/9*. Köln: Max-Planck-Institut für Gesellschaftsforschung.

McCahery, J. (1997) 'Market regulation and particularistic interests: the dynamics of insider trading regulation in the US and Europe', in G.R.D. Underhill (ed.) *The New World Order in International Finance*, London: Macmillan.

McCahery, J., W. Bratton, S. Picciotto and C. Scott (eds) (1996) *International Regulatory Competition and Co-ordination: Europe and the United States*, Oxford: Clarendon Press.

Milner, H.V. (1988) *Resisting Protectionism: Global Industries and the Politics of International Trade*, Princeton, N.J.: Princeton University Press.

Moran, M. (1991) *The Politics of the Financial Services Revolution*, London: Macmillan.

—— (1992) 'Regulatory change in German financial markets', in K. Dyson (ed.) *The Politics of German Regulation*, Aldershot: Dartmouth, for the Association for the Study of German Politics, 137–57.

OECD (1987) *International Trade in Services: Securities*, Paris: OECD.

—— (1996) *Financial Market Trends*, no. 63, February, Paris: OECD.

Porter, T. (1993) *States, Markets and Regimes in Global Finance*, New York: St Martin's Press.

Steinherr, A. (1994) 'Taming the wild beast of derivatives', *Financial Times*, 16 December.

Stubbs, R. and G.R.D. Underhill (1994) 'Global trends, regional patterns', in R. Stubbs and G.R.D. Underhill (eds) *Political Economy and the Changing Global Order*, London: Macmillan, 331–5.

Thurow, L. (1993) *Head to Head: The Coming Economic Battle among Japan, Europe and America*, London: Allen and Unwin.

Underhill, G.R.D. (1995) 'Keeping governments out of politics: transnational securities markets, regulatory co-operation, and political legitimacy', *Review of International Studies* 21 (3): 251–78

—— (1997a) 'The making of the European financial area: global market integration and the EU Single Market for financial services', in G.R.D. Underhill (ed.) *The New World Order in International Finance*, London: Macmillan.

—— (1997b) 'Private markets and public responsibility in a global system: conflict and co-operation in transnational banking and securities regulation', in G.R.D. Underhill (ed.) *The New World Order in International Finance*, London: Macmillan.

Index

advocacy coalitions 50
AFTA 51, 52, 56, 57
APEC 2, 3, 7, 10, 44, 48, 49, 50, 51, 52,
  53, 54, 55, 57, 61, 62, 64, 69, 78, 92, 223
ARF 51, 52, 56
Argentina 85, 92
ASEAN 2, 49, 51, 52, 53, 56, 75
ASEAN Free Trade Area *see* AFTA
ASEAN Regional Forum *see* ARF
Asia-Pacific Economic Co-operation
  forum *see* APEC
Asian culture 69, 70
Asianness 56, 60, 61
Association of South-East Asian
  Nations *see* ASEAN
Australia 61, 169
Austria 74, 111

Balladur, Édouard 32, 33
Banca d'Italia 177, 189
Bank for International Settlements 7, 9
banking 228, 230
Banking Directives, EU 225, 230–1, 232
banking supervision 227, 239
Banque de France 177, 188
Basle Committee on Banking
  Supervision 4, 224, 225, 226, 227, 228,
  238–43
Belgium 102, 111, 166, 180, 233
biotechnology 71
Brazil 85, 86, 88, 90, 92
Bretton Woods agreement 85, 87, 132,
  229
Britain *see* Great Britain *or* United
  Kingdom
BRITE programme 140, 144
Brittan, Sir Leon 167
Bundesbank *see* Deutsche Bundesbank
Bush, President George 28, 30, 145

business community 48; organization 75;
  relation with state in Asia 73–4, 76

Canada 2, 10, 28, 39, 61, 87, 93, 169,
  241; ratification of NAFTA 31–2
Canada–US Free Trade Agreement 28,
  87
capital adequacy 226, 228, 231–2, 239–43
Capital Adequacy Directive 225, 232,
  233, 235, 237, 241–3
capital controls 100
capital mobility 111, 122, 123, 134–5,
  174, 176, 179, 180; impact on
  macroeconomic policy 130–3, 135,
  174; impact on social democracy
  129–33
capitalism 3, 208; Asia-Pacific 69, 70,
  76–7; Asia-Pacific and Anglo-
  American compared 71, 72–3, 74, 76,
  77–8; social market 69
central banks 174, 189; and globalization
  178–9, 180, 181; credibility 182–3;
  ideology of independence 174, 175–8,
  181, 183, 186, 190, 191; theories of
  184–6
Cerny, Philip 6–8, 227
Chile 85, 90, 92, 93
China 54, 73, 86, 91; culture 70
Chinese, ethnic 74, 75, 76, 77
Christian democratic parties 106
Clinton, President Bill 31
Commission des opérations de bourse
  236
Committee of Central Bank Governors
  176, 177, 185
Committee of Economics and Finance
  Ministers 177, 191
Common Agricultural Policy 107, 108
comparative public policy 3, 4